Theory and Politics

Theory and Politics

Studies in the Development of Critical Theory

Helmut Dubiel

translated by Benjamin Gregg

with an introduction by Martin Jay

The MIT Press, Cambridge, Massachusetts, and London, England

This book was set in Baskerville by The MIT Press Computergraphics Department and printed and bound by Halliday Lithograph in the United States of America.

Library of Congress Cataloging in Publication Data

Dubiel, Helmut, 1946–
Theory and politics.

(Studies in contemporary German social thought)
Translation of: Wissenschaftsorganisation und politische Erfahrung.
Bibliography: p.
Includes index.
1. Frankfurt school of sociology—German (West)—History. 2. Horkheimer, Max, 1895–1973. Kritische Theorie. 3. Knowledge, Sociology of. I. Title. II. Series.
HM24.D8513 1985   301′.01   85-6612
ISBN 0-262-04080-8

Contents

Contents

Introduction

Martin Jay

Until the mid-1970s, the German reception of the Frankfurt School was marked by two competing, if ultimately complementary, tendencies. Political opponents from both ends of the spectrum launched increasingly shrill polemics against the role of Critical Theory in fomenting (or failing to foment with enough vigor) the German New Left, while supporters of the School, usually recruited from the ranks of its former students, defended virtually every aspect of its work with equal intensity. Impossible amid all the tumult was a dispassionate reconstruction of the School's intellectual trajectory from its beginnings in the 1920s through its exile in America to its triumphant return to postwar Germany. Ironically, this task was also hindered by the ambivalence felt by the School's leaders about what might be called their own unmastered past.[1] Outsiders from abroad, usually from Italy or America, thus found themselves in the unexpected position of having the field virtually to themselves.

After the deaths of Theodor Adorno in 1969, Friedrich Pollock in 1970, and Max Horkheimer in 1973, and the departure of Jürgen Habermas in 1971 for the Max Planck Institute in Starnberg, near Munich, the climate gradually began to change. Although those elements on the left who had gravitated to hard-line Leninism or Maoism continued to dismiss the Frankfurt School as irremediably revisionist, while its enemies on the right found new crimes to blame on Critical

Theory when the terrorism of the mid-1970s began, a space for serious discussion was finally cleared. The first scholars to occupy it came from the collective project on "theory formation as a group process" directed by Jürgen Frese at the University of Bielefeld. Taking as their object of study the Institute for Social Research, one of Frese's teams set out to investigate its transformation from an obscure Weimar academic outpost to the influential and embattled Frankfurt School of the Federal Republic. Among the members of this young and talented *Arbeitskreis* was Helmut Dubiel.

Dubiel had already completed his doctoral dissertation comparing Adorno and the conservative cultural anthropologists Arnold Gehlen, and he had begun work on an edition of Pollock's essays on the transition from monopoly to state capitalism.[2] He now focused his attention on the relationship between the historical events from 1930 to 1945 and the development of Critical Theory and the realization of its interdisciplinary goals. Drawing on previously untapped materials in the Pollock Archive in Frankfurt, he produced a tightly argued account that addressed these selected questions rather than attempting to provide an overview of the Institute's history as a whole. The results earned him his *Habilitation* in 1977 and were almost immediately published by Suhrkamp Verlag under the title *Wissenschaftsorganisation und politische Erfahrung: Studien zur frühen Kritischen Theorie.*[3]

The importance of the work was quickly registered by students of Critical Theory. Whereas the attention of most previous German commentators had been directed at the philosophical, cultural, or aesthetic concerns of the School in isolation from each other, it was now possible to understand the ways in which the Institute's work as a whole, including its social, political, and economic interests, fit together. It was also possible to see the extent to which the results of these common efforts responded to the changing events of the day. Such highly volatile questions as the Institute's attitude toward the Soviet Union, which still generates considerable passion,[4] were clarified as never before. As two recent commentators noted, the work successfully challenged both the assumption of those "who see Critical Theory as uniformly apolitical, idealist and anti-science and the affirmative conception of Critical Theory held by some of its epigones as uniformly radical and subversive."[5]

Aspects of Dubiel's argument were not, to be sure, without their critics. No less expert a witness than Herbert Marcuse expressed skepticism about the model of interdisciplinary research based on the dialectic of research and presentation posited by Dubiel.[6] According to his recollection, Horkheimer's role was not quite as dominant as the model suggested. Other commentators have suggested that an alternative approach to integrating the various disciplines represented at the Institute was offered by Adorno's less totalizing vision of the relation between theory and research.[7] Although not influential during the Institute's earlier years, it may have had an impact later, when Adorno's role became more central.

If Adorno's celebrated defense of the need for some exaggeration in every conceptual approximation of reality is taken seriously, then Dubiel's reconstruction of the Institute's interdisciplinary *modus operandi* can be appreciated for the insights it does provide. Moreover, it is clear that the work as a whole helped launch a series of investigations of the Frankfurt School's history by German scholars, most importantly Alfons Söllner's account of the contributions of Franz Neumann and Otto Kirchheimer and Wolfgang Bonss's treatment of Erich Fromm and the Institute's empirical work.[8] Other aspects of the Institute's past have been clarified in the work of Axel Honneth, Rolf Wiggershaus, Gerhard Brandt, Wolfgang Schivelbusch, Michael Wilson, and Moishe Postone, the last two being North Americans who did their dissertations in Germany.[9] Dubiel himself has continued to contribute to the process, most notably through his extensive interviews with Leo Löwenthal, which were published in 1980 as *Mitmachen Wollte Ich Nie*.[10] By the early 1980s, details of the Frankfurt School's history were finally well enough known in Germany to allow Eckhard Henscheid to publish a parody composed of half-invented anecdotes that drew on his readers' familiarity with the original story.[11]

Historical reconstruction has not, however, meant the relegation of Critical Theory to a museum exhibit in a gallery of outmoded ideas, as some critics had feared. The most telling evidence to the contrary is the frequent reconsideration in Habermas's work of his intellectual mentors, which have contributed to the clarification of his own continuing project.[12] The role of Dubiel, who collaborated with Habermas in Starnberg and recently moved with him back to Frankfurt, has also been exemplary in this respect. Contributing important papers to the 1979 Starnberg conference on the social-scientific potential of Critical Theory and the 1983 Frankfurt congress on Adorno,[13] he has shown how organic the transition from historian of the Frankfurt School to creative developer of its legacy can be. The remarkable revival of interest in Critical Theory, demonstrated by the unexpectedly large attendance at the Adorno conference—some estimates ranged as high as fifteen hundred people in the audience—and the widespread coverage it received in the German press, bears witness to the continued vitality of the ideas whose origins have scrupulously been recovered by Dubiel and other historians of the Frankfurt School. With this translation of his first major work, English-speaking readers thus gain access to a new and gifted participant in the ongoing reception and development of one of this century's most potent intellectual movements.

Notes

1. The expression *unmastered past (unbewältigte Vergangenheit)* was used by Germans to refer to their inability to come to grips with the meaning of Nazism. In the case of the Frankfurt School, which was instrumental in combating that particular amnesia, it can be used to mean the members' hesitancy in acknowledging their Marxist roots in the years after they returned to Frankfurt. Horkheimer in particular was very reluctant to resurrect his prewar writings, which were far more orthodox in their historical materialism than were his later efforts. When a reprint of the entire *Zeitschrift für Sozialforschung* finally appeared in 1970, Alfred Schmidt, Horkheimer's student, wrote a short historical introduction that concluded by emphasizing the inapplicability of many of its ideas to current problems. See his *Die "Zeitschrift für Sozialforschung" Geschichte und gegenwärtige Bedeutung* (Munich, 1970), p. 55.

2. Dubiel, "Ich-Identität und Institution," (Ph.D. diss., University of Dusseldorf, 1973); Friedrich Pollock, *Stadien des Kapitalismus*, ed. with intro. Helmut Dubiel (Munich, 1975). Dubiel also published an essay on the Frankfurt School's critique of Mannheim; "Ideologiekritik versus Wissenssoziologie. Die Kritik der Mannheim'schen Wissenssoziologie in der kritischen Theorie," *Archiv für Rechts- und Sozialpsychologie* 61, 2 (1975).

3. (Frankfurt, 1978); a summary of the second part had already appeared in *Kölner Zeitschrift für Soziologie und Sozialpsychologie* 26, 2 (1974).

4. See, for example, Lewis Feuer, "The Frankfurt Marxists and the Columbia Liberals," *Survey* 25, 3 (Summer 1980); Martin Jay, "Misrepresentations of the Frankfurt School," *Survey* 26, 2 (Summer 1982); G. L. Yulmen, "Heresy? Yes! Conspiracy? No!," *Survey* 26, 2 (Summer 1982); Lewis Feuer, "The Social Role of the Frankfurt Marxists," *Survey* 26, 2 (Summer 1982).

5. Douglas Kellner and Rick Roderick, "Recent Literature on Critical Theory," *New German Critique* 23 (Spring–Summer 1981), 145–146.

6. Marcuse et al., "Theory and Politics: A Discussion," *Telos* 38 (Winter 1978-1979), 128.

7. Wolfgang Bonss and Norbert Schindler, "Kritische Theorie als interdisziplinärer Materialismus," and Martin Jay, "Positive und negative Totalität. Adornos Alternativentwurf zur interdisziplinären Forschung," in Wolfgang Bonss and Axel Honneth, eds., *Sozialforschung als Kritik: Zum sozialwissenschaftlichen Potential der kritischen Theorie* (Frankfurt, 1982); for an English version of the second article, see *Thesis Eleven* 3 (1982).

8. Söllner, *Geschichte und Herrschaft: Studien zur materialistischen Sozialwissenschaft, 1929–1942* (Frankfurt, 1979); Bonss, *Die Einübung des Tatsachenblicks: Zur Struktur und Veränderung empirischer Sozialforschung* (Frankfurt, 1982). Söllner also edited and wrote an introduction for a collection of Neumann's essays, *Wirtschaft, Staat, Demokratie: Aufsätze 1930–1954* (Frankfurt, 1978), and Bonss edited and wrote an introduction for Erich Fromm, *Arbeiter und Angestellte am Vorabend des Dritten Reichs: Eine sozialpsychologische Untersuchung* (Stuttgart, 1980).

Introduction

9. Axel Honneth, "Von Adorno zu Habermas. Zum Gestaltwandel kritischer Gesellschaftstheorie," in Bonss and Honneth, eds., *Sozialforschung als Kritik*; Rolf Wiggershaus, "Die Geschichte der Frankfurter Schule," *Neue Rundschau* 89, 4 (1978); Gerhard Brandt, "Ansichten kritischer Sozialforschung 1930–1980," *Gesellschaftliche Arbeit und Rationalisierung, Leviathan*, Sonderheft 4 (1981); Wolfgang Schivelbusch, *Intellektuellendämmerung: Zur Lage der Frankfurter Intelligenz in den zwanziger Jahre* (Frankfurt, 1982); Michael Wilson, *Das Institut für Sozialforschung und seine Analysen des Faschismus* (Frankfurt, 1982); Moishe Postone, "The Present as Necessity: Towards a Reinterpretation of the Marxian Critique of Labor and Time" (Ph.D. diss., University of Frankfurt, 1983), chapter 3 of which appears under the joint authorship of Barbara Brick as "Critical Pessimism and the Limits of Traditional Marxisim," *Theory and Society* 11, 5 (September 1982).

10. (Frankfurt, 1980); chapters 4 and 2 appear in English in *Telos* 45 (Fall 1980) and 49 (Fall 1981), respectively.

11. Henscheid, *Wie Max Horkheimer einmal sogar Adorno hereinlegte* (Zurich, 1983).

12. See, for example, "The Inimitable *Zeitschrift für Sozialforschung*: How Horkheimer Took Advantage of a Historically Oppressive Hour," *Telos* 45 (Fall 1980); "Psychic Thermidor and the Rebirth of Rebellious Subjectivity," *Berkeley Journal of Sociology* 24 (1980); *Theorie des kommunikativen Handelns* (Frankfurt, 1981), vol. 1, chap. 4.

13. Dubiel, "Die Aufhebung des Überbaus. Zur Interpretation der Kultur in der kritischen Theorie," in Bonss and Honneth, eds., *Sozialforschung als Kritik*; "Die Aktualität der Gesellschaftstheorie Adornos," in Ludwig von Friedeburg and Jürgen Habermas, eds., *Adorno-Konferenz 1983* (Frankfurt, 1983).

I

The Integration of the Proletariat and the Loneliness of the Intelligentsia

Political Experience and the Process of Theory Construction in the Frankfurt Circle, 1930 –1945

The entire situation in Europe is quite sad. Even the fear of war itself forms but a moment within a social development in which, in any case, all cultural values of any significance are perishing with an uncanny necessity. Those few to whom the truth has fled appear as ridiculous, dogmatic persons speaking a bombastic language, as empty, completely without foundation. . . . The most unpleasant discovery to which materialism leads is that reason exists only as long as it is supported by a natural subject. Reason is possessed by this natural subject according to the way in which he could make use of it. He can also lose it through no fault of his own. (Horkheimer to Pollock, Paris, 20 September 1937, Pollock Archive)

Methodological Procedure

Those interested in the theoretical development of the Frankfurt Circle must at some point ask themselves, When a theory contains such internal disparities as those among the "materialism" of the early 1930s, the programmatic texts of the 1937 "Critical Theory," and the *Dialectic of Enlightenment* of 1944, where is one to locate a reference point that will define the theory's identity and continuity over the course of its development? Might it reside in the social base, the Frankfurt Circle, or in its central figure, Max Horkheimer? Or perhaps in particular stages of the theory's development, to which one might give normative status over and above other stages? Or, again, might it reside in a "genuine intention" of the theory as a whole, rather than in any particular individual or text? Present-day partisans of Critical Theory in large measure content themselves with imputing to the theory a specific, conventionalized, "true" intention that is independent of history. In similar ahistorical fashion they reduce all their positivist opponents to a single approach to the philosophy of science, out of the pluralistic ensemble of possible theoretical viewpoints.

The program of this book will, on the contrary, be to define the continuity of the theory's development from 1930 to 1945 precisely in terms of the discontinuity of its subject matter. We grasp its entire development as the reflective expression of a historical experience.

In critical opposition to the antihistorical philosophies of the time, the early Horkheimer's materialism sought its concepts and empirical orientation in intensely experienced historical constellations. Such a theoretical orientation could not seal itself off from the historical experience of its empirical subjects. An interpretation that seeks to continue this orientation must therefore take seriously comments such as Horkheimer's, as his essays of the 1930s were reissued, that he was compelled "under the pressure of world-historical events" to modify his earlier convictions. This is not to suggest that an interpretation of the early theory should subordinate itself to "autobiographical" assessments by Horkheimer or other members of the Frankfurt Circle, but rather that we undertake a systematic reading of the Circle's theoretical work as a theory-constitutive, self-reflective treatment of its own historical experience.

A procedure that grasps the immanent character underlying a theory in the course of its development as the self-reflective treatment of its external determinants is, in sociology's catalog of methodologies, a *sociology of knowledge*. We may characterize our methodology by comparing it briefly to the classical methodology of Karl Mannheim. Mannheim typically establishes a relation between cognitive structures and their social substrata, that is, social stratifications such as groups and classes. He considers cognitive structures as social structures, or, more precisely, as cognitive processes that transpire within social structures.[1]

In contrast, our methodology treats only those correlations of cognitive and social structures that the bearers of a particular theory themselves take up in relation to such structures and that thus become constitutive as such for the individual's or group's theoretical orientation.

The empirical focus of this procedure is significantly narrower than in the traditional sociology of knowledge. It is empirically rare that the people who are the object of a theory themselves reflect upon this theory. In clarifying the peculiar nature of this methodology, it may be helpful to first discuss, *via negationis*, relevant instances where such persons *cannot*, on our methodological premises, be found. They can seldom be found, if at all, in that branch of scientific production oriented toward basic research and professionally occupied with formulating theories. This is even more the case to the extent that idealistic and rationalistic ideologies prevail within a community of inquirers concerning the notion of progress in knowledge. According to the naive but popular linear-cumulative model of scientific development, the human agents of such development constitute an absolute subject, or at least an anonymous scientific community, that one may quote emphatically but that cannot be strategically reflected upon for the purpose of theory formation. If such reflection does occur in institutionalized scientific practice, it does so only as a symptom of crisis. As a rule, reflection on the social agents who produce theoretical sentences takes place only when there are breakdowns in scientific communication, that is, when there is extensive scientific critique and controversy concerning scientific foundations. In the code of scientific behavior, reflections on the subjects behind science are always the last means and the sharpest polemical weapons.

In the life-world, reflections by the social agents of cognitive structures on these very structures is even less probable than it is in science. The life-world is defined in part by the fact that the cognitive systems of orientation within which we always move are taken for granted prereflectively as a kind of social reality. To be sure, communication theory has shown that reflection on elements of communication processes at a metacommunicative level belongs to the social competence of persons. But it is important to note that metacommunication functions only against the background of a reliably institutionalized symbolic world, that is, one not grasped reflectively. We can see how very difficult it is to reflect on a culture's interpretation of the world and society as a whole by noting, for instance, the immense expenditure of effort involved in Michel Foucault's studies of our own culture.

We begin with the conjecture that this sort of self-reflective thematization of one's own cognitively orienting framework can be observed in small revolutionary groups. From the periphery of society, that is, outside all institutionalized forms of social influence, such groups conduct a radical struggle against the dominant understanding of social conditions. They consider their own theoretical orientation to be both the critical truth about the social structure from which they distance themselves and a utopian anticipation of a future mass consciousness. Because of this continual confrontation of profoundly differing conceptions of social reality, marginal political groups are existentially caught up in the contingency of political definitions of reality. Demonstrations of this contingency can in the long run prove fatal for group integration, and small, sectarian groups evade such demonstrations by "ontologically annihilating" those conceptions of political reality that they dispute. They grasp the distinction between their orientation and the dominant forms of social consciousness as one between "essence" and "appearance." Evidently the only possible escape for most politically marginal groups, in view of the overwhelming nature of society's "attempts at therapy and annihilation,"[2] is to envelop themselves in their own orientation toward reality in the manner of a *folie à la group*, that is, a collectively sustained madness.

We maintain that a marginal political group's level of consciousness may be determined by its ability to grasp continuously and self-reflectively the historical-political environment of its orientation. That is, the level of consciousness may be determined by the group's capacity to reflect upon itself—in much the same way as a sociology of knowledge—even as it orients itself.

The following examination traces the reflective process in a case study of the development of the theory of the Frankfurt Circle. We assume that the Circle's historical significance lies not so much in its political effect (which is in any case slight) or in its academic influence (which is declining) as in the enduring relevance of its theory-constitutive political and historical self-consciousness. The exemplary value of this reflective process cannot be isolated from its social content: Critical Theory's development is a central document of ths political and theoretical self-understanding of the German socialist intelligentsia in the successive historical contexts of the Weimar Republic, fascism, and war.

In reconstructing the historical process of a theory's internal, developmental alterations, philologists often distort various stages in the process by exaggerated suppositions of discontinuity. Thus, for example, the economism of Marx's mature writings is contrasted with the radical, democratic tenor of the young Marx or with the youthful humanism "decoded" in *Das Kapital*. An analogous danger, resulting from the major developmental permutations of Critical Theory during the period here examined, lies in concluding that particular stages formulated the "authentic" intention for the entire development. In this way other stages are made to appear as a learning process leading up to, or away from, this "true" motive. The following reflections on the difficulties posed by changes in theory are intended to eliminate such dangers.

We assume that theories which are not simply born of the same academic exercise to which they become assimilated, but rather provide practical orientation in political struggles, must be interpreted as a continuous and consistent theoretical whole—even if they are not, on a semantic level, immediately recognizable as such.

The a priori supposition of continuity and identity is less a matter of semantics than of function in an orienting frame of reference. Such political frameworks, whether of an individual or of a group, may be described as a slowly fluctuating potential for a specific cognitive attitude of anticipation or, more precisely, as an ensemble of highly abstract parameters and questions. The everyday processes of making decisions and evaluating experiences can then be interpreted as responses in light of these parameters and complexes of questions. The assumption of such an abstract, relatively invariant framework of relevance is lent support by the fact that, particularly in the context of political activity, one cannot assume a wholly indeterminate situation in which the political agent might remove himself from the continuity of historical self-understanding. The particular stage of a theory's development can be interpreted as continuous with respect to their identical function within a cognitive framework of political orientation, despite the considerable semantic discontinuities between stages. This implies, methodologically, that each of the various texts within a single theoretical tradition can be read as a historically varying answer to an identical, invariant framework of "points of inquiry."[3]

Thus the functional and the semantic continuity of politically orienting theories can be differentiated. For our analysis of the Frankfurt Circle's work, this means that we are not primarily interested in establishing a semantic connection between the early materialism and, for example, the critique of technology in the *Dialectic of Enlightenment*. Our initial interest lies rather in determining the theoretically orienting framework of points of inquiry underlying the entire period to be examined (1930–1945) in terms of which problems were isolated and which questions were posed.

Just as every good questionnaire is the result of a series of "pretests," the ensemble of these points of inquiry can be derived solely from an intimate knowledge of the texts to be examined. The single theoretically orienting framework underlying this ensemble that we can reconstruct and then ascribe to the Frankfurt Circle is by and large a model defined by topics abstracted from the Circle's various texts.

Our first concern was to isolate and systematize all direct and indirect allusions, in both published texts and unpublished letters (such as were available), to the *historical and political context out of which these texts and letters emerged*, and then to systematize these reflections, implicit or explicit, in this context. A threshold at which these reflections become theorems and theories could not be determined. Within one and the same section of our analysis we discuss, for example, both pretheoretical assessments of fascism documented in letters and conversation and nascent *theories* of fascism. But within that section we treat reflections and theories separately. At the same time, the spheres of historical and political interest were easily identified. On the one hand, attention was focused on conditions for possible socialist politics, that is, on the fate of the working-class movement in Germany and its communist and social-democratic wings, and on the development of Stalinism in the Soviet Union. On the other hand, attention was focused on the rise of national socialism, its coming to power, and its consolidation of that power, as well as on authoritarian tendencies in late capitalist countries.

The Frankfurt Circle's work in the 1930s aimed at the revolutionary transformation of society, even while it had doubts about the possibility of realizing its aims. Within its theory, then, the Circle reflected upon its own relation to political practice, even though the development of such reflections on theory and praxis into a theory of political organization was unlikely, given the Circle's remoteness from institutionalized groups. The Circle identified itself with the tradition of socialist theory, at least until the beginning of the 1940s. Characteristically, the socialist intelligentsia understood itself, not as the subject of its own theory, but as an instrument to articulate orientations already present in proletarian class consciousness. Hence the proletariat appeared as both subject and addressee of a theory tailored to its own social situation. And in fact the Frankfurt Circle's textual characterizations of the theory's subject, and its assertions about its addressee, were major indices of its position, at any given time, on the relation of theory and praxis.

A third sphere of the Circle's political and historical interests in the 1930s was an immanent determination of its theoretical position on particular issues, that is, on the formulation of its nature as an oppositional political theory and on its self-ascription to certain intellectual-political traditions. Also characteristic of the socialist tradition, within which the Frankfurt Circle understood itself, was a self-reflective relationship to its own theoretical work. It asked whether philosophical reflection, or empirical treatment within a particular social science, or a specific combination of both, was the most appropriate methodology for grasping a given object. These reflections about the form the theory was to take were in each case made in the context of deciding what relation philosophy should have to social science. Further, important considerations concerned the utopian reference point orienting the theory at any given stage of its development.

Our systematic representation of the early Frankfurt Circle is based on the following structure of points in inquiry:

Historical and political experience
> The labor movement
> The Soviet Union
> Fascism

Theory of the theory-praxis relation
> Subject and addressee
> Theory and praxis

Theoretical position
> Self-understanding within the tradition of historical and political theory
> Relation to Marxism
> Relation of philosophy to science
> Utopia

This schema, which we attribute to the Frankfurt Circle and which is the basis for our presentation, precludes the possibility of interpreting particular texts. With the exception of several programmatic essays by Horkheimer, few of the relevant texts respond to all our points of inquiry, and few sustain their original emphasis on a particular issue throughout the course of the Circle's theoretical development. We were therefore constrained to group together particular texts according to their temporal and textual coherence. We were guided by the parameters of political theory introduced by Horkheimer in his programmatic essays, which served as points of orientation for the entire Frankfurt Circle. This temporal structuring of the Circle's entire *Theorieproduktion* (proposed by Horkheimer himself) is particularly evident in the programmatic concepts of materialism (as of 1930) and Critical Theory (as of 1937). We characterize the theory production of the 1940s in terms of Horkheimer's concept of a critique of instrumental reason; in accordance with the theory's own initial self-structuring of its theoretical-political interests, we divide the entire process of its development from 1930 to 1945 into three sections and examine each independently of the others—in conformity with our general structure of points of inquiry:

Materialism: 1930–1937

Critical Theory: 1937–1940

Critique of instrumental reason: 1940–1945

It is not our intention to reify into static blocks these artificially differentiated stages of development, as if none of these stages were further developed within itself, and as if the caesuras, which we make for heuristic purposes, represented actual breaks in the theory's continuity. Rather, our procedure may be compared to the usual method of longitudinal studies, in which synchronistic cross sections are made at significant points in a process of development.

The First Phase: Materialism,
1930–1937

Historical and Political Experience

The Labor Movement

The Frankfurt Circle's assessment of the labor movement—up to the time of the Nazi seizure of power—is in part given in the conclusions to "Revolt of the Blue-Collar and White-Collar Workers," a study published in 1930–1931. Horkheimer had announced plans for this project in his inaugural address.[4] Because of the Circle's emigration and the attending circumstances, the evaluation of the study became so prolonged that it was still incomplete when *Studies on Authority and the Family* was published in Paris in 1936. The publication of the project's conclusions had been contemplated but never realized, apparently on account of differences between Erich Fromm, who directed the project's compilation, and the Institute's directorship. Only in May 1977 did preparations begin for publication of the results.[5]

The study dealt with the social-psychological structures of blue-collar and white-collar workers in the Weimar Republic. The original questions were organized into six categories (in addition to a social-statistical one): (a) political orientation, (b) general *Weltanschauung*, (c) personal taste, (d) specific character traits, (e) attitudes toward family and authority, and (f) use of leisure time. In the compilation available to me, these six categories had already been reduced to three: (a), (d), and (e).

The most significant result of the study was that only 15 percent of members of leftist political parties (the Social Democratic party of Germany, or SPD, and the Communist party of Germany, or KPD) displayed some degree of consistency in political orientation, character structure, and disposition toward active political engagement. These characteristics might have made militant resistance possible on the part of politically organized workers—against a fascist putsch attempt, for example. Forty percent of the politically organized workers who were studied displayed a much lower degree of consistency in the points mentioned. This led to the conclusion that the political influence of the leftist parties was significantly smaller than their numerical voter strength might suggest. Of those persons who displayed a higher degree of consistency, 27 percent were KPD members and 7 percent were SPD members. When further divided into active cadre members and inactive party voters, the data reveal a distinct decline in consistency. Character structure, antiauthoritarianism, and political orientation were highly consistent for the family and kin of KPD cadres, yet the same characteristics were found to be significantly lower for ordinary KPD *voters*, a large number of whom displayed authoritarian tendencies. This drop in consistency from cadre members to party voters was distinctly smaller for SPD members.

The portion of the completed study available to me suffered from a high degree of abstraction from the empirical, historical situation to which it referred. Only through a detailed historiographical commentary could the study be made significant.

Horkheimer's political reflections on the situation of the German working-class movement in *Dämmerung* [Twilight] may be read as this sort of commentary. It is a collection of aphoristic notes written between 1928 and 1934. In the section entitled "The Powerlessness of the German Working Class," Horkheimer gives a materialist interpretation of the labor movement's development in the Weimar Republic. His thesis is that the labor movement's split into KPD and SPD follows from changes in the relations of production:

There is today a gulf between those employed regularly and those employed irregularly or not at all—a chasm similar to the one between the entire working class and the lumpen-proletariat in earlier days. . . . Work and misery become separated and fall to the lot of two groups. . . . Yet, unlike the prewar proletariat, *these* unemployed, the most directly and urgently interested in revolution, do not possess the capacity for

education and organization, the class consciousness and the depend-
ability of those who as a rule were incorporated into a capitalistic
enterprise. . . . The capitalistic process of production thus realizes a
separation—of a worker's interest in socialism, from those human
qualities necessary to its realization. . . . (1974a:283)

Horkheimer criticizes the politics of the KPD and SPD on precisely
these grounds.

His central criticism of the KPD aims at the dogmatization of its
theoretical program:

The impatience of the unemployed is found, on an intellectual level,
only in the mere repetition of Communist party slogans. Because of
the sheer mass of theoretically treated material, the principles do not
assume a contemporary form but are understood undialectically. . . .
Faithfulness to materialist teachings threatens to become an insipid
and empty cult of words and persons. . . . The communists have far
too few reasons, that is, they often refer not to reasons but to simple
authority. Convinced that they possess the entire truth, they are not
too particular about individual truths, and bring their overwise opponent
to his senses with moralistic arguments and, if necessary, physical
violence. . . . (1974a:283, 285, 286)

This turned out to be the case: In the final phases of the Weimar
Republic, the KPD had its mass base in the unemployed.

The massive increase between 1928 and 1932 in the number of
votes received by the KPD paralleled the ever-growing unemployment.
The connection perceived by Horkheimer between the "mentality of
the unemployed" and the KPD's dogmatization of its political orientation
is disputed by some contemporary historians, including Sigmund Neumann,[6] at least as a causal connection. This dogmatization was indeed
caused not so much by the mentality of those unemployed, who
supported the KPD, as by a structural change within the KPD between
1924 and 1929. This phase of development has been characterized
by Hermann Weber as the KPD's "Stalinization."[7] With this concept
Weber characterizes the acceptance of the organizational principles of
the Soviet Communist party, that is, the creation of a rigid, centrally
organized, and dogmatically homogenized party apparatus. The so-
called Stalinization began in 1924 with the repression both of any kind
of internal party opposition and of all alternative theoretical orientations. This process is identical to the total coordination of the KPD's

central committee with the Soviet-dominated EKKI (*Exekutivkomitee der Komintern*, or Executive Committee of the Cominterm).[8]

Although Horkheimer was indeed closer to the KPD than to the SPD in the late Weimar Republic, he was certainly not a member of the KPD. Aside from the lack of any evidence to support this suggestion, and apart from his own energetic denial,[9] the very generality of his criticism of the KPD's dogmatizing process clearly indicates that he was not a party insider.[10]

To the critique of the KPD's political dogmatization cited above, Horkheimer adds this remark:

Political praxis is thus deprived of exploiting given opportunities of strenthening its political positions. . . . (1974a:283)

He is obviously alluding here to the KPD's revolutionary restraint during the world economic crisis, a restraint noted by several historians. Their interpretation of the KPD's restraint is controversial: Sigmund Neumann maintains that it was dictated by Moscow (1970:92–93), whereas Hermann Weber traces it to the weakness of the party's military defense troops (1969:343). When I asked Horkheimer in 1973 about the meaning of the sentence quoted, he explained that it was an allusion to the KPD's strictly anti–Social-Democratic politics, whose axiom about "social fascism" had hindered a popular front against fascism.

The form of theoretical orientation that was decisive for the Frankfurt Circle would have had no place in the KPD, particulary in the Weimar Republic. A differentiated, critical relationship to the culture of bourgeois science, a demanding examination of the tradition of materialist theory, and an unclosed dialectical approach were, if not in open conflict with the orientation of official party intellectuals, at least beyond their horizons. Thoroughly incompatible with the dogmatic propositions of the KPD line was Erich Fromm's conception, central to the Circle's theory, of an analytical and materialistic social psychology—that is, the attempt to provide a more nuanced theory of historical materialism through the introduction of psychoanalytic considerations. Although Fromm's ideas were developed in the context of criticizing similar ideas of Wilhelm Reich, the difference between the two falls within psychoanalytic theory itself. Hence the "papal edict" of the "Stalinized" KPD against attempts to integrate psychoanalysis and Marxism is directed at Erich Fromm's efforts as well, even though his views were less expounded than were those of Reich.[11]

The Soviet Union

An examination of the KPD's appeal to the socialist intelligentsia must also consider the intelligentsia's assessment of the situation in the Soviet Union. This is not an external criterion, since, in the late 1920s, recognition of the archetypal nature of the Soviet path to socialism was the central ideological criterion for membership in the KPD. Moreover, by 1926 the KPD was under the direct command of the Soviet-dominated Comintern and hence was only a section of the Comintern.

Surprisingly, the Soviet Union is not named explicitly in a single writing of the Circle—with the exception of Rudolf Schlesinger's thorough, if merely narrative, report entitled "New Soviet-Russian Social Research" (ZfS 7, 8). Yet more or less indirect references to political conditions in the Soviet Union form a central background element of the Circle's political-theoretical self-understanding throughout the period under examination. Horkheimer expressed this in 1931 with a directness that would later become unusual:

In the year 1930, the way a person views Russia tells much about the way he thinks. The situation there is quite difficult. I do not undertake to know where that country is going; without a doubt, there is great misery. Who among the educated does not have intimations of the great efforts now being made there, and unthinkingly places himself above it all—he who on this point evades the necessity of thinking—is a miserable comrade whose company is worthless. He who has eyes for the senseless injustice of the imperialist world—which cannot simply be explained away as technical powerlessness—will view the events in Russia as a continual, painful effort to overcome this frightful social injustice, or he will ask with beating heart whether this effort still endures.

In 1934 Horkheimer distanced himself from this skeptical solidarity by replacing it with a searching, theoretically deliberating stance:

There is such a thing as an enlightened, even revolutionary despotism. Its character is determined by its relationship to the true interests of those it dominates. Even if an unconditional standard does not exist, in light of which this relationship might be judged in various periods—

for the simple reason that despotic harshness and injustice are to be explained not solely in terms of the despotism itself but also with reference to the general degree of development of the masses it dominates—still its social function, its progressive or reactionary significance, is determined in most recent times by the extent to which its exercise corresponds to the interest in universality or to some privileged particularity. . . . (1934b:36)

Horkheimer confirmed in a conversation with me that this passage refers to the USSR. When asked, from the distance of more than forty years, about his estimation at that time of conditions in the Soviet Union, he responded by further relativizing the skeptically distanced sympathy that is unmistakable in the quotations above. The Soviet Union was not publicly criticized by Institute members at the time, said Horkheimer, because they considered it, on an ideological level, the most powerful opponent to fascism. It is significant that this restraint was abandoned in 1939, after the Stalin–Hitler pact.

Friedrich Pollock's purely analytical stance toward the USSR's attempts to organize a planned economy would also have been incompatible with membership in the KPD. He considered these attempts to be so marked by peculiarly Russian conditions that nothing could be learned from them that might be applied to overthrowing capitalist relations in Western Europe.[12]

Pollock was the Frankfurt Circle's general authority for information on which they based their mostly implicit judgments of Soviet politics. In preparation for his *Habilitationsschrift*, published in 1929 as *The Experiment in Planned Economy in the Soviet Union, 1917–1927*, Pollock traveled extensively in the Soviet Union in 1927. His most important contact in Moscow was Riazanov, director of the Marx-Engels Institute. Letters Pollock wrote to Horkheimer reveal that Riazanov introduced Pollock to several members of the internal Bolshevik opposition who were later liquidated in the purges. (Riazanov was himself banished by Stalin.) Pollock's reserve toward the government of the USSR is understandable in light of this information, and his attitude is evident in the dispassionate presentation of his information. Absent are all paeans to the achievements of Soviet socialism typical of pro-Bolshevik literature. Instead, central aspects of Soviet economic planning are uncompromisingly criticized. For example, Pollock criticizes forced industrialization (1929:366), and with regard to the kulak problem he conjectures that even such a radical government as Stalin's could not risk using, against the farmers, the formal state power of disposition over land (1929:374). That Stalin did in fact take this risk is known, and one can easily imagine how Pollock must have judged this solution to the problem. He closes his book on a sober note:

> In the course of this work we have become acquainted with the theoretical and practical starting point of the Soviet Union's attempts in planned economy.... Where they will lead, only history can tell. (1929:382)

Again, such dispassionately formulated judgments of political conditions in the USSR—which, according to Horkheimer,[13] were decisive for the Frankfurt Circle of the early 1930s—would hardly have been reconcilable with membership in the KPD.

Yet for all the critical distance from the KPD's politics, a critical solidarity with the "revolutionary wing of the working-class movement" was decisive for the Circle's political orientation. This solidarity was the result, not of a positive assessment, despite all reservations, of the KPD's actual policies, but rather of principled considerations about the socialist intelligentsia's political role. In *Dämmerung* Horkheimer wrote, in 1932:

> The shortcomings of the revolutionary leadership may indeed be quite unfortunate. The political struggle against the inhumanity of contemporary conditions is—however poorly led—nonetheless the form assumed in this historical moment by the will to a better social order, and is understood as such by many of the oppressed and tormented in the whole world. Each and every shortcoming of the leaders thus negates the fact that they form the head of the struggle. Anyone who, in immediate alliance with an actively engaged party, can under certain circumstances influence its course, whose unity with a party in theory and praxis is beyond question, may be capable of fruitful if external criticism of the party's leadership.
>
> But a proletarian party cannot allow itself to be made the object of a contemplative critique, for each of its errors is a product of the circumstance that it cannot be protected from such critique by the effective participation of better powers. Whether the contemplative critic might have strengthened these powers through his own active work in the party cannot be gauged by his remarks on party activities after the fact, for it remains unclear whether his opinion was helpful to the masses in a given situation, whether his theoretical superiority was combined with necessary organizational skills—in short, whether

or not his politics were at all realizable. An easy objection would be that the leaders controlled all of the party's means of power, that the party apparatus did not allow the individual any responsibility, and that it therefore deprived rational persons of all prospects for success from the very beginning. As if a political will were not in every historical moment met by sufficient barriers to its realization! Today such barriers pile up precisely before the intellectuals; yet who else but those who *practically* overcome difficulties can demonstrate that such barriers, in due consideration of all given conditions, are not indeed the least of the difficulties? Bourgeois criticism of the proletarian struggle is a logical impossibility. (1974a:257)

Horkheimer's criticism of the Weimar Republic SPD is disproportionately sharper than his criticism of the KPD:

In contrast to communism, the reformist wing of the working-class movement has forgotten that it is impossible to improve human conditions substantially within capitalism. It has lost all elements of theory, and its leadership is an exact image of those members who are the most secure: Many seek, with all available means and even at the expense of the simplest loyalty, to maintain their party positions; the fear of losing their position gradually becomes the sole explanation for their actions. (1974a:294)

The passage quoted makes three implicit charges. First, the formulations "reformist wing" and "forgotten . . . within capitalism" both allude to the fact that, while the SPD captured the role of state-sustaining political party in the Weimar Republic, it did not once use this power to start doing away with the private enterprise system. The justification for this charge, often made by leftist critics of social democracy in the Weimar Republic, is still controversial for historical interpretation. Even those historians who concede a revolutionary will to Weimar's Social Democratic government find it significant that key positions in the executive apparatus were filled with royalist, reactionary elements.[14]

The second charge is that Weimar's Social Democratic government "lost all elements of theory." We cannot here sufficiently treat the shortcomings of the theoretical portions of the Social Democratic party program, from that of Erfurt in 1891 to that of Heidelberg in 1925. But Horkheimer's charge of theoretical deficiency is a harsh blow simply because, from Erfurt to Heidelberg, the SPD dissociated any radical theoretical orientation from its daily political affairs. This paradoxical juxtaposition of theoretical radicalism and pragmatic opportunism found *philological* expression in all party programs, in the separation of its statement of principles from its program of action.[15] It was expressed *sociologically* in the marginalization of theoreticians within the party itself.

Horkheimer's third accusation, that "many [party members] seek, with all available means . . . to maintain their party positions," was well founded. Sigmund Neumann speaks of a "strikingly modest fluctuation of party membership" (1970:34). The bureaucratization of the Social Democratic party apparatus and institutionalization of party favoritism "now and then revealed caricatures of the worst Wilhelminian times."

In the first years following the National Socialist seizure of power, the publications of the Frankfurt Circle no longer mentioned the Weimar Social Democratic government by name. In conversation, Horkheimer attributed this to an awareness of their mutual fate in defeat. This reserve toward the SPD was entirely abandoned by 1936, when it finally became evident, after three years of consolidation of fascist rule, that the Weimar Republic had become a historical phenomenon. Yet the intense and frequent criticism in the *Zeitschrift für Sozialforschung*, by 1936, of Social Democratic tenets—and particularly of Social Democratic cultural politics—was, according to Horkheimer, entirely representative of the Circle's position in the years during which the Social Democrats were responsible for the Weimar state.

The Circle's criticism of the SPD's theoretical and political orientation aimed above all at its cultural politics. Marcuse, for example, took SPD *Kulturpolitik* to be a striking instance of what he terms a culture's "affirmative" character. The demands of the Görlitzer Program of 1921 for an egalitarian distribution of *cultural* as well as material goods, the "holding of cultural property in common," or the "right of all countrymen to cultural goods" (1937a:91; 1968:132), served, according to Marcuse, only to win over the "masses once again for the social order" that is affirmed by the "entire" culture. Walter Benjamin argues in a similar vein in a critique of SPD workers' education programs. The orientation of these programs toward the standard of bourgeois culture

implied that the same knowledge that secured the bourgeoisie's domination of the proletariat would also enable the proletariat to liberate itself from this domination. But in reality a form of knowledge with no access to praxis, and unable to teach the proletariat as a class anything about its situation, was of no danger to its oppressors. (1937:352; 1978:246)

And Horkheimer, correspondingly:

The history of German social democracy should serve to warn against a love for culture. In place of a critical attitude toward the dominant culture—which alone might have provided the chance for future preservation of its elements—could be seen the repeated endeavor to flaunt yesterday's bourgeois wisdom as a showpiece, much as peasants mimic the bygone fashion of their masters. (1938b:380)

Fascism

The Institute first began the project of planned studies of National Socialist fascism in a comprehensive and systematically coordinated fashion at the beginning of the 1940s. In the period under discussion here (1933 to 1937), there were at most a fundamental theoretical assessment and several disparate research programs. The existential reality of fascist Germany was surely too close for these emigrants to be able to define it systematically as an object of inquiry. But aside from these philosophical conjectures, the Institute's own evaluation of national socialism was itself an obstacle to its formulation as an object of inquiry. To put it in a formula, national socialism was understood as the political form corresponding to advanced monopoly capitalism. The group around Horkheimer by no means perceived the National Socialists' seizure of power as the historical caesura it appeared to be from the perspective of 1945, especially in bourgeois historiography. This theoretical estimation also determined the temporal horizon of the Circle's perception: They saw only a continuous historical context. In their eyes, the final years of the Weimar Republic and the first years of the Third Reich formed a continuum.[16] On the one hand, this chronology, laden with theoretical premises, was the basis for the enduring topicality of conditions in the Weimar Republic until late into the Frankfurt Circle's emigration period. On the other hand, it hindered formulation of the phenomenon of fascism as a clearly defined object of research. The "theory of the historical process" envisaged by Horkheimer in 1932 was not differentiated from the Circle's theory of fascism in the period under discussion.

The Frankfurt Circle's analysis of fascism in this period can be divided into three thematic forms: (1) a political-economic analysis formulated by Pollock; (2) complementary to this analysis, Marcuse's critiques of ideology and culture as well as Horkheimer's culture-critical study of the early history of the cult of the führer; and (3) a social-psychological analysis by Erich Fromm in *Studies on Authority and the Family* (which, in comparison with studies of authority in the 1940s, remained quite fragmentary). In the following, we will confine ourselves to analyses of Pollock and Marcuse, since both arrive from disparate points at essentially the same conclusion, which subsequently achieved consensus within the Circle. All later Institute studies of fascism begin with this thesis.

In his essay "Remarks on the Economic Crisis," conceived at the end of 1932 and written in the early part of 1933, Pollock advocated the thesis that the structural cause (in addition to other, contingent factors) of the world economic crisis lay in the monopolistic structure of late capitalism, and more recisely in the incongruity between the liberal organization of relations of production and the de facto liquidation of the market. In Pollock's eyes, the alternative is clear. The "partial organization" already practiced in the monopolies should be repeated by comprehensive planning on the part of the state. For Pollock, it is decisive that this economic planning need not necessarily be socialist. The organization of society on the basis of a planned economy is possible within a capitalist system:

To begin with, such an organization would imply that the most powerful capitalist groups, which dominate the state, dictate to all other groups the conditions of their economic activity. . . . This organization presupposes an understanding among the most powerful groups, to the benefit of a capitalistic common interest, on a politics of planned economy. . . . (1933:348)

After reviewing the objections one might expect to this capitalism-immanent economic planning, Pollock remarks:

But should the difficulties in the capitalist system continue to worsen, then these obstacles, too, will probably be overcome, in the interest of saving the system—even if it takes terrible struggles to accomplish this. Such a reorganization of economic methods would necessarily be accompanied by a complete transformation of society's political organization. Events of the past few years have demonstrated the nature of those political forms corresponding to monopoly capitalism. (1933:349)

What exactly those "events" were, to which Pollock alludes, is apparent: von Papen was chancellor as of May 1932. His pro–National Socialist acts are well known; we need here only mention his lifting of Brüning's decree prohibiting the SA. There followed the transitional cabinet of Schleicher, and in January 1933 Hitler became chancellor. In February followed the Decree for the Protection of the People and State (*Verordnung zum Schutz von Volk und Staat*, also called the *Reichstagsbrandverordnung*, or Decree in Response to the Arson at the Reichstag), which suspended all constitutional rights. Finally in March came the "empowering law" (*Ermächtigungsgesetz*), which abolished the division of power by extending legislative functions to the cabinet.

Pollock interprets these events as symptomatic of a process in which society was politically "disciplined." The need for this, according to Pollock, resulted from the "contradiction" between the monopolistic structure of productive relations, on the one hand, and the political form of society, on the other. Fascism, and in this context particularly German national socialism, is then the political form corresponding to highly developed monopoly capitalism.

Marcuse gave a critique of ideology corresponding to this political-economic interpretation of national socialism. His essay, "The Struggle against Liberalism in the Totalitarian View of the State" (1934), thematizes the ideological-political *Weltanschauung* of German fascism. In his view, the fascist critique of liberalism essentially was restricted to a critique of the liberal "superstructure," that is, the cultural self-interpretation of liberalism. Fascism understood itself as an alternative to this cultural self-portrait. The idolization of man went against the bourgeois insistence on freedom for the individual; collective universalism went against the atomism of bourgeois social doctrine; and the irrationalism of folk traditions went against the rationalism of early bourgeois society. According to one of Goebbels's most suggestive propaganda sayings, national socialism "annuls 1789." Marcuse's thesis is that the National Socialists, for all their criticism of liberalism, not only respected the actual social and economic premises of liberalism, but indeed guaranteed and strengthened them:

But supplanting the real content of liberalism with a *Weltanschauung* is in itself decisive in what it conceals and leaves unsaid. The concealment points to the true battlefront: It avoids the economic and social structure of liberalism. (1934:165; 1968:10)

Marcuse maintains that liberalism can be essentially defined as the private ownership of the means of production. We know today, from historiography, that Hitler, from his early "struggles" up to the Röhm affair, sharply attacked trends within the NSDAP (National Socialist German Workers' Party) that sought to extend criticism of liberalism to economic and social spheres. Even non-Marxist historians agree that in the early 1930s Hitler considered no inner-party sacrifice too great to maintain the interest and support of big capital.[17] With this in mind, Marcuse joins with Pollock's thesis:

The turn from the liberal to the totally authoritarian state occurs on the basis of one and the same economic order. With regard to the unity of this economic base, we can say that it is liberalism that "produces" out of itself the total-authoritarian state—as its own consummation at a more advanced stage of development. The total-authoritarian state brings with it the organization corresponding to the monopolistic stage of capitalism. (1934:174ff.; 1968:19)

Theory of the Theory-Praxis Relation

The Subject and Addressee of the Theory

The intellectual vanguard of the labor movement assumed that the theory it produces, while not immediately identified with proletarian class consciousness, is nonetheless mediated by identifiable links to it. This assumption was essential for its political identity. According to this assumption, theory is mediated by a continuum that can be established by connecting agitation with worker education—by means of a general theory derived from the worker's typical everyday experiences. By its own claims, socialist theory has its basis, point of reference, empirical source, and legitimation in the world of those experiences. Only insofar as the education of workers by intellectuals results in their own enlightenment is such education more than mere dogmatic indoctrination; and only insofar as theory is communicable, and is indeed communicated to the worker's actual consciousness, does theory have a political—more precisely, socialist—identity. Yet proletarian class consciousness is not identical with the diverse orientations actually found within the proletariat. According to the socialist intelligentsia, proletarian class consciousness is more of a transcendental phenomenon. It is a possibility of knowledge that intellectuals ascribe to the proletariat, and through which the subjectivity of the proletariat is raised to consciousness of its objective class position. Despite this transcendental conception of class consciousness, the mediating connection to empirical class consciousness—even if not always historically synchronic—must not be broken. Otherwise the socialist intellectual would no longer have a criterion by which to determine whether his political-theoretical work is simply indoctrination, academic theory, or in fact a moment of proletarian self-enlightenment. Reference to the "proper class standpoint" is, for this reason, always the ultimate "legal argument," the last "court of appeal" in the theoretical-political disputes of the socialist intelligentsia.

This ascription of a continuum—that is, of a mediated identity between proletarian class consciousness and socialist theory—unites even such divergent positions as those of Rosa Luxemburg and Lenin. Whether the self-enlightenment of the masses is possible only if theory is "imported" into the masses, or whether the construction of socialist theory must always take as its point of departure that class consciousness which is present before all theory, such a continuum is always imputed, in any case, even if there is disagreement about the extent to which the continuum mediates proletarian class consciousness and socialist theory.

George Lukács formulated this conception in *History and Class Consciousness* (1932). Although this idea was traditionally held by the socialist intelligentsia, Lukács expressed it with a metaphysical hyperbole that repulsed even those who otherwise shared his view. In a neo-Hegelian manner, he maintains a speculative identity between a transcendentally conceived class consciousness and Marxist social theory. According to Lukács, from the class standpoint of the proletariat, historically produced through the development of the forces of production, a perspective is established that makes transparent capitalist society as a totality. Only with the development of a commodity economy does bourgeois society become totalizing. Bourgeois scientists such as Adam Smith could potentially understand this society in theory. But only for the proletariat do conditions for emancipation coincide with theoretically recognized conditions for the overthrow of capitalist society. This coincidence of social theory and a (proletarian) practical, political orientation—of the subject of knowledge with the object of knowledge—establishes for Lukács the immediate unity of proletarian theory and praxis. In the proletariat are both subject *and* addressee of the theory; they are in fact identical.

For all the criticisms (including those of its own author), this rather pointed, speculative identity of class consciousness and social theory formed the self-consciousness of those socialist intellectuals who were not integrated into the SPD or the KPD in the 1920s. This must be borne in mind when analyzing the political influences on the Frankfurt Circle's theoretical development. In 1929 Horkheimer clearly stood in the tradition of this thesis when he wrote, in his then characteristically expressionistic language:

[It is] not today's legislator, but rather those groups that themselves experience need as a consequence of their social status . . . [who] are naturally invested with knowledge of the root of the problem. . . . (1930a:90)

In his later texts (those written between 1932 and 1936), Horkheimer shifts this viewpoint. The proletariat's qualification as a carrier of historical truth is not for Horkheimer, as it was for Lukács, the result of giving metaphysical status to the proletariat's social situation. He views the proletariat's aptitude as a carrier or subject of historical truth solely in terms of social psychology:

This portion of mankind, which because of its (social) circumstances must necessarily confront this change . . . already possesses powers and attracts even more. . . . This portion is psychologically prepared as well, since its role in the process of production prohibits it from the hope of fruitless accumulation of wealth. . . . In any case, mankind's collective efforts, guided by knowledge, contain . . . great disinterest for individual existence . . . and scant interest in possession and property. (1933b:190, 191)

This psychologizing of class-consciousness theory—which distances itself strikingly from the subsequent history of Lukács's thesis—is expressed in the Circle's subsequent research. One example is Fromm's cautiously maintained thesis that the proletariat is the potential carrier of the matriarchal principle (1934:225; 1970:108). The study of blue-collar and white-collar workers, already mentioned in *Studies on Authority and the Family*, is based on the following correlation of character with party membership: "authoritarian" = DNVP; "revolutionary" = KPD; "ambivalent" = SPD (Fromm 1936:256).

Lukács's thesis was thus made less metaphysical. This led not only to a modification of the class-consciousness theory in the form of the psychologization described above, but also, as the theory was modified, to a limitation of its sphere of application, particularly as it took into account the historical situation of the German workers' movement in the final period of the Weimar Republic. The above-mentioned revolt, begun in 1930, indicated that only 15 percent of the German workers could be classified as "revolutionary." In his estimation of the ability of the labor movement to resist fascism, Pollock wrote:

As we know from experience, this ability to resist has been overestimated in the past. The revolutionary advances in arms technology and the stupendous refinement in psychological methods to control the masses suggest for the immediate future that resistance would develop only as a result of the greatest disasters. (1933:350)

Marcuse wrote in 1934:

The fate of the labor movement is clouded with uncertainty. (1934:194; 1968:42)

The crucial experience of the defeat of the labor movement in the last years of the Weimar Republic, along with criticism of the SPD's and KPD's respective theoretical orientations, led to a thesis significant for the Circle's political and theoretical biography, and one that broke radically with the socialist intelligentsia's traditional self-understanding. According to this thesis, a social theory adequate to the proletariat's historical and political circumstances is no longer in any way connected to the proletariat's political consciousness through a mediating factor. This uncoupling of Marxist socialist theory from proletarian class consciousness (taken to ever-greater lengths in the years between 1936 and 1939) would appear, on a literary level, to oppose Lukács; on a historical and empirical level, it would appear to oppose the grotesque denial of reality by those who, even as late as summer 1933, when the leading functionaries of the German labor movement were already behind bars, still conjured up the myth of proletarian class consciousness.

The thesis of a discontinuity between social theory and class consciousness made necessary a reexamination, within the tradition of socialist theory, of the extent to which "materialist thought is relevant to efforts to create a better society" (Horkheimer). According to the Frankfurt Circle, the connection between materialist thought and the proletariat can no longer be based on the a priori assumption that theory has its real origin in the proletariat's class consciousness. For Horkheimer, this means that the Circle is related to the proletariat solely on the basis of a moral decision made by the social bearers of the theory, even further relativized by a skeptical attitude. Horkheimer remarks on the ethos of the "materialist fighter":

. . . he would prefer to risk his life rather than accommodate himself to the existing social reality and to a career within it, not because of an external command or an inner voice full of promises, but simply on account of his wish and his desire, which will themselves one day disappear. In one manner of speaking, this context bespeaks skepticism and nihilism. (1935b:8)

The Circle's theory continues to be addressed to the proletariat not only by force of moral decision but also by orientation toward the proletariat's imputed "objective interests." Horkheimer repeatedly maintained in the early 1930s that the relevance of theory lies essentially in its connection to generalizable interests of "struggling social groups":

The value of a theory is decided by its relation to the tasks taken up at a certain point in history by society's most progressive forces. It is not immediately valuable for all humanity but in the first instance only for that group interested in these tasks. (1934b:26)

Alluding to the disintegration of intelligentsia and proletariat, of theory and class consciousness, he continues:

The fact that, in many cases, theory has completely distanced itself from the struggling masses is one reason among others for their suspicion toward the intellectuals. If this estrangement has its origin, not in untutored consciousness, but solely in the convincing demonstration that all connection to the decisive questions of the moment has been lost, then the charge against the apparently unconditioned intelligentsia . . . is correct. It is correct insofar as thought, lacking all connection, implies not freedom of judgment but the insufficient control of thought with respect to its motives. (1934b:26f.)

This assessment of the relation between political and theoretical orientation—programmatically formulated by Horkheimer in every essay of this period—was binding for the Circle. Leo Löwenthal, for example, qualified the concept of "theoretically informed consciousness":

Where criticism of existing social relations and a proposal for better ones are undertaken without the theoretically informed consciousness that the struggle, as well as the goal, is bound up with the historical interests of suffering groups. . . . (1936:354)

Marcuse also defines the Circle's theory as "aligning itself with progressive forces" (1936a:28; 1968:76).

Theory and Praxis

Thus, according to Horkheimer, one cannot and should not presume under contemporary historical conditions that a consciousness, theoretically adequate to the situation of socially disadvantaged groups, will indeed be present in such groups. With no empirical basis, Horkheimer assumes a "process of estrangement" between a theory adequate to this situation, on the one hand, and the existing theoretical orientations of the political representatives of the labor movement, on the other. On the basis of his assessment of the Weimar Republic's socialist parties, Horkheimer apparently suspects that in political struggles—whether because of dogmatic goals of integration (KPD) or pragmatism in everyday politics (SPD)—an optimal theory will either be abandoned as a goal or be subordinated to mass agitation and party integration. Horkheimr proposes the opposite thesis (constitutive for his Circle): Under the present historical conditions, successful political struggle requires orientation according to the best available social theory:

The demand to remain at the highest level of knowledge possible at any given time is, for progressive social groups, not rationalism, but rather a compelling conclusion drawn from their social situation. (1934b:46)

Under the prevailing social organization, humanity has neither voice nor consciousness—except possibly in the form of theory. (1933b:173)

If materialist thought proves to be a psychological aid precisely in such times as these, then only . . . because many emotional fetters in which people today suffer are sundered when the appropriate word is heard—and also because this word can to a great extent overcome the present massive isolation of people from each other. This is the power of truth. . . . (1934b:50f.)

To be consistent, Horkheimer can attribute revolutionary potency only to those social groups whose theoretical orientation has become the primary factor determining their actions. In the context of a social-psychological argument in which he deplores the intellectual and political indolence of "persons of a particular social stratum," he maintains:

. . . sudden world-historical transformations are often actively brought about by groups in which established psychic makeup does not play a role, as much as that knowledge has become a vital force. (1936a:21; 1972b:67)

These strong statements give the mistaken impression that Horkheimer considers theory itself a form of political praxis. He does indeed suggest a different emphasis among the various factors (mentioned above) in political struggle—toward a more theoretical, scientific orientation. This means that he opts for a relative separation of theory from praxis, of theory's scientific development from the practical, political struggle.

. . . as much as theory and praxis are linked to history, there is no preestablished harmony between them. (1935b:343–344; 1978:427)

In this sense, a differentiation of theory from praxis means that the "truth" of a revolutionary theory cannot be identified with its "scientific correctness." A political theory is "true" in the achievement of its revolutionary realization in given historical situations, whereas the objective conditions giving rise to a revolution may be determined by scientific criteria of "correctness." If one obliterates this distinction by a precipitate identification of theory and praxis—as does Lukács, for example—then the historical success of the labor movement becomes the sole criterion for the theory's verification. If success is never achieved, then the theory is refuted—or else the reality that falsified the theory must be dogmatically denied.

The firmness with which Horkheimer always advocates the criterion not only of historical success but also of scientific "correctness" is understandable only against the historical background of the demise of the German labor movement. This demise was evident by 1935.[18]

In such a process of verification, those individuals or groups struggling for more rational conditions might succumb completely and human society develop retrogressively, a conceivable possibility that any view of history that has not degenerated into fatalism must take into account. This would refute the trust in the future. . . . The direction and content of activity, along with its success, are more closely related to their theory for the historically progressive groups than is the case with representatives of naked power (their talk functions only as a mechanical aid to their rise to power and is revealed in the language of open violence). . . . But the knowledge of those who have struggled in vain, insofar as it reflects the structure of the present epoch and the possibility of a better one, is not dishonored because humanity succumbs to bombs and poison gas. . . . Truth is a moment of correct practice, but whoever identifies it directly with success passes by history. (1935b:345; 1978:428–429)

Horkheimer's main thesis, then, is that in the prevailing historical conditions, a consciousness equal to the situation of "historically progressive" forces is no longer present as class consciousness, but only as scientifically developed theory. This should not be misunderstood as idealist. In this period Horkheimer always emphasized the historical and social relativity of science, just as he stressed that theory can play a historically powerful role only in common struggle with social groups, interests, and tasks:

The bridges to the future will not be built by individuals but through organized mutual effort . . . in which the will to humanity fuses with an explicit and highly developed theory of society. (1935b:16)

Nor should this alliance of "social theory" and "organized mutual effort"—maintained during the Circle's "materialist" phase—be misunderstood as being instrumental, as if the bearers of the theory would act as a kind of scientific advisory board for political matters for the proletariat. Rather, Horkheimer postulates that the political and practical qualification of a theory must lie within the theory itself. This program appears in negative form in the Circle's methodology, as the critique of ideology. The tradition of ideology critique in general, and in particular Horkheimer's emphasis on it, proceeds from the conviction that the ideological content of political statements is embodied not only externally, in the scholar's partiality, but also internally, in the cognitive structures of scientific propositions themselves,

... in its lack of clarity, its perplexity, its obscure language, its manner of posing problems, its methods, the direction of its research, and above all what it closes its eyes to. (1932a:6; 1972:8)

The unmediated duality of a *Lebensphilosophie* style of metaphysics and narrow-minded, specialized science typified the scientific scene in the Weimar Republic. This represented to Horkheimer a scientific institution whose very structure was so pathological as to be incapable of grasping developmental tendencies within society as a whole—and was thus unable to serve social needs. He considered this pathological form of science the source of prefascist hostility toward intellectuals and of the depoliticization and fascist turn of the scientific intelligentsia in the last years of the Weimar Republic. To put it positively, when Horkheimer speaks of social theory or of materialist science, he does not mean the state of philological research on texts by Marx and Engels reached by 1933. He means, rather, the program to unify philosophy and science—a program within the tradition of Hegel and Marx. This is a project for an interdisciplinary, "materialist" super-science that can integrate the theoretical with the empirical. Contrary to bourgeois, specialized science, and in opposition to the socialist scientism of Kautsky and Stalin, this projected science would function at such a high level of theory, method, and research that its distance from social praxis would be made obsolete by its own immanent standards.

Theoretical Position

Self-Understanding within the Tradition of Historical and
Political Theory

Horkheimer and his co-workers[19] characterized the Circle's political-theoretical orientation as materialist. This self-description never appears as an explicit appellation. But the materialism of the Circle's theoretical work appears implicitly in a specific interpretation of the history of philosophical materialism, in the Circle's declared affinity with a very selectively interpreted tradition of Marxism, and in the materialist postulate of the unity of philosophy and science.

Like those of many pre-Marxist materialists, Feuerbach's theory was constitutively situated in the context of enlightenment, social criticism, and politics. Horkheimer projects into the entire history of old European materialism a link between such materialist positions and the corresponding political conflicts. Accordingly, the atomism of Democritus, the "materialistically" interpreted Aristotelianism of Averroes, and the technical utopias of the Renaissance or of bourgeois mechanistic materialism are appropriate theories for their respective eras, just as Marx's critique of political economy represents an adequate theory of nineteenth- and twentieth-century capitalism.[20]

This perspective implies a historical relativization of Marxist social theory, though (until 1937) Horkheimer and Marcuse did not take this into account, either as an explicit interpretation of Marx or in a revised historiography of materialism. Marcuse, however, did say in a private conversation (San Diego, December 1975) that the Institute in the early 1930s had a project to write a history of materialism.

In Horkheimer's interpretation of this history, the objects of materialist theory vary; they derive in each case from a particular social conflict. The enlightening and critical function of this theory has, however, an almost suprahistorical meaning. Horkheimer is therefore wholly consistent when he submits his Circle's theoretical orientation to the law of historical relativity:

The theory that we regard as correct may one day disappear because the practical and scientific interests that played a role in the formation of its concepts, and above all the facts and circumstances to which it referred, have disappeared. (1935b:337; 1978:421–422)

This relativist position—which refers to the *objects* of materialist theory and not to their social function—is directed explicitly against Hegel and, one may assume, implicitly against certain aspects of Lukács's Hegelianized reappropriation of the Marxist theory of class consciousness. Characteristic of Hegelianism—with its logic of identity—is the fundamental assumption that true knowledge can only be the result of a supersubject's self-knowledge, regardless of whether this supersubject is conceived as World Spirit or as a class-conscious proletariat. The Circle's materialism is directed against this idealist identity of subject and object, and identity that produces itself within a process. To Horkheimer's program belongs a conception of human thought as the empirically situated thought of individuals. Even the collective, everyday experiences of individuals in political struggle cannot, according to this program, be hypostatized into a class consciousness separable from these experiences. This nonidentity of thought and being, of subject and object, cannot ultimately be eliminated but only lessened, by means of science, and only in terms of particular epochs. This nonidentity defines the epistemological position of materialism:

In the knowledge of the irreducible tension between concept and object, materialism . . . possesses a critical weapon to ward off the belief in the infinity of the mind. This tension is not everywhere the same in intensity. Science is the distillation of efforts to overcome this tension in various ways. . . . (1933a:17; 1972:28)

To this fundamental, epistemological assumption corresponds the historical-philosophical assumption of the nonidentity of subject and object in the historical process. This second assumption in turn forms a critical foil to Hegel's historical-philosophical principle: to grant ontological reality to individual historical facts only insofar as they are moments of the historical totality imputed to them. Here, Horkheimer criticizes the form of knowledge that is supposed to create a totality within the historical process and to give this totality an immanent teleology. According to "materialism," to the contrary, there exist no prognostic instruments derivable from some absolute knowledge:

Materialist theory . . . is not a metaphysics of history but a picture of the world that changes and develops in the context of practical efforts to improve it. (1933a:192)

Accordingly, even historical prognoses cannot be made without considering the resources of political power at any given moment. Equally unallowable is the historical fixation of the most progressive, contemporary theoretical orientation and the consideration of preceding epochs as, at best, windows on the Absolute.[21] This fundamental, historical-philosophical assumption of the nonidentity of subject and object in history is directed against all attempts—by Lukács as well as by bourgeois philosophy of the 1920s—to impute a subject to the historical process. Such attempts, which hypothesize such collective identities as Spirit, folk, or race, glorify this subject, falsely generalize particular interests, and historically rectify ex post facto contingent political decisions.

Relation to Marxism

According to Horkheimer, epistemological relativism does not follow from the nonexistence of criteria for the truth of scientific judgments. These criteria would hold true for successive social formations. Nor does epistemological relativism follow from the impossibility of conceiving of such epoch-specific standards in a Hegelian manner: as stages in the self-reflection of a supersubject:

All theories are not equally true; only that theory is true which can grasp the historical process so deeply that it is possible to develop from it the closest approximation to the structure and tendency of social life in the various spheres of culture. . . . (1935b:339; 1978:434)

The Circle's Marxist orientation is characterized by a theory—designed to grasp the structure of given historical epochs—whose potential insights lie neither in a "free-floating intelligentsia" nor, à la Lukács, in a proletariat in whose class standpoint social theory is semiotically concentrated. Rather, these potential insights are held by a group of scientists,[22] at first anonymous, whose theoretical research has as its organizing principle the proletariat's objective interests:

Because the solution to crucial problems depends, particularly at the present moment, upon the outcome of the struggles between social groups, the significance of a theory lies, above all, in the extent to which its principle of construction is determined by the goals of such a group. (1943b:26)

That form of materialism most adequate to the historical situation is the "economic theory of society":

Materialism is characterized by its content: the economic theory of society. (1933a:33; 1972:45)

When the Circle's texts up to 1936–1937 speak of an "economic theory of society," they do not allude to the theory of *Das Kapital* or of other critical economic writings—which presume to have answered all the questions—and certainly not the history of their dogmatic influence in the Second and Third internationals. What is meant, rather, is the reformulation of Marxist theory under the historically changed conditions of capitalism and the labor movement—a reformulation that the texts do not themselves realize but only suggest as being realizable.

During its materialist period, the Circle's most palpable revision of orthodox Marxism was its reconceptualization of the relation of base and superstructure; the Circle integrated psychoanalytic models of explanation into historical materialism. In "History and Psychology," Horkheimer criticizes the crudeness of the base-superstructure theory. The thesis of the ontological primacy of the economic base and the complete dependency of the superstructure must be refined by means of social psychology:

To the extent that we do not know how structural changes in economic life transform all aspects of an individual's life—by means of the given psychological disposition of individuals from the various social groups— the doctrine of the dependence of an individual life on economic life contains elements that strongly prejudice their hypothetical value for explaining the present. (1932b:134)

Erich Fromm developed in outline this program for a materialist social psychology in "On the Method and Function of an Analytical Social Psychology" (1932). The essay was, like corresponding passages in *Studies on Authority and the Family*, only programmatic in nature. Horkheimer's definitions of materialist dialectics form the other, less apparent revision (or better said, refinement) of the Marxist theoretical tradition.[23] These unsystematically developed definitions of dialectics— scattered throughout practically all the essays of the Circle's materialist period—encouraged a tendency already present in Lukács's work: greater emphasis on the operative and methodological aspects of dialectics.[24]

Relation of Philosophy to Science

In his inaugural address as director of the Frankfurt Institute for Social Research in 1931, Horkheimer criticized contemporary social research for its juxtaposition of two unconnected spheres: speculation unconcerned with questions of feasibility and overly specialized, scientific work. He maintained in other writings that the state of German social research was only a particular instance of the prevailing dissociation of philosophy and the specialized sciences. He considered philosophy's tendency to discredit knowledge drawn from the specialized sciences and neopositivism's reification of physical science to be complementary expressions of the pathology of contemporary science.[25]

The materialist position of Horkheimer's group was inaugurated in the following oppositional program:

Materialism requires the unification of philosophy and science. Of course, it recognizes technical differences between the more general research of philosophy and the more specialized research in the sciences, just as it recognizes differences in method between research and presentation but not between science and philosophy as such. (1933a:23; 1972:34)

This postulate is expressed in the research plans Horkheimer formulated in his inaugural address:

What matters today . . . is to organize investigations on the basis of current philosophical problems that unite philosophers, sociologists, economists, historians, and psychologists in an ongoing research community that can do together what in other disciplines one individual alone does in the laboratory, what genuine scientists have always done: pursue those questions aimed at the view of the whole, using the most refined scientific methods; reformulate the questions in the course of work as demanded by the object; make more precise and develop new methods without losing sight of general considerations. (1972c:40)

After Horkheimer assumed the directorship, the Frankfurt Institute's global program became one of interdisciplinary social research, in which philosophy was to assume the role of a problem-sensitive, integrative medium for the specialized sciences, which were splintered into various disciplines. The program resulted from a dialectical critique of the relation between the sciences and philosophy, a critique based on Hegel's *Philosophy of History* and Marx's *Kapital*. A dialectical critique of the sciences requires, first of all, that its claims be limited; according to Horkheimer, the analyses of the sciences are not yet knowledge but serve only to splinter the social objects of research according to the limits of each particular discipline. The essence of the "dialectical method" consists in crossing the boundaries between specialized scientific analyses. Although this method begins with the analytical and statistical data provided by the specialized sciences, it subsequently organizes them through a procedure that Marx called presentation— in distinction to the "research" carried on by the sciences. This procedure makes possible the reconstruction of the social object in its "concrete" historical process.[26]

Utopia

The Frankfurt Circle's concept of utopia in the 1930s is entirely within the tradition of the "concrete utopia." Here, *utopia* is not understood as a fantasy of ideal political conditions quite beyond real society, as it was in early bourgeois political philosophy. *Utopia* in the Marxist sense defines a point of identity within society from which strategies for that society's revolutionary overthrow can be studied. For the Frankfurt Circle, the point at which to approach the revolutionary overthrow of capitalism is the private ownership of the means of production, and the economic order based on it. In his critique of Kant's theory of a "perfect constitution" (in *On Perpetual Peace*), Hork-heimer writes:

This ideal is in fact a utopia. . . . In order to overcome the utopian character of the Kantian conception of a perfect constitution, a ma-terialist theory of society is needed. The individual's various interests are not eternal facts, but have their source in material conditions. . . . The irreconcilable differences of interests result from differences in property relations. . . . The convergence of private economic goals will cease to appear as a wonder only when this particular organization of the economy—whose introduction at one time represented an extraordinary progress, including the possibility of the development of self-conscious individuals—is detached from a form of society in which productive property is administered, not according to good intentions, but according to rational necessity, and in the general interest. In a future society, in a society as moral consciousness intends it to be, the blind mechanism of economic struggle . . . will be replaced by the goal-oriented application of the immeasurable wealth of human and technical powers of production. (1933b:175–176)

Engels suggested that the socialist reorganization of society would provide at a single stroke such an abundance of goods that social conflicts could no longer result from their distribution. Horkheimer, by contrast, advocates a historically relativizing view: The revolutionary reorganization of society means that economic scarcity would be a function solely of the parameters of the stage of historical development of the productive powers. He therefore defines the "basic content of the concept of justice" in such a way that

... at the very least, the inequality in the individuals' living conditions would be only as large as unavoidably necessitated by the maintenance, at the current level, of society's supply of goods. (1933b:187)

The concreteness of the Frankfurt Circle's concept of utopia is demonstrated by the existence of an independent research program within the Institute in the early 1930s on planned economy and carried out by Pollock together with his colleagues Mandelbaum and Gerhardt Meyer. Among the results of this research, the essay "On a Theory of Planned Economy" by Mandelbaum and Meyer most clearly developed these ideas. Its significance for the Circle's political orientation is expressed in a detailed "Prefatory Note by the Editor," written by Horkheimer expressly for this essay to emphasize once again the political relevance of research on planned economies:

Yet if theory cannot solve the problem by itself, at least certain intellectual efforts form a necessary moment in progressive praxis. These are the efforts that provide orientation in the struggle for the creation of a rational economy. This is true not only with regard to research into the developmental tendencies of the present social form. It is true concomitantly as the demonstration of a planned economy's possibility, and of how it is possible. Above all, mankind's present significant experiences with planned economies must be taken into account; today, theoretical orientation as well as terminology must be based on these experiences. (ZfS 3:228)

Yet Mandelbaum and Meyer abandoned this amazing postulate to orient themselves on the Soviet Union — a postulate, incidentally, that directly contradicts Pollock's conception (cited above). Their essay offers merely a typology of conceptions of a planned economy, as well as a critique of liberalist doubts about the very possibility of such an economy. These doubts are based on the problems, in socialism, of accounting methods, methodicalness, productivity, freedom in consumption, and the organization of revenue. Mandelbaum and Meyer also outline sociological and political conditions — albeit purely formal ones — for the possibility of a new social order based on a planned economy.

The Second Phase: Critical
Theory, 1937–1940

Historical and Political Experience

The Labor Movement

In contrast to the views expressed in essays written from a materialist
position, in the subsequent Critical Theory period (1937–1940) the
German labor movement was seen solely in terms of its defeat in
1933. This defeat of "progressive strivings," along with their theoretical
orientation, was given as the practical reason—along with theoretical
ones—for taking, under the name of Critical Theory, a new position
within the Marxist theoretical-political tradition:

But what if the events anticipated by theory do not occur? What if
the forces that were supposed to bring about radical change are sup-
pressed and appear to have been defeated? Little as the truth of the
theory is thereby contradicted, it nevertheless appears in a new light,
which illuminates new sides and aspects of its object. . . . In the new
situation, the transformed function of the theory accords it, in a more
intensive sense, the character of a "critical theory." (Marcuse 1937b:637;
1968:142)

Beginning in 1937, the politics of the Weimar KPD were criticized
only indirectly, through criticism of its political model, the Soviet Union.
The SPD was now criticized solely with regard to how its politics
unintentionally paved the way for the National Socialist seizure of

power. In 1938 Siegfried Marck published in Zurich a book entitled *The New Humanism as Political Philosophy*. An amalgam of almost all nonfascist ideologies of the Weimar Republic, this book served as a philosophical platform of the ideologically splintered German emigrant groups, hence at the same time as a proposal for a political orientation in a postfascist Germany. In "The Philosophy of Absolute Concentration" (1938), Horkheimer subjected Marck's program to a devastating critique. In an unpublished letter to Leo Löwenthal he characterizes it ironically as "being homesick for the Weimar Republic." A renewed orientation toward Weimer's political culture, especially its Social Democratic culture, would be more than illusionary:

Marck misunderstands national socialism because he misunderstands the Republic in which he grew up. . . . Even the most extreme odiousness of today has its origin, not in 1933, but in 1919, in the shooting of workers and intellectuals by the feudal accomplices of the first Republic. The socialist governments were essentially powerless. Instead of getting to the root of the problem, they preferred to remain at the unsteady, ever-shifting level of mere facts. Indeed, they considered theory to be nothing but a fad. The government made freedom into political philosophy rather than political practice. Even someone with strong personal reasons should never wish upon mankind that repetition; it would turn out as badly as the original. (1938b:384)

For Horkheimer, the behavior of the trade unions at the end of the Weimar Republic threw an even harsher light on the SPD's politics. In the first hour of the National Socialists' seizure of power, on 30 January 1933, the chairman of the Free Trade Unions offered to cooperate with the National Socialists,[27] while the other trade unions called for calm and order. Horkheimer interprets this orientation toward the letter of the law, on the part of trade unions close to the SPD, as a politics of accommodation:

The trade unions wanted to transform themselves from organs of class struggle into organs of the state; they wanted to serve in the distribution of state aid, in training the potential recipients of this aid to be submissive; in short, they wanted to contribute to the domination. (1939a:119)

The Soviet Union

The political development in the Soviet Union from 1936 to 1939, that is, from the start of the purges to the Stalin–Hitler pact, was for the West European socialist intelligentsia an *experimentum crucis* for their political convictions. During these years many members of the former KPD and of other European communist parties either quit their party or became dogmatic Stalinists, ready to sanction every fluctuation in the party line. The renegades' memoirs clearly document this historical process.[28] Those best known to the German-speaking world were, incidentally, more or less well disposed toward the Frankfurt Circle, either while in Frankfurt or later in emigration; they include Arthur Koestler, Karl August Wittfogel, Franz Borkenau, and Alfred Kantorowicz, among others.

Open terror, culminating in the show trials, began at the end of 1934 with the reaction by Stalin and the NKVD to the murder of Kirov, the Leningrad party secretary. In 1935 Stalin formed a central control commission for the "extermination of all enemies of the people," and the subsequent campaign led to the deportation and murder of countless Soviet citizens. But it was the Trial of the Sixteen in August 1936 that first attracted worldwide publicity, for this was the start of the liquidation of the entire Bolshevik old guard, beginning with Zinoviev and Kamenev. The Trial of the Seventeen in January 1937 was extensively covered by the Western press, in particular by the *New York Times*. In June 1937 there was a secret trial of Red Army generals, including Marshal Tukhachevski, all of whom were convicted and subsequently executed. And in March 1938 there followed the Trial of the Twenty-One, in which Bukharin, among others, was confronted with outrageous charges.

The unpublished correspondence of the Frankfurt Circle available to me contains almost no reference to the show trials. In a letter dated 7 September 1937, Friedrich Pollock calls Stalin a gangster. Walter Benjamin's published correspondence with Horkheimer contains several relevant passages. On 31 August 1936, one week after the conclusion of the Trial of the Sixteen, Benjamin wrote:

In other respects it is—and here we are surely of a mind—a dark summer. Of course I have been following the events in Russia with great interest. And it seems to me that I am not the only one who doesn't know what to make of them. . . . (1966, vol. II:722)

On 31 January 1937, one day after the conclusion of the Trial of the Seventeen, he wrote to Horkheimer:

I can't make heads or tails of present events in the Union (1966, vol. II:728)

On 20 July 1938, Benjamin wrote to Gretel Adorno from Denmark, where he was staying with Brecht:

Here I come across more party-line literature than in Paris, and thus it was that I recently saw an installment of *International Literature* [a German-language, Stalinist literary magazine published in Moscow]. . . . The anguish in this literature is great. I think you will be able to guess how Bloch interprets it. As for Brecht—he tries to make out the motives of Russian cultural politics as best he can. But that obviously does not prevent him from recognizing the theoretical line as catastrophic for all that which, for twenty years, we have been fighting for. His translator and friend was, as you know, Tretyakoff. Most likely he is no longer alive. . . . (1966, vol. II:722)

Aside from Rudolf Schlesinger's review of recent literature in "New Soviet-Russian Social Research"—which contains, by the way, euphemistic allusions to Stalinist cultural politics—the term *Russia* or *Soviet Union* does not appear in the theoretical texts published in the Institute's *Zeitschrift* in volumes 6, 7, or 8. In a letter by Horkheimer referring to the editing of his essay "The Jews and Europe," he states:

I have even further softened passages dealing with Russia. . . . (20 July 1939, Pollock Archive)

In the printed version of the essay, in which Horkheimer—according to the letter—intended to draw an analogy between Bolshevism and fascism, all allusions to the Soviet Union were removed. For whose sake, I do not know.

As one of the political reasons for rechristening the Circle's theoretical orientation as Critical Theory, Marcuse names the defeat of the "forces that were to have brought about radical change" (1937b:636f.). Further,

In the new situation, the transformed function of the theory accords it, in a more intensive sense, the character of a "critical theory." (1937b:637; 1968:142)

One of the results of socialist theory's transformed political function—in the face of the defeat of the German labor movement—is the immanent critique of attempts to realize socialism in other countries, that is, criticism of the Soviet Union:

> Its critique [i.e., that of Critical Theory] is also directed at any avoidance of its full economic and political demands by those who invoke it. (1937b:637; 1968:142)

Horkheimer's and Marcuse's criticism concentrates on one particular problem: Has a socialist revolution been realized by the socialization of the means of production and by the reorganization of the economy into a planned one? In my opinion, the problem was relevant not so much because of contemporary developments in the Soviet Union, where the Stakhanov movement had just begun and the second five-year plan was approaching its end. Its relevance to the Frankfurt Circle resulted much more from the immanence of the Circle's theoretical development in this materialist period. As already shown, its utopian point of reference was the "planned organization of society," whose economic and political realization would consist, first of all, in the abolition of the private ownership and management of the means of production. Now, in 1936, Horkheimer and Marcuse expressly emphasize that a change in property relations implies merely a negative precondition for the building of a socialist society. The socialization of the means of production, and the forcing of industrial production onto a new organizational basis, would not be immediately identical with this society's socialist transformation.

> Not that the labor process is regulated according to a plan, but rather which interest determines this regulation becomes important: It is rational only if this interest is the freedom and happiness of the masses. . . . Without freedom and happiness in the social relations of men, even the greatest increase in production, even the abolition of private property in the means of production, remains infected with the old injustices. (Marcuse 1937b:638; 1968:143)

And again,

> The placing of industrial production under state control is a historical fact, whose significance is of primary importance for any critical theory. Whether it is a question of socialization in this sense — that is, to what extent a higher principle is developed in this socialization — depends not simply on the alteration of certain property relations, or on increased productivity in new forms of social cooperation, but just as

much on the nature and development of the society in which all this occurs. (Horkheimer 1937b:629)

In the following passage Horkheimer develops a catalog of political criteria for the identification of genuine socialist societies. These criteria seem to negate elements of Soviet-Russian development:

The problem of what will be produced and how; of whether relatively unchanging groups with special interests exist; of whether social differences will be maintained or even heightened; further, the problem of the individual's active relation to the government; of the relation between all important administrative acts and the knowledge and will of the individuals they affect; of the dependence of all conditions, controllable by man, on real consensus—in short, the degree to which the essential aspects of real democracy and association have been developed also lies within the concept of socialization of the means of production. (1937c:630)

Fascism

The years 1936 to 1939—more clearly than the preceding years—are marked by the consolidation of power by the National Socialist party in Germany and by the spread of fascist governments in Europe. The Nuremberg Race Laws were enacted in September 1935. In March of the following year Hitler's troops occupied the demilitarized zone in the Rhineland; Germany renounced the Locarno Treaty and extended the military enlistment period. In Morocco in July 1937, Franco's revolt touched off the Spanish Civil War. Germany and Japan established a pact, joined by Italy in 1937, against the Communist International. Austria was annexed by the German Reich in March. In April began the Sudeten crisis, which would end, to Hitler's advantage, at the Munich Conference. The Reich's *Kristallnacht* of 9 and 10 November 1938 caused a greater public outcry, particularly in the United States, than all previous anti-Semitic crimes.[29] In March 1939 German troops marched into Prague. The Poland crisis began. Germany renounced the German–British naval agreement and concluded the Iron Pact with Italy. The Spanish Civil War was won by the fascists, with German and Italian aid. Despite the warnings of Chamberlain and Daladier, Hitler invaded Poland in September 1939.

In published letters, particularly by Walter Benjamin, and in the unpublished letters by Pollock and Horkheimer available to me, there are numerous references to particular elements in this chain of events leading to World War II. These references are difficult to systematize. They are often—for example, in Benjamin's letters—quite enigmatically formulated, apparently on account of the censors.[30] In some cases, references to particular events are formulated in terms so specific to the daily politics of the time that they can hardly be coordinated within a historiographical reconstruction of events.[31] The particularity of the event often disappears behind the generality deduced from it. Thus a letter from Horkheimer to Pollock, dated 25 August 1937 (Pollock Archive), contains reflections on fascist cultural politics that were prompted by a visit to the Paris World Exhibition, where Albert Speer's colossal architecture was awarded a first prize. And yet all letters written from 1935 onward share a more or less latent conviction of a monstrous, apocalyptic tendency permeating the particular facts of daily politics and legitimizing at the same time a "philosophical" distance from the particular results.

Pollock to Horkheimer (12 April 1936): "Geneva is in full bloom. The entire environment contributes toward making life more pleasant. I know that this is nothing but the setting for a frightful reality. . . ."

Horkheimer to Pollock (22 April 1936): "The situation in general is disgusting. I read the newspapers only fleetingly; after all, one can always anticipate what is in them. . . ."

Horkheimer to Löwenthal (21 July 1937): "One hardly dares to look at the newspapers any more. . . ."

Horkheimer to Pollock (20 September 1937): "The entire situation in Europe is quite sad. Even the fear of war itself forms but a moment within a social development in which, in any case, all cultural values of any significance are perishing with an uncanny necessity."

The "continuity thesis" formulated by Pollock and Marcuse in 1933–1934, that fascism is the political form corresponding to developed monopoly capitalism, was further radicalized and refined until 1939. Horkheimer expressed this thesis incisively and suggestively in "The Jews and Europe."

The thesis maintains that fascism is a political consequence of problems of the reproduction of capital in the developed monopolistic period:

The pride of liberalism—technically highly developed, advanced industry—thwarts its own principle, since selling labor power becomes impossible for large portions of the population. Reproducing the status quo via the detour of the labor market becomes uneconomical. Earlier the bourgeoisie was economically decentralized, a many-headed ruler; the expansion of one's business was for every entrepreneur the condition for increasing one's share of the social surplus product. One needed the workers in order to survive the competition. In the age of the monopoly, unlimited investment of new capital no longer promises a great increase in profits. (1939a:116)

The inclination of Social Democratic state administrations to steer these tendencies, on the one hand, by means of social legislation (especially unemployment benefits) and, on the other hand, through a politics of economic management simply meets the economic resistance of big capital:

The economic programs of those good European statesmen are illusory. In liberalism's final stage, they want to compensate a collapsing market economy's inability to feed people through state contracts; with the consent of the economically powerful, they want to stimulate the economy so that it provides everyone with a livelihood. They forget that the aversion to new investments is no mere whim. The industrialists have no desire to set their industries in motion via the detour of taxes, which they must pay to an all-too-impartial government, merely to pull bankrupt farmers and other unemployed from their difficulties. . . . Their efforts are absurd: They want to subordinate to the universal that class whose particular interests essentially contradict the general interest. (1939a:116)

Big capital organizes its resistance politically in fascist or fascistic parties, or it finds in these parties agents of its own interests:

The relations of production realize their aims despite the efforts of humanitarian governments to prevent this. The pioneers from the entrepreneur associations create a new apparatus. Their legal advisers undertake the organization of society; in place of the scattered commandos in the individual factories there arises the totalitarian domination of the entire people by particular interests. (1939a:118)

The phenomenon of anti-Semitism, particularly that of national socialism, is also explained in political-economic terms. The contraction in the market's function, characteristic of late liberalism, also affects the role of money capital and of the sphere of circulation. Their classical social bearers were, in European capitalism, merchants of Jewish heritage. Horkheimer sees a causal connection between the persecution of the Jews and the elimination of the sphere of circulation in late capitalism:

Jews were displaced as agents of circulation because the modern economic structure essentially retired the entire sphere. They are the first victims of the dictate of those in power that takes over the function eliminated. State manipulation of money, having the necessary consequence of robbery, turns into the brutal manipulation of its representatives. (1939a:131)

The Frankfurt Circle's continuity thesis—that late capitalism necessarily turns into fascism—was confirmed by events in the period between the wars. This thesis also maintains that German national socialism is not specifically a German problem but rather a generalizable tendency of social development. In September 1939 Horkheimer wrote:

The confrontation between liberalism and the totalitarian state no longer occurs simply within national boundaries. (1939a:128)

Indeed, in Europe at the start of the Second World War, only nine countries were still governed by parliaments, and there, too, strong fascist movements had developed, such as the Action Française. In Italy, Lithuania, Latvia, Estonia, Poland, Hungary, Romania, Austria, Greece, Turkey, Portugal, Spain, and Germany, fascist dictatorships were in power. Even bourgeois historians concede that by 1939—even before Hitler spread fascism throughout Europe with his troops—"a fascist Europe was certainly within the realm of possibility."[32]

According to the logic of the continuity thesis, even the "nontotalitarian countries in Europe" (Horkheimer) could not be excluded from the suspicion of this tendency. Obviously playing upon Daladier's and Chamberlain's concessions to Hitler at Munich, Horkheimer remarks:

The skeptical diplomats of the nonauthoritarian countries in Europe are backed by dogmatic bankers anxious about their balances. (1938b:33)

He cites in "The Jews and Europe" the opinion of an official of the Whaley-Eaton Foreign Service that if it came to a choice between inflationary development and totalitarian economic and social control, the British government would surely choose the latter (cf. 1939a:129). As for the United States, Horkheimer addressed himself to (Social Democratic) German emigrants who, on the basis of the American social order, had been drawn into becoming anti-Marxist apologists of capitalism:

. . . the literary opponents of totalitarian society are now praising the conditions upon which their existence depends, and denying the theory that articulated their secret while there was still time left. No one can expect the emigrants from that world which produced fascism to hold up a mirror in the land where they have been granted asylum. But whoever avoids the subject of capitalism should keep silent on the subject of fascism. (1939a:116)

From 1935–1936 until well into the first two years of the war, the Frankfurt Circle's estimation of fascism was characterized by a fear, bordering on panic and fed by theoretical forebodings, of the globalization of fascist systems of rule. Horkheimer wrote in 1939:

The confrontation between liberalism and the totalitarian state no longer occurs simply within national boundaries. Fascism conquers from without and from within alike. For the first time the entire world has been pulled into the same political development. India and China are no longer mere border zones, historical entities of the second rank; they are filled with the same tension as that within the developed capitalist countries. (1939a:128)

And in a statement directed at the Jewish groups within the general population in Germany, whose hopes since 1939 were set on the allied war powers, Horkheimer radicalized in a gloomy prognostication his conception of the globalization of fascist rule:

The Jewish hope in the Second World War is a wretched one. Wherever it may end, complete militarization is leading the world further into authoritarian, collectivized forms of life. . . . Mobilization brings the columns of workers—charged with the armaments industry, with the construction of ever newer roads, subways, and municipal buildings— nothing new except perhaps a mass grave. The ineluctable conscription of the Earthly Kingdom in peacetime was itself static warfare. . . . The resettlement of the peoples into foxholes is Hitler's triumph, even should he someday be defeated. (1939a:132f.)

Horkheimer and his co-workers were not alone in this apocalyptic vision of the fascist era. All of the German emigrant literature dealing with fascism, from Rauschning's *Revolution of Nihilism* to Franz Neumann's *Behemoth* to Hannah Arendt's *Origins of Totalitarianism*, concur—despite considerable theoretical-political differences—in its judgments of the fascist epoch as one of universal historical significance.

Theory of the Theory-Praxis Relation

The Subject and Addressee of the Theory

Even as early as its materialist period, the Frankfurt Circle held that the historical circumstances required the continued development of materialist social theory beyond all proletarian class consciousness. In Horkheimer's essay "Traditional and Critical Theory" (1937), which introduces the Critical Theory period, this conviction is unmistakably radicalized. Taking up again the argument of his book *Dämmerung*—that a unified class consciousness equal to the situation is hindered by stratification within the wage laborers' social structure (labor-aristocracy versus lumpen-proletariat)—Horkheimer now expresses directly what he had formulated circuitously in his earlier writings:

But it must be added that even the situation of the proletariat is, in this society, no guarantee of correct knowledge. The proletariat may indeed have experience of meaninglessness in the continuing and increasing wretchedness and injustice of its own life. Yet this awareness is prevented from becoming a social force by the differentiation of the social structure that is still imposed on the proletariat from above and by the opposition between personal and class interest, transcended only at very rare moments. Even to the proletariat the world superficially seems quite different from what it really is. Even an outlook that could grasp that no opposition really exists between the proletariat's own true interests and those of society as a whole, and would therefore derive its principles of action from the thoughts and feelings of the masses, would fall into slavish dependence on the status quo. (1937c:268; 1972b:213–214)

He consistently criticizes the principles of "Luxemburgian" intellectuals who—through a schematic, or historically fixed, hypothesis of the masses' spontaneity—think they have found an ultimate guarantee for theoretically correct knowledge: in its subordination to the proletariat's particular orientation at any given moment. Horkheimer maintains, on the contrary, that in the proletariat's given political situation, those theoretical subjects who count themselves among the socialist intelligentsia must, for the proletariat's sake, distance themselves cognitively from the proletariat's consciousness:

The intellectual is simply satisfied to proclaim with reverent admiration the creative strength of the proletariat, and finds satisfaction in adapting himself to it and in canonizing it. He overlooks that such an evasion of theoretical effort (which the passivity of his thought spares him) and of a temporary opposition to the masses (which active theoretical effort might force upon him) only makes these masses blinder and weaker than they need be. . . . By completely subordinating himself to the current psychological disposition of that class, he enjoys a professional optimism and the blissful feeling of being linked with a mighty force. When the optimism is shattered in periods of crushing defeat, then many intellectuals risk falling into a pessimism and nihilism that is just as ungrounded as their exaggerated optimism had been. *They cannot bear the thought that precisely the kind of thinking that is most topical and has the deepest grasp of the historical situation must at times isolate its subject and throw him back on himself.* (My emphasis; 1937c:268; 1972b:214)

For Horkheimer, this consciously undertaken process of achieving cognitive distance from the proletariat is, in the given historical-political situation, the mark of a critical intelligentsia conscious of its political role. Another mark of this sort is the intelligentsia's self-chosen "loneliness" (Horkheimer), its isolation from the masses. According to the correspondence available to me, this explanation of Critical Theory's "loneliness" motivated Horkheimer's co-workers to identify with the positions taken in "Traditional and Critical Theory." Pollock wrote Horkheimer on 16 August 1937:

I have finally been able to read the "Theory" essay to the end. . . . Nowhere in the world has "Critical Theory" been further developed as in these pages, and the fact of its loneliness, which is so incisively founded, should not be permitted to move us to abandon the theory. (Pollock Archive).

Walter Benjamin wrote to Horkheimer in August 1937:

I have finally read your essay "Traditional and Critical Theory," and, as you may well imagine, am in complete concurrence. The way in which you characterize the atmosphere in which our work is done, and your explanation of the causes of its isolation, move me particularly. . . . (1966, vol. II:736)

Horkheimer's explicit distinction between the German proletariat's class consciousness and the "theory of society" equal to this proletariat's political situation in 1937—that is, the presupposition that the proletariat, even in the most mediated form, is no longer the subject of a theory equal to its own situation—required theory construction to find a new candidate for the role of the subject. While there is no explicit subject in the earlier essays, as of 1937 and the "Theory" essay, this role is occupied by the "subjects of critical activity" (1937c:262). In other formulations, "critical activity" is itself made into a subject, in which Horkheimer speaks of the "structure of the critical activity" or the "specific nature of critical behavior" (1937c:264). As indicated, the identifying criterion of the "subjects of critical activity" is the ability to endure, for the sake of theoretical adequacy, social marginalization even from that group for whom the theory was being developed: the proletarian masses. Horkheimer establishes the political-historical conditions of the possibility of such a theoretical work in formulations that give the impression that the Frankfurt Circle conceived of itself as the subject of the "theory of society":

Under conditions of monopoly capitalism and the impotence of workers in the face of the repressive apparatus of authoritarian states, truth has sought refuge among small groups of admirable individuals. But these have been decimated by terror and have little time for refining theory. . . . In the general historical upheaval, truth can reside in numerically small groups. History teaches that such groups, hardly noticed even by those opposed to the status quo, outlawed but imperturbable, may take the lead at the decisive moment. (1937c:288, 291; 1972:237–238, 241)

This conjecture is strengthened by the pathos and emphasis, particularly in Horkheimer's letters of the time, that appear in discussions of the historical-political significance of the Circle's work. Horkheimer wrote to Pollock from Paris on 20 September 1937, about six weeks after completing the essay "Traditional and Critical Theory":

Those few to whom the truth has fled appear ridiculous, dogmatic persons speaking a bombastic language, as empty, completely without foundation. The solace that certain figures in the Old Testament experienced the same thing is all the less helpful given that the prophets' success was not overwhelming in the long run. The most unpleasant discovery to which materialism leads is that reason exists only as long as it is supported by a natural subject. . . . The repercussions for the subject are never so strong and sustained that the subject might lose the character of naturalness. Hence things never arrive at that famous identity from which idealism lives. Yet we must of course attempt to realize this identity as far as possible. . . . (Pollock Archive)

The argument that the segregation, isolation, and marginalization of a group of intellectuals not only does not restrict but rather confirms the validity of its theoretical work appears in the years from 1937 to 1940 in all of the theoretical texts and in numerous letters. There exists, nonetheless, no textual evidence demonstrating that the Frankfurt Circle identified itself immediately with the potential subject of historical truth. Yet the sentences quoted above should certainly be taken as an approximate qualification of the actual sociological and historical conditions of possibility for the formation of a theory equal to the historical situation. And given these conditions, the Frankfurt Circle would itself have been the most likely candidate for the role.

It would be easy to dismiss the Frankfurt Circle's self-interpretation—at a time when its academic and political prominence by no means corresponded to that of today—as megalomaniacal messianism. Yet that would be unhistorical; for this self-interpretation was the result of a specific historical constellation, which, in Horkheimer's view, exhibited itself in the following way:

At a time in which a tidy elite of economic and other leaders plots to strike down the masses with blindness, and the intellectuals with a firm sense of dimension, theory is identical with the attempt to maintain the understanding to which mankind must come if it is not to have to start from the beginning again. (1938b:386)

The historical-political constellation was specific in that fascist Germany, with a methodicalness and thoroughness unique in the modern age, had banished the entire progressive intelligentsia, humanists as well as social scientists. The methodicalness of the banishment and the open terror in the Third Reich legitimized the emigrants and resistance fighters in their self-understanding as the genuine representatives of an oppressed political culture, hence as the designated bearers of a postfascist society in Germany. One finds between 1933 and 1945 the thought of this political-moral mandate in numerous organized emigrant groups. And certainly it is only in the context of such groups that one can understand the Frankfurt Circle's messianic stance. In one text, Horkheimer identifies in this way one of the subjects of "critical activity":

. . . it is Critical Theory and the historical struggles to which it belongs. It can be found concretely among those who are building, in authoritarian states and in states striving to become authoritarian, the cells of a new world. (1938a:47)

Here, Horkheimer may have had the group named New Beginning in mind. This group had been founded in the Weimar Republic by members of the leftist SPD and a marginal wing of the KPD, and it agitated conspiratorily within these parties. In fascist Germany, New Beginning was, until 1938, one of the most important resistance groups. After having been destroyed in Germany by the Gestapo, it was reconstituted in America as the avant-garde of a postfascist, socialist Germany, and it soon won such influence that it is treated, in the histories of the emigrant scene, on a par with the organizations in exile of the SPD and KPD. The group's orientation was left-socialist until the Stalin–Hitler pact; thereafter it drew nearer to the SPD.[33] There were connections between this organization and the Frankfurt Circle: In 1937 the chief theoretician of the group, Richard Löwenthal, under the pseudonym Paul Sering, published in the *Zeitschrift*. Arcadius R. Gurland, a co-worker in the Institute in the late 1930s and early 1940s, was also a member of New Beginning.

Theory and Praxis

By 1937, the subject and addressee of revolutionary theory are separated much more clearly in the Frankfurt Circle's political self-interpretation. Horkheimer maintains repeatedly that, for the sake of the adequacy of the theory, the critical intellectual must be able to endure marginalization from the addressee of his theoretical work. He warned intellectuals not to overlook

that any evasion of theoretical effort . . . or of a temporary opposition to the masses (which active theoretical effort may force on him) only makes these masses blinder and weaker than they need be. (1937c:268; 1972:214)

This is merely a negative determination of the relation between intelligentsia and proletariat. It is supplemented, positively, by considerations about the organizational mediation of socialist intelligentsia and party-organized proletariat—a mediation that, even if it remained on a metalevel, is nonetheless the single explicit *organizational* linkage of theory and praxis to be found within the entire period examined here. The relation of socialist intelligentsia and proletarian class is presented in this organizational reflection as a "dynamic unity" whose elements consist of both theoretical subjects and some members within the proletariat as well as within other classes; they are related to each other in a mode vaguely described as "mutual interaction." This "dynamic unity" is supposed to guarantee that the intelligentsia's radical marginalization from those to whom the theory is directed occurs to the latter's benefit:

If . . . the theorist and his specific object are viewed as forming a dynamic unity with the oppressed class, so that his presentation of social contradictions appears, not merely as an expression of the concrete historical situation, but just as much as a stimulating, transforming factor within it, then the real function of Critical Theory emerges. The course of the conflict between the most advanced elements within the class and the individuals who articulate the truth about it, as well as of the conflict between the most advanced elements with their theoreticians and the rest of the class, is to be understood as a process of mutual interactions, in which consciousness, with its liberating power, develops at the same time its own motivating, aggressive, and disciplining powers. The trenchancy of this conflict is revealed in the ever-present possibility of a tension between the theoretician and the class his thought is to serve. (1937c:269; 1972:215)

This kind of solidarity with the proletariat, with the theoretician's simultaneous distancing of himself from the proletariat's empirical consciousness, is precarious, to the extent that such solidarity no longer assumes—and is no longer able to assume—any practical organizational form. Where the empirical, political unity of critical intelligentsia and proletariat exists only in the heads of the former, the criteria for the specifically socialist identity of a political position become diffuse. This would suggest, above and beyond systematic reasons, that the Frankfurt Circle's extremely sharp criticism of the bourgeois intelligentsia was a function of its fear of being identified with that group. Yet this critique of the bourgeois intelligentsia's relation to politics continues at the same time as the line developed in Horkheimer's materialism essays, in which he defined the relation between science and politics. This relation was determined *negatively* within the program of ideology critique, and *positively* within the interdisciplinary reorganization of institutional research. The core of this distinction is that no threshold of indifference can be established between science and politics; science has political implications even in its content—in its selection of a subject, its definition of problems, and its methodology and research techniques. Whereas bourgeois science is defined precisely by its assertion of the opposite, "critical" science for Horkheimer recognizes the intrinsically political nature of science, analyzes it through ideology critique, and introduces into theoretical work the consciousness of its internal capacity to be politicized. Horkheimer saw one hostile opponent of this postulate in Max Weber's thesis that ultimate theoretical foundations lie outside all theory, and that scientific knowledge is related only externally to the form of its political instrumentalization. Horkheimer places the notion of intellectuals' classlessness—suggested by Alfred Weber and Karl Mannheim's concept of the "free-floating intelligentsia"—in the theoretical political tradition of Max Weber. Such a tradition rejects Horkheimer's ultimately Hegelian conviction that the "chaotic surface of events" is based on a "structure . . . capable of being grasped conceptually" (1932a:I), within reach of a science reorganized on dialectical principles. Thus intellectuals do not enjoy the privilege of neutrality toward historical-political processes, for such a neutrality could conceivably serve for any political orientation whatever. Equally ideological is the gesture, by academic science, of reflective distance with which it presumes itself relieved of any political partisanship:

Critical Theory rejects the formalistic concept of mind that underlies such a conception of the intelligentsia. According to this concept, there is only one truth, and the positive predicates of honesty and internal consistency, reasonableness, and the pursuit of peace, freedom, and happiness cannot be ascribed in the same sense to any other theory or praxis. There is also no theory of society, including that of the sociologist concerned with general laws, that does not contain implicit political interests; and the truth of these interests can be determined, not in a supposedly neutral reflection, but in personal thought and action, indeed, only in concrete historical activity. (1937c:275; 1972:222)

A pronounced characteristic of the bourgeois intelligentsia is its distanced, reflective attitude (e.g., the attitude of a sociology of knowledge) toward political movements:

It is disconcerting that the intellectual should represent himself in this way, as though a difficult labor of thought, which he alone could accomplish, were the prime requirement for the choice between revolutionary, liberal, and fascist goals and means. (1937c:275; 1972:222–223)

In Horkheimer's view, the postulate of the unification of theoretical and political activity cannot be replaced, and is an urgent necessity in concrete historical constellations. The intellectual's apolitical or neutral attitude assumes, in view of fascism's success, absurd dimensions:

At a time when the forces of freedom in Europe are themselves disoriented and seek to form themselves anew . . . the conception of the intelligentsia, which claims to be nonpartisan and is therefore abstract, represents an understanding of the problems that actually only obscure them. . . . What the vanguard needs is prudence in the political struggle, not academic instruction as to its so-called position. . . . (1937c:275; 1972:223)

Yet Horkheimer's thesis about the unavoidable partiality of science was not based on the argument described, the force of which derives from the specific historical situation. More central to his argument is a systematic construction: In that tradition of Marxist theory adopted by Horkheimer, scientific labor is only one moment in the total process of social labor. Theory, even of the critical kind, is a moment in the process by which society reproduces itself in the productive appropriation of nature. The development of science therefore can be reconstructed, in any particular instance, only in terms of a specific social-historical development. Accordingly, the objects of scientific labor can constitute themselves only within the spectrum of socially organized labor. The subject and object of scientific labor are socially constituted. According to Horkheimer, on the one hand bourgeois science characteristically represses consciousness of these facts, and on the other it pragmatically transforms this consciousness into social and productive technologies. For critical science, it follows, from insight into the social origin of its objects, as well as from its interconnection with the social labor process, that the scientifically analyzed facts are in principle mutable and accessible for political disposal by a "rationally organized society." The acutely experienced historical process is grasped as a process to be given shape and presented theoretically. The form taken by such theoretical work is, according to Marx, "critique." Critique is a form of theory that self-consciously demands of itself an internal connection to an extratheoretical, practical, political movement.

Theoretical Position

Self-Understanding within the Tradition of Historical and Political Theory

In August 1937, Horkheimer introduced the Circle's new political-theoretical self-definition in the essay "Traditional and Critical Theory." From that time onward almost all of the Circle's members assume the label Critical Theory: Wittfogel (1938:339), Adorno (1938:90), Marcuse (1937b:570), Pollock (in a letter of 16 August 1937, referring to Horkheimer's essay), as well as Leo Löwenthal (in an undated letter in the Pollock Archive).

The philosophical adversaries of Horkheimer's programmatic texts of the materialist period in the early 1930s were the Hegelian philosophy of identity and the folk-collectivist ideologies contained in the philosophy of the Weimar Republic. The adversaries of the Circle's structural orientation were redefined in 1937. The critique of the philosophy of identity and of collectivist ideology was replaced by nothing less than a critique of the orientation of modern theory in general—the critique of "traditional theory."

According to Horkheimer, traditional theory takes the form of logically consistent, hypothetical propositions. Each particular hypothesis is deducible from the highest principles, depending on the particular philosophical orientation, as the result of induction from experiential processes (sensualism), or as evident insights (rationalism, phenomenology), or as conventional premises (axiomatics). Despite the diversity of the ways in which they achieve their highest principles, these various forms of traditional theory share the same conviction about the nature of "theoretical explanation." A fact or state of affairs is considered to be explained if, after abstracting it from its context in reality, it is possible to subsume it under a particular hypothetical system of applied propositions. Theoretical explanation here presupposes a strictly maintained separation between subject and object; explanations signify the interrelating of the various independent levels of theoretical propositions with sense data. Horkheimer maintains that this form of theory is determined by its function as one moment within the total process of man's appropriation of nature (conditioned by the division of labor):

The manipulation of physical nature, like the management of certain economic and social mechanisms, demands the formation of a body of knowledge—such as is given in an ordered framework of hypotheses. (1937c:250; 1972:194)

Without elaborating, Horkheimer suggests that the theories instrumentalized for the production process are characterized by an ability to transform observed causal or functional links between a succession of events into purposive strategies; this strategic transformation of experimentally produced observations then affects the form of theory itself. "Traditional theory" is characterized precisely by its forgetting, suppressing, or repressing just this fact—that it is a moment (within a division of labor) of the politically organized social process of production. It is symptomatic of this state of affairs that changes in scientific paradigms are attributed only to ingenious researchers, and not to the changing requirements of production. Another symptom is the hypostatization of the scholar in the liberal era.

Critical Theory, in contrast, is characterized by the consciousness of the limitations of scientific and theoretical activity, and hence of its own limitations. It considers scientific activity a "partial process" within the total social labor process. Theory is itself a "critical" element of the process by which society reproduces itself in its productive appropriation of nature. Because theory itself is part of the social labor process, science cannot be separated analytically from other social activities:

The isolated consideration of particular activities and branches of activities requires for its validity an accompanying concrete awareness of its own limitations. A conception is needed to overcome the one-sidedness that necessarily arises when limited intellectual processes are detached from their matrix in the total activity of a society. (1937c:254; 1972:199)

Critical Theory further distinguishes itself from traditional theory by relativizing the division, strictly maintained in the latter, of the scientific subject from the particular object of scientific examination. Hork-heimer's idea, that

the facts given us through our senses are socially pre-formed in two ways: through the historical character of the perceived object and through the historical character of the perceiving organ. . . . (1937c:255; 1972:200)

means that science can be sufficiently understood only in the context of social life—just as the objects of science appear only within the horizon of the relevant structures of socially organized labor. This thesis of the twofold social constitution of the subject and object of science may seem trivial in view of its own specialization and division into various specialized sciences, such as the theory of science, social-psychological research into social perception, or Marxist discussions of the objectively constituting role of human praxis. Yet, above and beyond its contemporary originality, which cannot be emphasized enough, this thesis is an important element in the context of Critical Theory's political self-justification. The awareness that science, like Critical Theory, is socially constituted is not simply exploited prag-matically as a reflective mechanism, that is, as a technocratic attempt to make the productive process itself function better:

The aim of critical activity is not to be found either in conscious intention, or in its objective meaning, or in the aim of improving the functioning of any part of this structure. (1937c:261; 1972:207)

The programmatic indifference of Critical Theory to scientific and political action results from an awareness of its being firmly established in the continuum of the social labor process. It considers itself a moment within this process and, at the same time, a political reflection upon the organizational form proper to this process. It is "immanent to human labor" (Horkheimer, 1937c:267; 1972:209), and "it champions a reorganization of labor" (1937c:264; 1972:212). Although the theo-retical labor of "subjects of critical activity" is only one aspect of the social process of production, it does have *theoretical* power over the totality of the social context and thus is able to represent this context as, in principle, capable of the process of revolutionary transformation:

In recognizing the present form of the economy and the whole culture that it generates to be the product of human labor as well as the organization that humanity was capable of and has provided for itself in the present era, those who adopt the critical attitude identify themselves with this totality and understand it as will and reason; it is their own world. At the same time, they discover that society can be compared to nonhuman natural processes, to pure mechanisms, since the cultural forms that are supported by war and repression are not creations of a unified self-consciousness; that world is not their own, but rather the world of capital. (1937c:262; 1972:208–209)

Relation to Marxism

The model for Horkheimer's concept of critique is Marx's *Critique of Political Economy*. As Horkheimer introduces the term *critical attitude* in the essay under discussion, he remarks in a footnote:

The term is used here less in the sense it has in the idealist critique of pure reason than in the sense it has in the dialectical critique of political economy. It denotes an essential characteristic of the dialectical theory of society. (1937c:261; 1972:206)

Marx developed the concept of critique in the *Critique of Political Economy* as an alternative to Hegel's type of reflection, which, in constituting a philosophy of history, gives the very act of this reflective understanding of a historical process the character of a subject, so as to substitute the act, in the form of the "Idea," for the historical process itself. This tendency, present already in the analytical form in which history is approached, to glorify, through reflection, social relations as the result of historical becoming is expressed, for example, in Hegel's identification of the categories in the *Philosophy of Right* with the Prussian state of his time. Because Marx's method, by contrast, strictly separates the reflection upon the historical process in which social relations are generated from the historical process itself, it arrives at a nonmystifying, but instead "critical," concept of theory:

For Hegel, the process of thinking, which he even transforms into an independent, self-sufficient subject and then calls the "idea," is the demiurge of the real world, and the real world is merely the external, phenomenal form of the "idea." . . . In its mystified form, dialectics became the fashion in Germany, because it seemed to glorify the present state of things; in its rational form it is a scandal and an abomination for the bourgeoisie and its doctrinaire spokesmen, because in its affirmative understanding of the present state of things it includes, at the same time, an understanding of the negation of that state, of its necessary decline; because it comprehends every historically developed form as in fluid movement and therefore takes into account its transitory nature; because it allows nothing to impose upon it; and because it is in its essence critical and revolutionary. (Marx, 1974:27ff.; 1906:19–20)

Horkheimer articulates, as a program, this—Critical Theory's—paradigmatic orientation according to Marx's method of a "critique of political economy," and further illustrates it in the following allusions to Marx's *Kapital*:

[Critical Theory] considers the economic categories of labor, value, and productivity precisely as they are interpreted in the existing order, and considers every other interpretation as simple Idealism. (1937c:262; 1972:208)

The concepts that originate under its influence are ones critical of the present situation. Class, exploitation, surplus value, profit, pauperization, and social collapse are moments of the conceptual whole whose meaning is to be sought, not in the reproduction of present society, but in its remaking. (1937c:271; 1972:218)

In the writings of the period under discussion, the concept and indicated characteristics of Critical Theory are projected back onto the entire theoretical and political tradition of Marxist theory. This is not simply an act of renaming; on the one hand it is an act of determining where Critical Theory itself stands within the tradition of Marxist theory, and, on the other hand, it is a critical act of making Critical Theory independent of undue influence by this tradition. For example, Horkheimer distinguishes Critical Theory from its distorting and adulterating instrumentalization by the German Social Democrat movement and by Bolshevism (1937b:630), the concept of Critical Theory functions as a standard or guiding principle that perseveres throughout all historical and political developments and is concerned with the adequacy of the form of the theory to the situation with which it deals; for this reason, this standard is considered the single reliable guarantor of a rational choice in political strategy. Thus *Critical Theory* is the name for the Circle's theoretical-political orientation, a mark of belonging to the tradition of Marxist theory, and—significantly—the expression of the claim of representing the real substance of the authentic tradition.

The form of *Theoriepolitik* (practiced already in the materialism phase) that establishes the identity of one's own theory in terms of its place within a certain tradition of theory also characterizes the form of presentation of Critical Theory. Further, it is characteristic that the fulfillment of Critical Theory's claim—of adequately rendering, in theoretical and historical terms, the "orthodox" structure of Marxist theory—is in fact exhausted in nothing more than a few allusions, in claims to providing an adequate Marxist interpretation of late capitalism. Horkheimer's program of a critical science guiding political action—one patterned on Marx's method of economic critique—nonetheless possesses its own originality. This program is original in comparison with the contemporary interpretations of Marx's critique of economy, that is, in the context of the 1920s controversy over the "theory of collapse." In these interpretations *Das Kapital* was considered paradigmatic, but as only one book among other, worse books on economics, and not as the methodologically reflective and material realization of a specific, "critical" form of science.

Those passages from Horkheimer's texts referring to the methodology of *Das Kapital* formulate the stimulus to disentangle the restriction of positiveness and negativeness that is uniquely characteristic of Marx in order to decipher the material execution of the work itself; thus they are an attempt to render transparent the possibility of the revolutionary transformation of capitalism by a critical phenomenology of its structure of reproduction.

Critical Theory claims to be the standard that preserves the "orthodox" structure of Marxist theory, and not just in opposition to the dogmatic and reformist instrumentalization of theory on the part of the Second and Third internationals. It also claims to represent the adjustment of theory, made necessary by historical development, to changed social conditions, even as it maintains the postulate that the *basic* structure of capitalist development remains unchanged. Taking as an example the developmental process of liberal to monopoly capitalism, Horkheimer attempts to show that "such changes . . . do not leave the structure of Critical Theory untouched" (1937c:286; 1972:236). This example demonstrates once more that Horkheimer interpreted fascism as the political form of developed monopolistic late capitalism. He combines in this example economic, structural changes, such as the tendency toward monopolization and the division of ownership and control, with changes in the superstructure. The latter changes include the annihilation of liberalist individualism through the ideology of the Führer; the distinction, intended in an anti-Semitic sense, drawn between "parasitic" and "productive" capitalists; the increasing autonomy of positivist law from its foundations in natural law; and the technological production of meaning by the propaganda apparatus of authoritarian states. Horkheimer not only draws a parallel between these two forms of structural change and imputes a causal connection between them; he also maintains that these changes have affected the relation between superstructure and base to the extent that a Marxist theory of culture must be defined anew:

Explanations of social phenomena have become simpler but also more complicated. Simpler, because the economic factors more directly and consciously determine human life, and because the power of resistance and substantiality of the cultural sphere are disappearing. More complicated, because the uncontrolled economic dynamism—in relation to which most individuals are reduced to mere media—quickly brings about ever new visions and portents. (1937c:288; 1972:237)

This quotation suggests a direction in which Marx's theory of the superstructure might be reinterpreted, and Horkheimer considers the suggested direction exemplary for structural change within a theory, and one that takes into account changed social-historical conditions. Such an alteration of theory is not merely an external correction but the realization of its principle of "critique": the identification of a political alternative to existing conditions only in a phenomenology of the present society.

The Frankfurt Circle thus identifies its theory *within* the Marxist tradition more clearly and more radically in this period than in earlier phases—yet without reducing its theory to the political and theoretical tradition of Marxism. The theory maintained, in its self-interpretation, a vaguely defined distance from this tradition, and claims precisely on account of this distance to preserve the "orthodox" form of Marxist theory.

Relation of Philosophy to Science

In its earliest years the Frankfurt Circle defined the relation between philosophy and science as one of programmatic indifference: "Materialism requires the unification of philosophy and science" (Horkheimer 1933a:23; 1972:34). Horkheimer planned for philosophy the role of a problem-sensitive, integrative medium for the specialized sciences, now fragmented into various disciplines. He intended a research process based on an organizational maxim derived from the distinction, present in Hegel and formulated by Marx, between one plane of "research" and another of "presentation." In 1937 one finds hardly any traces of this program.

The elements of a Marxist economic critique, as Horkheimer previously interpreted them—quite pointedly and selectively—served only as the foundation for a research program still to be developed. Now, in Critical Theory, the proposed relation of philosophy to science is immediately identified with the relation already present—according to Horkheimer—in Marx's economic critique. What Marx saw as the significance of classical bourgeois economics is interpreted by Horkheimer primarily as the significance of the ensemble of untheoretical specialized sciences, which can be used in the ultimately philosophically and theoretically oriented Marxian method of dialectical presentation. The specific difference between classical political economy and—despite its own designation—the ultimately philosophical critique of political economy is that, while critique incorporates the conceptual, analytical, and empirical material provided by other theories, it interprets the functional context of capitalist production as a totality. But in doing so, those (analytical and empirical) elements of the specialized sciences gain a new theoretical significance, as moments within a theoretically reconstructed totality:

Das Kapital is in its analyses no less precise than the national economy that it criticizes, yet the driving motive, right up to the most subtle accounts of isolated and periodically recurring processes, is knowledge of the historical course of the whole. (Horkheimer 1937b:627)

According to Horkheimer, the Critique of Political Economy interpreted in this way is "philosophical" not only with regard to the methodological and operative aspect of the analysis of totality. For Horkheimer—as already for Lukács—the operative aspect cannot be separated from the political aspect, according to which any science with theoretical mastery of the social totality would bring under control social relations as a whole.

According to Horkheimer, the critique of political economy redeems the materialist claim, even if formulated by Hegel, that "philosophy is its own epoch grasped in thought." What distinguishes the "critique" of the *Critique of Political Economy* is a peculiar coincidence of philosophy and specialized science:

In contrast to the institutional form of the modern, specialized sciences, however, the Critical Theory of society has remained philosophical even as an economic critique; its content is formed by transforming the concepts that predominate in the economic sphere into their opposites: equitable exchange into the deepening of social injustice, free economy into domination through monopoly, productive labor into the fetters of the relations of production, the preservation of the life of society into the pauperization of the nations. (1937b:627)

Marcuse accentuates somewhat differently the thesis that the *Critique of Political Economy* represents a coincidence of philosophy and science. In a philological correction he points out to Horkheimer that the young Marx maintained that, for "philosophy, there remains merely the task of elaborating science's most general conclusions." Marcuse points out that Critical Theory (taken as the essence of the history of the theoretical influence of Marxist theory) violates the postulate of the coincidence of philosophy and science. Clearly he is alluding to the fact that in the Soviet Union, for example, the specialized sciences in the form of "Soviet physics" had been fettered by philosophy, whereas in the Second International, the positivistically pursued specialized sciences were fetishized at the expense of philosophical orientation. When Marcuse then says that Critical Theory must also be critical toward itself (1937b:646), the bearers of this critical approach to the effective history of Marxist theory are the members of the Frankfurt Circle—who define themselves as marginal within the labor movement, yet nonetheless as bearers of a theory that is both philologically and situationally adequate. In the following quotation (which does not make clear whether it refers to German Social Democratic philosophy or to the Bolshevik praxis of materialist theory), Critical Theory's philosophical accent is characterized as a reaction to recent "economism" on the part of Marxists:

Critical Theory is not only critical toward itself, toward its own social bearer. The philosophical element within the theory is a form of protest against the new "economism": against an isolation of the economic struggle, against the division maintained between the economic and the political. (Marcuse 1937b:646)

Utopia

In the materialist period of the Frankfurt Circle's theoretical development, the point of reference for its political orientation had been the reorganization of the capitalist economy along the lines of a planned economy. This is no longer the case in the period considered here; the research on planned economy, intensively pursued in earlier years, was also discontinued. The relation of this shift to the critique of socialism in the Soviet Union, discussed above, cannot be overlooked. Horkheimer and Marcuse now insist that the abolition of private control over the means of production, their reorganization in the form of a planned economy, and the push toward industrialization are only negative preconditions for the establishment of a socialist society. The Frankfurt Circle's utopian point of reference clearly shifts—as early as 1935, though explicitly only in the programmatic writings on Critical Theory—from a scientifically pursued technology of the planned economy (Meyer/Mandelbaum/Pollock) to a philosophical treatment of the various *interests*, at work in a given transitional society, that participate in the reorganization of a capitalist economy into a planned economy. As Marcuse wrote in "Philosophy and Critical Theory":

Not that the labor process is regulated according to a plan, but rather which interest determines this regulation becomes important. (1937b:638; 1968:144)

This act of "making more abstract" the utopian frame of reference occurs in a context of critiques of attempts to give substantial form to the anticipated utopian social order, to depict utopia. According to Marcuse,

Critical Theory is not at all engaged in depicting a future world. . . . (1937b:645; 1968:154)

And Horkheimer:

The goal that [critical thought] seeks to reach—the bringing about of a rational order—is founded upon the needs of the present. Yet we do not find within the existence of this need the image of its being overcome. The theory that it suggests does not operate in the service of a reality already present; it expresses only its secret. (1937c:270)

The refusal to anticipate the "future world" or "future society" is well established—Marcuse emphasizes—in the tradition of Marxist theory, and Critical Theory views itself as the authentic expression of this tradition. Marx's critical economic analyses were indeed a critical phenomenology of the capitalist process of reproduction, not theoretical anticipations of a socialism with a planned economy.

Utopia is now "made philosophical," that is, transcendentalized. According to the suggestive phrase that "in the bourgeois economic organization, social activity is blind and concrete, that of the individual abstract and conscious" (Horkheimer, 1937c:256), what now matters is to make the transcendentally conceived bourgeois subject the orienting paradigm of the "future social order." In Horkheimer's words:

Critical thought is today motivated by the attempt to overcome the tension and to abolish the opposition between individual purposefulness, spontaneity, and rationality, and those relations of the labor process on which society is built. According to critical thought, man will be in conflict with himself until this identity is achieved. (1937c:264; 1972:210)

In the theoretical-political terms of the materialist period, the proletariat was the designated social bearer of the utopian guiding principle. After the definition of utopia had been changed, as described, its bearers could no longer be an empirically identifiable group. The subject of utopia is now itself altered; the bearer of utopia becomes the "fantasy" or "imagination" of a transcendental subject:

In order to retain what is not yet present as a goal, fantasy is needed. The essential connection of fantasy with philosophy is evident from the function attributed to it by philosophers under the title *imagination*. . . . Because of its unique capacity to 'intuit' an object even without its being present, the imagination has a considerable degree of independence from the given, of freedom in a world of unfreedom. In surpassing what is present, it can anticipate the future. (Marcuse 1937b:644; 1968:154)

The Third Phase: The Critique
of Instrumental Reason,
1940–1945

Historical and Political Experience

The Labor Movement

Adorno wrote in 1944:

Sociologists ponder the grimly comic riddle: "Where is the proletariat?"
(1951:258; 1974:194)

When Horkheimer, Pollock, and Adorno examine from the perspective
of the 1940s the demise of the German labor movement, all of their
relevant considerations are founded on the then-current judgment
that the proletariat had disintegrated as a class-conscious, and therefore
politically effective, subject of history. According to this judgment, the
political function of Critical Theory could now consist only in reflecting
upon the determinants of this disintegration.

Their basic thesis maintains that the proletariat has been integrated
into the context of bourgeois domination or that it reproduces this
context of domination in the structures of its own organizations. The
authoritarian-bureaucratic structure is described—without any historical or sociological differentiation, and without considering the particular
situation of individual socialist parties and labor unions—as characteristic of the proletarian organization before 1933. Thus, from the
apocalyptic perspective of the Frankfurt Circle after 1943, the political
orientation and structural organization of the ADGB [*Allgemeiner*

Deutscher Gewerkschaftsbund, German General Trade Union Congress], the SPD, the KPD, and indeed the Soviet Communist party and the Comintern appear ultimately to be the same. In the following discussion of the contexts in which the argument was made, it is often impossible to determine clearly whether, for example, Horkheimer's judgments about the labor organizations are aimed more at their Social Democratic or at their Bolshevik versions. The reasons given in support of the central thesis—that the proletariat as the bearer of political emancipation has dissolved—vary in the different theoretical contexts in which they appear. The most common argument maintains that the perverting of the labor organizations into an authoritarian, bureaucratically structured apparatus was brought about by the proletariat's integration into the capitalist system of the Weimar Republic. This charge is addressed to the responsible bearers of the Social Democratic policies in the Weimar state; it is also aimed at the legal right, also enjoyed by the proletariat and guaranteed in the Reich's constitution, to freely form coalitions; and it is aimed at the Republic's welfare-state character. Horkheimer:

Integration is the price that individuals and groups must pay in order to flourish under capitalism. Even those trade unions whose program opposed all forms of parliamentarianism have, as their membership has increased, significantly departed from the extravagances of general strikes and direct action. By accepting the Ministry of Munitions, they demonstrated in the First World War their readiness for peaceful cooperation. Even the maximalists after the Revolution were unable to cope with the fact that the ignominious sociology of the party system won out in the end. (1972a:16; 1978:99)

As a consequence of this integration, the capitalist structures of authority reproduced themselves even in the anticapitalist mass organizations. Horkheimer formulates explicitly the strong thesis of a structural approximation between the top management of capital and labor.

The top man and his clique become as independent in the labor organization as the board of directors in an industrial monopoly is from stockholders. The means of power—on the one hand, the party's or trade union's till, on the other, the factory's stocks—are at the management's disposal in the fight against troublemakers. . . . In extreme cases the dissidents are beheaded, bought off at the stockholders' convention, or expelled from the party convention. (1972a:15; 1978:98)

The separation of de jure titles of possession from the de facto power of disposal (a separation characteristic of monopoly capitalism) and the party leadership's bureaucratic autonomy from its base in proletarian mass organizations are different expressions of the same phenomenon: the implementation of the Führer or leader principle in all social mass organizations, even before the Führer existed as a historical reality.

Adorno:

Proletarians must assimilate if they want to live. [The principle of self-preservation] is everywhere forcing itself through the collective to the conspiratorial clique. Of necessity, the division reproduces itself below— between leader and followers—just as it realizes itself within the ruling class itself. (1972, vol. I:380)

And Horkheimer:

To the extent that the proletarian opposition in the Weimer Republic did not destroy itself through sectarianism, it became the victim of the spirit of the administration. The institutionalization of the leadership of labor and of capital had the same motive: the transformation of the mode of production. Monopolized industry, which makes the mass of shareholders into victims and parasites, condemns the bulk of the workers to a passive life and the public rolls. (1972a:15; 1978:98)

The radical thesis, which Marcuse and other members of the Circle maintained together with Horkheimer and Adorno, follows consistently: Fascism surpassed the conditions that prevailed before its coming to power, not in a negative sense, but rather in their positive continuation. Because it is maintained only with regard to the organizational form of proletarian mass organizations, this thesis is not to be confused with the charge of "social fascism" that the KPD leveled against the Weimar social democracy for complicity with the fascists.

In an aphorism from *Minima Moralia*, written in 1944, Adorno qualifies more precisely what Horkkheimer called the transformation of the mode of production, which supposedly prepared the ground for the leader principle: Progress in the technologies of production in late capitalism has led to such an elimination of the various kinds of skilled labor that the selection of leadership positions within the production process can no longer be made according to criteria of rationality with respect to technical aspects production:

The quantification of the technical processes, their dissection into minute operations that are largely independent of education and experience, makes the expertise of the new-style managers quite illusory. . . . Membership in the elite seems attainable by everyone. One merely waits to be co-opted. . . . They are experts only in control. The fact that now anyone can do as much has not led to their demise but to the possibility that any can be appointed. . . . One's downfall is decided, not by one's incompetence, but by an opaque hierarchical system in which no one, and scarcely even those at the top, can feel safe: It is an egalitarian threat. (1951:257; 1974:194)

In a letter to Paul Tillich, in which Horkheimer analyzes Tillich's objections to the essay "Reason and Self-Preservation" (written in 1941), Horkheimer also explains—in terms of a variant reading of a Max Weber thesis—the integration of the proletariat into the sphere of capitalist domination. The influence of the Protestant culture on the capitalist economic ethic expresses itself not only in the mentality of the capitalist entrepreneur but also clearly in the mentality of the working class:

And so it seems to me that the religious influences of the early and mature medieval Church on the intellectual structure of the European industrial proletariat have not been sufficiently demonstrated. . . . European workers were driven into the factories by the whip of hunger and other terrors. There can be no doubt on this point. The fact that they did not always run away whenever the opportunity was provided by an easing of the draconian laws (and as was still the case at the start of the Bolshevik industrialization in Russia) demonstrates, as I see it, the very significant role played by the new religiosity. It unleashed, as did the cultural policies of the Russian bureaucracy, the goal-oriented rationality of the modern worker. (19 August 1942, Pollock Archive)

Finally, the thesis of the integration of the proletariat appears again in the *Dialectic of Enlightenment*, as one illustration among many that technological domination of nature does not lead to human emancipation, but rather is reproduced in the form of a "second nature," that is, in forms of social intercourse:

The impotence of the worker is not merely a stratagem of those in power but rather the logical consequence of an industrial society in which the fate of antiquity is finally changed by trying to escape it. (Horkheimer and Adorno 1944:36; 1972:37)

We will consider this line of argument more thoroughly in the subsequent course of our discussion.

For the present it is to be borne in mind that the thesis of proletarian
integration, as well as that of the transformation of proletarian mass
organizations into an authoritarian apparatus—more an expression of
the leader principle than of proletarian solidarity—was not the product
of new experiences, new information, or a change in historical sources.
Rather, the thesis is simply the radical intensification of a pessimistic
view of socialism's chances in Germany—a judgment characteristic of
the Circle's political orientation as it developed in the final period of
the Weimar Republic.

The Soviet Union

The American press reported amply on those events of the 1930s that
were decisive for the Soviet Union's political and moral image in the
outside world: the show trials, the Comintern's policies with respect
to the Spanish Civil War, Stalin's pact with Hitler, and the entry of
Russian troops into those parts of Poland subjugated by the Germans.
Yet, after Hitler's invasion of the Soviet Union, these impressions,
according to historians, began to fade in the minds of Americans. And
in the United States of the early 1940s there was, not least because
of Roosevelt's pro-Soviet foreign policy, no resolute stand against communism aimed at Russia.[34] This rather well-disposed indifference toward the Soviet ally, particularly on the part of the liberal American
intelligentsia, contrasts sharply with the passionate discussion of Soviet
politics within the German and European socialist émigré circles in
the United States. The literary and theoretical treatments of the show
trials and pact began in émigré circles only in the 1940s. Franz Borkenau's *The Spanish Cockpit*—among other things, a settling of accounts
with the Comintern's policies regarding Spain—appeared at the end
of 1939. Arthur Koestler's *Darkness at Noon* appeared in London in
1940; a novelistic documentation of the antecedents to the show trials,
it was partially reprinted in 1941 in the New York German exiles'
newspaper *Neue Volkszeitung*, together with anti-Stalinst articles by Ig-
nacio Silone. To this day, Koestler's and Silone's writings of the time
are considered the most responsible and best-founded critiques of
nascent Stalinism. The Stalinist apologia (e.g., Maurice Merleau-Ponty's
Humanism and Terror) is based particularly on these texts.

The literary and journalistic presentations of the key political developments in the Soviet Union could not have gone unnoticed by the Frankfurt Circle members. Moreover, in Paul Massing, who left Moscow for New York as late as 1939, the Institute's members had an eyewitness to the Stalinist terror.[35] In 1943 Koestler wrote an article for the *New York Times Magazine* on the failure of "horizontalism"—the group of ideas and organizations that in the late nineteenth and early twentieth centuries promised to put an end to the political chaos of national-state egoisms. Above all, this meant the international solidarity of the left, which the Soviet-guided Comintern believed it represented until 1942. Koestler writes:

The outstanding feature of our days is the collapse of all horizontal structures. . . . Seen from the melancholy angle of a Continental (or rather of that bunch of homeless Leftists to whom I belong, and whom the Stalinists call Trotskyites, the Trotskyites call Imperialists, and the Imperialists call bloody Reds), the bankruptcy of Left horizontalism is becoming increasingly apparent. The corpse of the Comintern, in an advanced stage of decomposition, has at last been officially interred . . . in Russia the wheel is coming back full circle to the traditional values of the Fatherland, the Cadet Schools, and the Orthodox Church. . . . (1940:101–102)

Pollock sent this article to Horkheimer in November 1943, and Horkheimer replied:

Before I close this letter, your handwritten lines with the article of Koestler have arrived. I glanced through it and think it has some similarity with our own thoughts. . . . The article seems to be congenial and is welcome. Do you know Koestler personally? It might be most worthwhile to talk to him if he ever comes to this country, for he could prove to be one of the few to understand what we are doing. . . . (19 November 1943, Pollock Archive)

In his writings of the early 1940s Horkheimer characterized the Soviet system—without, even now, explicitly naming it—as "integral statism." This concept means the Russian Revolution's being limited (a limitation criticized as early as 1937) to a *nationalization* (*Verstaatlichung*) of the means of production, without any realization of the emancipatory potential of socialism. Horkheimer's 1942 essay "The Authoritarian State" contains phrases that condemn the political situation in the Soviet Union, where the uncompromising rejection of the Stalinist system could not be clearer. Alluding to the authoritarian structure of trade unions in the Western democracies, he remarks:

In the remaining democracies the leadership of the large working-class organizations already finds itself today in the same relationship to their members as the executives of integral statism have to society as a whole; they keep the masses, whom they take care of, under strict discipline, maintain them in hermetical seclusion from uncontrolled elements, and tolerate spontaneity only as a result of their own power. (1972a:16; 1978:98)

On the development of Stalinism in the Soviet Union, he notes explicitly:

As long as the vanguard is able to act without periodic political purges, the hope for a classless condition lives on. The two phases, in which (according to the prescription of tradition) a classless society is supposed to be realized have little to do with the ideology that today serves to perpetuate integral statism. Since an unlimited amount of consumer goods and luxury items still seems like a dream, the ruling class, which should have withered away in the first phase, is able to reinforce its position. Safeguarded by poor harvests and a housing shortage, it proclaims that the reign of secret police will disappear when the land of milk and honey has become reality. . . . (1972a:29; 1978:111)

Horkheimer even places the Soviet system near the fascist one:

Whether revolutionaries pursue power as one pursues loot or criminals is revealed only in the course of events. Instead of ultimately dissolving into a democracy of councils, the group might constitute itself as the ruling body. Labor, discipline, and order can save the republic and tidy up the revolution. Even though abolition of the state was written on its banner, the party transformed its industrially underdeveloped fatherland into the secret vision of those industrial powers that were growing sick on their parliamentarianism and could no longer survive without fascism. (1972a:17; 1978:99)

Such formulations being unmistakably within the larger context of the totalitarianism thesis as it was developed in a great number of contemporary studies on national socialism, such as Franz Borkenau's *The Totalitarian Enemy* (1940), Emil Lederer's *The State of the Masses* (1940), Sigmund Neumann's *Permanent Revolution* (1942), and particularly Hannah Arendt's writings of that time. And yet neither Horkheimer nor Pollock, nor Adorno, ever explicitly formulated the totalitarianism thesis, nor did they ever expressly acknowledge its symptomatic elaboration by American political science (C. J. Friederich). While Horkheimer, in his essay "The Authoritarian State," subsumes both Germany's fascist system and Russia's Bolshevik system under the category of fascism, he nonetheless distinguishes their respective political-economic structures. The Soviet Union's "integral statism" and Hitler-Germany's "state capitalism" are, despite all phenomenological similarities (single-party system, secret police, centralized economy), structurally distinct versions of the "authoritarian" state.

Fascism

The Frankfurt Circle's political and historical experiences between 1939 and 1945 were strongly marked by the events of the war, even though the chronology of the Second World War received only indirect expression in the development of the theory. In terms of the Institute's scholarly treatment of the National Socialist system—which in the early 1940s eclipsed all other research interests—the war brought together the historically determining conditions that propelled fascism to its purest and most developed form.

The Frankfurt Circle never identified with the Allies' war aims or, in particular, with the political philosophy that acknowledged these aims. Not even those members, such as Marcuse, Löwenthal, Neumann, and Pollock, who in the final years of the war worked full- or part-time for the American authorities, identified with these aims. On 1 September 1939, the day the war began, Horkheimer wrote in a letter:

The frightful thing about this situation is that, given the present constellations and rallying cries, there is not a single one toward which one could feel even distantly sympathetic. (Pollock Archive)

This remoteness from the Allies' ideological war goals (which can be documented up to 1945) was in the first two years of the war, and particularly in Horkheimer's case, an expression of a socialist interpretation—and still recognizable as such—of the economic structures of the adversaries. Thus Horkheimer even interpreted Chamberlain's politics of appeasement against the background of the English financial aristocracy's sympathies for Hitler's politics. He considered England's military restraint during the Polish campaign as support for his thesis, which he maintained until 1941, that the British *grande bourgeoisie* sought a settlement with Hitler. Horkheimer thought he found the ultimate proof for his views in Rudolf Hess's attempt to mediate between England and the Third Reich at the expense of the USSR:

Hess was the leader of the entire fifth-column work. His personal presence in London indicates just how far along matters were. His argument to the aristocratic dissidents there was most probably the following. What you are going to win at best through war is a liquidation of the social hierarchy and the transformation of England into an American province. "We" are not enthusiastic about giving Stalin the opportunity for Russia to win on account of our having to fight America. Therefore we offer you our hand. . . . (21 May 1941, Pollock Archive)

In the subsequent course of the war Horkheimer rejected this tendency (also common among other socialist emigrants in the early war years) to interpret the arrangement of national states into two adversarial groups as an overlapping of an internationalized class struggle and as its consequence[36] — an interpretation similar to the interpretation of the First World War by left-wing Social Democrats.

We cannot say to what extent the Circle concurred with this view. What did not change, right up to the end of the war, was the Circle's nonidentification—maintained in spite of all radical opposition to the fascist war powers—with the political philosophy of the Western war powers. What did change was the complex of arguments on which this ideological distance was based. It came to be based on the technology-critical philosophy of history sketched in "Reason and Self-Preservation" and then developed in the *Dialectic of Enlightenment*; according to this argument, fascist state capitalism merely completed the historical logic of late-capitalist industrial societies. Horkheimer and Adorno considered National Socialist Germany only a forerunner of a tendency inherent in all Western industrial nations—a tendency obscured, to be sure, by the Allies' military stand against Germany. They write in 1944:

Fascism triumphed in Germany. . . . Now that fascism is devastating the earth, the nations are forced to fight it, for they have no alternative. But when it is all over, no spirit of freedom will necessarily spread across Europe; its nations may well become just as xenophobic, hostile to culture, and pseudocollectivistic as was the fascism against which they had to defend themselves. Even fascism's defeat will not necessarily stop the movement of the avalanche. (1944:197; 1972:221)

The highly technical manner of fighting the war forms one of those historical impressions that led to the technology-critical philosophy of history developed in the 1940s. Horkheimer and Adorno considered military technology, not as an ideologically neutral instrument that legitimates itself through the political goals toward which it is applied, but rather as an expression of a monstrous apparatus that has made itself autonomous of all nontechnological goals. Adorno wrote in 1944, after seeing a newsreel report on the war in the Pacific:

The impression is not of the battles, but of road construction and blasting operations, undertaken with boundless vehemence—also of "fumigations," the extermination of insects on a tellurian scale. Operations are conducted until grass no longer grows. The enemy functions as patient and cadaver. Like the Jews under fascism, he simply serves as the object of technical-administrative measures, and when he resists, his resistance immediately takes on the same character. (1951:66; 1974:56)

National socialism's system of government, law, and economy, as well as its cultural policies, formed at the beginning of the 1940s the unequivocal focus of the Institute's research. First, there were the preparatory studies for a project, never realized, on the "cultural aspects of national socialism"; then the preliminary studies for various projects on anti-Semitism, studies that later became part of the *Studies in Prejudice*; as well as the following individual works, which might be loosely ordered as follows:

by Pollock: "State Capitalism," "Is National Socialism a New Order?"

by Kirchheimer: several essays on the National Socialist legal system

by Neumann: *Behemoth*

by Gurland: work regarding National Socialist policy on technologies and on the middle class

by Marcuse: "The State and the Individual in National Socialism"

by Horkheimer: the programmatic essays "The Jews and Europe" and "The Authoritarian State"

Taken together, these studies are to this day unequaled in terms of their theoretical sophistication, empirical content, and interdisciplinary orientation. That they nonetheless have been forgotten—precisely as a group—results not only from the circumstances of their publication but also from the fact that these individual works cannot be considered the initial elements of a comprehensive theory of fascism. This is less because of their heterogeneity in method and discipline than because they are informed by controversial assessments of fascism's capitalist character. These assessments led to the division of the Institute's members into two camps in 1940–1941.

The two fronts consisted of Franz Neumann, Gurland, Kirchheimer, and Marcuse on one side and Pollock, Horkheimer, Adorno, and Leo Löwenthal on the other. On the basis of detailed empirical analyses, the first group (particularly Neumann, Kirchheimer, and Gurland) advocated the old continuity thesis, formulated in 1933, according to which the fascist system—even in its most advanced war-capitalist form—is the form of political organization most appropriate to highly monopolized capitalism. By contrast, Pollock, Horkheimer, and Adorno advocated, on the basis of Pollock's theory of state capitalism, the thesis that a fully developed fascist system—in the concrete historical case of the National Socialist system—tends to annul the Marxist primacy of economic factors over political factors. In a perversion of socialist goals, the fascists in Germany had already implemented political control and guidance of the economic process.

With his concept of state capitalism Pollock attempted a theoretical systematization of trends that he considered peculiar to national socialism but also present in the United States. He finds the concept of state capitalism more useful for describing these trends than such forms as "state socialism," "guided economy," or "neomercantilism." The concept of state capitalism is designed to express several ideas: that the state-capitalist system is the successor to the private-capitalist one; that the state has taken over central functions of the capitalist; that profits still play a (subordinate) role; and that the system is not a socialist one. The state-capitalist system can be roughly characterized as follows. The market, as an indirect instrument coordinating supply and demand, is replaced by a system of direct planning. This planning system rests in the hands of a powerful bureaucracy, itself the product of a fusion of state bureaucracy and top industrial management. The total economic process takes place within the framework of a general plan with guidelines for production, distribution, consumption, savings, and investments. The plan is to be realized by fiat of the state executive, and prices should gradually lose their function as indices of scarcity.

Although the profit system will not (yet) be completely abolished, interests concerned with profit must nonetheless submit to the general plan. The trend (which became manifest in the period of monopoly capitalism) toward separating possession of the means of production from the actual power to dispose over them will have been completed; the tendency is then to reduce the traditional capitalist to the role of a mere government pensioner. Although most industry would remain in private possession, it would be state-supervised. The top leadership of industrial monopolies will have become government commissioners—similar to the way in which the institutions of guilds, chambers of commerce, and chambers of labor, originally organized in terms of civil law, were transformed into official authorities. Pollock assumes that a state-capitalist system is thoroughly capable of securing such imperatives of modern economic policy as steady growth and full employment. He clearly considers an authoritarian and a democratic state capitalism possible, but he makes it clear in the essay "Is National Socialism a New Order?" (1941) that he considers the authoritarian version the more likely alternative and that in drafting a theory of state capitalism, he ultimately oriented himself on National Socialist development. This essay is nothing other than application of the state capitalism theory to National Socialist conditions.

Franz Neumann considers the concept of state capitalism to be self-contradictory, even at the analytical level. He maintains that the theory is untenable, mainly on empirical grounds. In detailed analyses in legal and political theory and in economics, he demonstrates that the possibility of harmonious coordinating the elements of the entire political-economic process—presupposed by Pollock's state capitalism theory—does not correspond to actual national socialism. The "contradictions" of monopoly capitalism originating in its prefascist era have not been overcome; indeed, they exist in a politically critical, that is, totalitarian form. He opposes Pollock's programmatic concept of state capitalism with the concept of totalitarian monopoly capitalism. Neumann concedes that the National Socialists developed, into the beginnings of a "command economy," the Weimar Republic's political instruments of economic management. But he maintains that the top industrial bureaucracy's influence, the maintenance of the profit motive, and a concentration of capital, which even increased as of 1933, have established only the private-capitalist identity of the National Socialist economic order. To support his thesis Neumann analyzes the 1933 legislation for the obligatory formation of cartels; the Reich's 1934 labor law; the 1936 four-year plan; the distribution of power in the self-administering corporate bodies of the war industry; and the Third Reich's policies concerning expropriation and technology. Gurland studied these last-mentioned policies in an essay published in 1941, and Kirchheimer analyzed in detail modifications to the law concerning stock. Neumann sums up his theory as follows:

What, however, is the generating force of that economy: patriotism, power, or profits? We believe that we have shown that it is the profit motive that holds the machinery together. But in a monopolistic system profits cannot be made and retained without totalitarian political power, and that is the distinctive feature of national socialism. (1944:354)

The point at which the controversy became critical between the two camps in general, and between Pollock and Neumann in particular, was a methodological one: the question of the primacy of the political over the economic sphere. Horkheimer and Adorno, in any case, interpreted Pollock's theory of state capitalism in this way and adapted its argument to their own theory in *Dialectic of Enlightenment*. Pollock's thesis provided the theoretical description of a social order in which the *political* administration so thoroughly controls the entire economic process that one may speak of a primacy of the political over the economic sphere under nonsocialist conditions. Adorno and Horkheimer found in Pollock's theory the political-economic refinement of their own thesis (a refinement they themselves never accomplished), namely, that domination in highly developed, industrial societies no longer assumes an economic form, as in liberalism, but rather an immediately political form, as in the pre-bourgeois era. Pollock's theory provided them with the economic justification for considering an economic analysis of society no longer necessary or even possible.

Theory of the Theory-Praxis Relation

The Subject and Addressee of the Theory

The culture industry of late capitalism and the propaganda apparatus of the fascist states have made the politically significant development of a proletarian class consciousness so very unlikely, according to

Horkheimer and Adorno, that they can no longer treat the proletariat as the subject of a social theory suited to that class's historical situation. In his "Reflections on Class Theory" of 1942, Adorno remarks with resignation:

The complete organization of society by big business and its omnipresent technology has so totally filled the world and people's heads that the thought "It could in any way be different" has become an almost hopeless exercise. The infernal image of harmony, the invisibility of the classes in the petrification of their condition, gains a real power over the consciousness only because the idea—that the oppressed, the workers of all countries, should unite as a class—seems hopeless in view of the present distribution of impotence. (1972, vol. I:376)

In his programmatic essay of 1937, "Traditional and Critical Theory," Horkheimer developed the idea that a social theory adequate to the contemporary historical situation is still possible only in the social form of a marginal group—marginal not only in relation to society but also in relation to the proletarian masses. This judgment—which might be classified in terms of a sociology of knowledge—about the conditions for the Circle's own theoretical work is radicalized in the 1940s to the point of nullifying itself self-referentially. Now, only individuals—completely isolated politically, not members of any political organization, "lonely" individuals—are capable of anticipating collective interests theoretically. By the end of 1938, Adorno had written in his essay "On the Fetish Character in Music":

In the sphere of music, too, the collective powers are liquidating individuality, which is irrecoverable—but against them only individuals are capable of consciously representing the aims of collectivity. (1938:355; 1978:299)

In 1944 he wrote:

Inviolable loneliness is the sole form in which the intellectual can in some way preserve his solidarity. Participation in any form . . . merely masks a tacit acceptance of inhumanity. (1951:22; 1974:26)

These judgments represent an implicit critique of all forms of organized political activity. Their literary form is significant in that they are not presented as the product of an informal analysis of contemporary political organizations, but rather as conclusions drawn from a pessimistic anthropology, experienced as though it were evident. None of Adorno's texts reveals the point of reference for his all-embracing pessimism in existing political organizations—whether organizations for political emigrants, political parties in the Weimar Republic, American trade unions, or resistance groups in the Third Reich.

The same can be said for the manner of presenting the problem that constituted the political identity of the Circle from the very beginning: its cognitive distance from proletarian class consciousness. In the early 1930s Horkheimer thought that this distance resulted in part from social-psychological factors and in part from the low theoretical sophistication of the Weimar Republic's socialist parties; in 1937 he thought it resulted from the fascist political repression of the working class. In 1944, in the form of an aphorism on the sociology of language, Adorno again discusses the relation between proletarian class consciousness and scientific social theory. Their relation appears in this context as that between proletarian dialects and the standard written language—the relation, to use modern diction, between a "restricted" and an "elaborated" code. Adorno's argument is based on Horkheimer's critique of a "Luxemburgian" intelligentsia. The proletariat's orientation has been perverted through its domination. The intellectual would only make himself subject to this domination if, in his theoretical-political work, he were to adopt the proletariat's orientation:

To oppose workers' dialects to written language is reactionary. Domination alone has left its mark on the language of the oppressed, and has even robbed from them the justice promised by the unmutilated, autonomous word to all those free enough to pronounce it without rancor. . . . If written language codifies the alienation of classes, redress cannot lie in regressing to the spoken language, but rather only in the consistent exercise of the strictest linguistic objectivity. (Adorno 1951:129ff.; 1974:102)

The proletariat's class consciousness and the development of a critical social theory can no longer be at all mediated in terms of the Frankfurt Circle's political models of the 1940s. Above and beyond this, domestic power relations in National Socialist Germany and in fascist-controlled continental Europe raised doubts about whether, under the given political-historical conditions, the proletariat could still be considered the *addressee* of revolutionary theory-construction. This was the perspective of emigrants who had no real opportunity to mediate their political work with the consciousness of those to whom their theory was originally addressed:

It is completely naive to think that one could exhort the workers, from an external position, to overthrow the system. Anyone who can only play at politics should let it alone. (Horkheimer 1939a:135)

Then, in 1944, Horkheimer and Adorno openly acknowledged in *Dialectic of Enlightenment* that their theory—which, when they initially developed it, was interpreted programmatically as a theoretical support for proletarian struggle—had completely lost sight of its addressees:

If there is today anyone to whom we can bequeath the message, it is neither the so-called masses nor the individual who is powerless, but rather to an imaginary witness—lest it perish with us. (1971:228; 1972:256)

Horkheimer was referring to his essay "Reason and Self-Preservation" when he wrote in 1942 to Paul Tillich:

We can hope for no more than that, would day ever break, our writings will be recognized as a very little star that had shown, though barely perceptible, in the horrible night of the present. (12 August 1942, Pollock Archive)

In a remark contained in his *Eclipse of Reason*, and probably written in the final days of the war,[37] for which there are further examples in the writings of the 1950s, Horkheimer suggests that the proletariat is no longer the addressee or even the subject of the Circle's work. The Circle's theory now interprets itself as an attempt to break through the silence of fascism's victims, to give these victims a voice:

The anonymous martyrs of the concentration camps are the symbols of the humanity that is striving to be born. The task of philosophy is to translate what they have done into a language that will be heard even though their finite voices have been silenced by tyranny. (1947:161)

Theory and Praxis

According to Marx, revolutionary theory becomes practical by seizing the masses. Horkheimer and Adorno maintain that such a form of political praxis is now displaced in the long run, on the one hand, by the conditioning of social experience through propaganda and through the culture industry, in fascism as in the United States, and, on the other hand, by the transformation of Marxism into a Stalinist science of legitimation. In the programmatic introduction to *Dialectic of Enlightenment*, they write:

when the public sphere has reached a state in which thought inevitably becomes a commodity, and language the means of promoting it, then the attempt to detect such degenerations must avoid all allegiance to current linguistic and conceptual conventions, lest their world-historical consequences thwart it entirely. Were these consequences nothing more than the obstacles resulting from the self-oblivious instrumentalization of science, then social analysis could at least join with trends opposed to "official" science; and yet these too have been taken over by the total process of production. They have changed as much as the ideology at which they were directed. They suffer what has already occurred to the triumphant form of thinking. If it willingly abandons its critical element and allows itself to become merely an instrument in the service of the status quo, it then tends, despite itself, to transform the positive, which it desires, into something negative and destructive. (1944:1ff.; 1972:xi–xii)

Despite the political-historical claim that they make for their theory with all the pathos of a philosophy of history, Horkheimer and Adorno could give only a negative determination to the practical-political role of their theoretical work—given the conditions prevailing in the public sphere. Horkheimer wrote in 1939:

The confusion has become so widespread that the truth has a greater practical value the less it yearns for some supposed praxis. Theoretical insight is needed, along with the transmission of this insight to those who will one day at last be able to lead the way. The optimism of a political call to action, today, is born of a lack of courage. (1939a:135)

But with no prospective bearer for theoretical insight, the capacity of theory to orient political action can now be determined only negatively: in the form of resisting the political instrumentalization of theory. In 1945 Horkheimer wrote in the introduction to *Eclipse of Reason*:

In so doing the author is not trying to suggest anything like a program of action. On the contrary, he believes that the modern propensity to translate every idea into action, or into active abstinence from action, is one of the symptoms of the present cultural crisis: action for action's sake is in no way superior to thought for thought's sake, and is perhaps even inferior to it. (1947:vi)

This option for a purely theoretical critique incapable of being joined to political action; this clear preference—given the alternative of political activism—for a self-sufficient critique, represents a self-hypothesization of theoretical work that, because it no longer has a political addressee, can now be only self-referential. If the texts of the 1940s still speak of a (para-)political praxis on the part of theory, it is only programmatically in the form of philosophical "discourse" or of the culture-critical "maxim" that merely reverberates around itself.

Horkheimer and Adorno formulate explicitly this rather theoretical form of a praxis of theory, and they do this in the manner of a philosophy of language—or, more precisely, in a reflection on the relation of philosophy, language, and truth. These very unsystematic considerations, confined to a purely theoretical domain, form the positive foil for a critique of the instrumentalization of language in the culture industry. Yet they were directly motivated by the apparently traumatic experience of fascist radio programs. In a letter dated 21 July 1940, Horkheimer wrote to Pollock:

On the trip over here I listened to Hitler's speech. His words speed across the plains and seas of the world; they penetrate into the most distant mountain valley. But I had a strong feeling that these indeed are not words, but a natural force. The word is concerned with truth, but this is a means of war, and belongs to the shining armaments of Martians. (Pollock Archive)

Yet—according to this line of thought—a purely theoretical language, not instrumentalized for purposes of domination, gains in political significance precisely because it is misused as propaganda; it gains in political significance even if those still able to speak it are isolated and powerless. In his 1942 essay, "The Authoritarian State," Horkheimer writes:

The isolated individual who is not appointed or protected by any power cannot expect fame. Nonetheless, he is a force, because everyone is isolated. His only weapon is the word. The more it is bandied about by barbarians within and cultural sophisticates without, the more it regains honor. . . . One's integrity is revealed again in the betrayal of language to commerce. (1972a:30; 1978:112)

The extreme instrumentalization of language in fascist propaganda furnishes the negative image of a "pure" language, the idea of the word as something that *means*, not as something that spurs to action.

Behind this notion of a pure language, of the word not abused for purposes of manipulation, stands the old conception of truth as the identity of name and object, of word and thing, and the decoding of their identity as the task of philosophy:

Philosophy is the conscious effort to knit together all our knowledge and insight into a linguistic structure in which things are called by their correct names. (Horkheimer 1974a:167)

The rationalization of language in the course of the Enlightenment, and even more so its conditioning by mass communication in the form of propaganda and the culture industry, have buried layers of experience that were still found in the immediate identity of word and content—in words, for example, such as *Wehmut* [melancholy], *Geschichte* [history], *Geduld* [patience] (Horkheimer and Adorno 1944:147; 1972:164). Horkheimer and Adorno considered the sign theory of language an intertheoretical reflex of the process of the separation of word and content, the reduction of the word to a mere sign, a mere formula. Striking examples can be found in the culture industry and in fascist propaganda for the fact that "the word that only still signifies is no longer allowed to mean anything."

The outer left wing in football, the black shirt, the Hitler Youth, and similar types are nothing more than their names. If, prior to its rationalization, the word is burdened with lies as well as with yearning, the rationalized word has become a straitjacket even more for yearning than for lies. (1944:148; 1972:164)

Jay (1976:306) has pointed out the affinity of these linguistic considerations to Walter Benjamin's theory of language, as developed in his essay "The Task of the Translator." Benjamin presupposes a distinction between divine and human language. Divine names are identical with the essence of the things signified, whereas human words are related to things inadequately, imperfectly. The task of the translator is the identification in human language of those elements of divine language, and the mediation of the human with the divine. Similarly for Horkheimer and Adorno, the task of philosophy is to decode language's truth potential, made inaccessible through the sundering of words from their contents. This hermeneutics for a language deformed by the culture industry and propaganda is, for Horkheimer and Adorno, the political praxis of their theory—indeed, the single praxis possible and adequate under the prevailing historical circumstances.

Theoretical Position

Self-Understanding within the Tradition of Historical and Political Theory

The *materialism* and *Critical Theory* periods of the Frankfurt Circle's theory development were each inaugurated by a programmatic essay by Horkheimer. In these essays Horkheimer developed certain programmatic concepts which then reappeared in a great number of individual studies by Circle members. The developmental period now to be discussed is not characterized by any such clearly identifiable program for a theory.

First, there is no longer a precise name for the collective theoretical-political orientation. We will therefore adopt the German title of *Eclipse of Reason* [*Kritik der instrumentellen Vernunft*] and call this period the *critique of instrumental reason*. The concept of Critical Theory is still used in writings of the early 1940s (particularly in volume 9 of *Studies in Philosophy and Social Science*), but, in comparison with 1937, it has completely different connotations. To the extent that the concept appears at all in *Dialectic of Enlightenment* and *Eclipse of Reason*, it has largely the same meaning as the concept *philosophy*.

Second, there is no programmatic piece by Horkheimer to introduce this period, and there is also no clearly identifiable caesura between this period and that of Critical Theory. The most concise formulation of theory development in the 1940s is *Dialectic of Enlightenment* of 1944; yet the themes developed there are already intimated in the writings of Horkheimer and Adorno as early as 1939, and most clearly in Horkheimer's essay "Reason and Self-Preservation," published in 1942.

Third, individual texts issuing from the Circle's work can be ascribed far less to a collective effort in the 1940s than in the 1930s. *Dialectic of Enlightenment*, however, arose not only out of a co-authorship by Horkheimer and Adorno. This book documents a close context of work and discussion—a context in which Marcuse and Löwenthal originally participated, and the results of which clearly correspond to Pollock's theory of the state.

The materialism and Critical Theory periods had definite cultural-political identities, in that each identified with an existing theoretical tradition and the corresponding friend-enemy constellations. For the period we shall call the critique of instrumental reason there is no longer an intellectual-political tradition on which the Circle's position might be based. Its identity becomes even less clear, since the identity of its adversary takes on universal dimensions. The stated opponent, the main object of criticism, is nothing less than the entire Western rationalist tradition, from its earliest mythological origins to the present age of a world war unleashed by fascists. Horkheimer and Adorno maintain that precisely the fascist era provides the world-historical possibility of gaining insight into the pathogenesis of the Western rationalist tradition:

Beneath Europe's known and recognized history there exists another, subterranean history. It comprises the fate of the human instincts and passions repressed and distorted by civilization. From the perspective of the fascist present—an era in which the hidden side of things comes to light—manifest history reveals itself in its connection with its dark, subterranean side. . . . (1944:207; 1972:231)

This line of argument is structurally analogous to Marx's assertion that only from the perspective provided by the zenith of fully developed capitalism do the precapitalist forms of production become theoretically accessible. Texts of both the materialist and Critical Theory periods developed an argument against separating nature from history, according to which the human species deals with nature solely in terms of the specific form of the social division of labor. This argument is now radicalized and historically derelativized. It is radicalized in that historically definable periods of forms of production are no longer viewed as the real object of theory—as is the case in Marxist theory; instead, the proper theoretical object is now considered to be the entirety of the world-historical process of active confrontation between man and nature. Furthermore, the earlier argument is historically derelativized, so that nature—above and beyond all historically iden-tifiable, organized forms of human labor—is itself conceived of as a quasi-subject, as the alter ego of the human species, increasingly al-ienated from the species through technological exploitation designed to enhance its self-reproduction. Horkheimer and Adorno interpret the beginning of history—the constitution of the human species in the act of self-empowering assertion over nature—as an act of violent differentiation of itself out of its previous self-identity with nature. Technics and technology, the systematized forms of the productive self-assertion of the species vis-à-vis nature that were considered throughout the modern rationalist tradition as a vehicle of progress, are now considered by Horkheimer and Adorno as a vehicle for world-historical regression. Habermas has pointed out the mystical Jewish tradition in which such a conception of nature stands, which Adorno and Horkheimer share with other speculative Marxists, such as Bloch and Walter Benjamin.[38] Behind the implicit identification with this *topos* is the surrendering, never made explicit, of Marx and Engels' prognosis that the emancipation of the human race will be achieved by perfecting human domination of nature. The claim made by the industrial age—to have achieved emancipation from the domination of nature through a high level of technological development—is interpreted as signifying the deepest fall into nature. Hence the conviction, of the old European, rationalist tradition, of the primacy of spirit over nature, is dialectically turned against itself: A view of reason restricted merely to improving the technology of self-preservation is still a part of that nature which actually instrumentalizes reason to even the score. This critique of technical control over nature is the programmatic theme integrating all of the specific analyses made in *Dialectic of Enlightenment* and other writings of the 1940s:

A philosophical reconstruction of world history would have the task of showing how the consistent domination of nature, despite all deviations and resistance, has been continuously and increasingly successful and has integrated that which is intrinsically human. Economic forms, forms of authority, and cultural forms could also be derived from this perspective. (Horkheimer and Adorno 1944:200; 1972:223)

The development of this perspective, especially in *Dialectic of Enlightenment* and *Eclipse of Reason*, is far less systematic than this formulation would suggest. In these writings the following individual theses are inextricably conflated:

1. The constitution of the human race at the beginning of all history by violent differentiation from its context in nature, with the productive "exploitation" of nature for the purpose of self-reproduction.

2. The reproduction of this domination over the "primary nature" into "second nature," that is, into the forms of social organization in

which nature is dominated; the development and refinement of technological domination over nature in the modern era and in the industrial age has its political expression in the totalization of political repression, whose most extreme and advanced form is fascism.

3. The constitution of the personal self by controlling its inner nature. This construction is developed on both phylogenetic and ontogenetic levels. For Horkheimer and Adorno, the development of modern subjectivity stands in phylogenetic relation to the technical unshackling of the bourgeois form of production; and ontogenetically, in the Western tradition of education; the base-line criterion of successful socialization is the individual's ability to domesticate the demands made by his internal biology.

4. The deformation of all forms of cognitive orientation toward the world. Repressed nature reproduces itself precisely in that medium considered by the Western rationalist tradition to be its most extreme opposite: in mind itself. It is not in Western philosophy and science that Horkheimer and Adorno see the first appearance of this process, but rather in historically early forms of human orientation in the world: in magic, mythology, theogony, and theology.

By a metaphorical generalization, Horkheimer and Adorno characterize the entire pathogenesis of Occidental rationality, from its early historical origins to the age of the culture industry, with the concept of enlightenment. This concept is closely related to what Max Weber called rationalization, as well as to Lukács's use of the concept of reification (a usage itself based on Weber). According to Horkheimer and Adorno, all historical forms of cognitive world-orientation played the role of politically integrating society. Horkheimer takes logic as the paradigm of this thesis. Basing himself on the analysis of the classificatory schemata used in primitive cultures, according to Durkheim's sociology of knowledge, he shows how relations of social domination are mirrored in the hierarchies of formal logics (cf. 1974a:106).

This propensity, inherent in all the cognitive systems created in the course of Western history, to become instruments of political integration and repression is palpable in the most advanced forms of these systems — in the mass communication of the culture industry and in fascist propaganda. In these forms, according to the argument, the Occidental rationalist tradition has assumed its contemporary form.

In the critique of the culture industry, the consciousness of all members of society is seen as so completely filled with a reality prefabricated by mass communication that the individual's every cognitive act is only the ratification of a social decision made long ago. Previous social experience is so dominant in relation to all cognitive acts that their performance merely confirms that they belong to the system:

Life in the late capitalist era is only a continuous initiation rite. (Horkheimer and Adorno 1944:138; 1972:153)

The original relation of the means of mass communication to empirical reality has been perverted into something absurd: While journals and newspapers in the nineteenth century, and radio and cinema in the 1920s, at least offered additional information, commentaries, and parodies of reality as grasped by the senses, in the technologically highly developed, late-capitalist era, reproduction of reality by the culture industry and mass communication has become so encompassing, hermetic, and totalitarian that the individual's sense experience now merely illustrates previous social experiences.

Horkheimer and Adorno thought even the social order of the Allies to be prefascist. As clear evidence of this view, they compared fascist propaganda with the omnipresent advertising in the "remaining democracies of late capitalism":

The advertising of the same commodities over and over, merely marketed under different brand names, the praise—based on scientific tests—for a laxative in the radio or television announcer's soothing voice, between the overtures of *La Traviata* and *Rienzi*: All this has become indefensible simply because it is so ridiculous. In these times, at last, industry's dictates—camouflaged by the pretense of free choice—have become the unconcealed commands of the Führer. (1944:143; 1972:159f)

Relation to Marxism

Earlier discussions have clearly shown that in the 1940s, Horkheimer and Adorno depart from the Marxist theoretical tradition. Their theory no longer takes as its object the forms—particularly the capitalist forms—of social intercourse by which the human species reproduces itself in appropriating nature. Instead, their concern is the world-historical drama of the active confrontation of the human species with nature. Those writings we have discussed abandon that decisive utopian theme of socialist philosophy which views emancipation from nature as an essential aspect of political emancipation. Horkheimer and Adorno suggest that the technically produced domination over *natura naturans* reproduces itself in the West's social institutions and forms of consciousness. Their abandonment of the Marxist theoretical tradition is also demonstrated by their explicit renunciation of its methodology of economic critique. Pollock, Horkheimer, and Adorno, in their presentation of considerations derived from their theory of fascism, develop the assumption that political domination in fascism and in advanced late capitalism is no longer economically mediated, and that social analysis consequently cannot continue with the methodology of the economic critique. This departure from the economic critique as the methodological paradigm of social theory is typified in Horkheimer's essay "The Social Function of Philosophy," written at the end of 1939. The programmatic concept of critique and dialectic is, after 1937, no longer conceived in terms of *Critique of Political Economy* but in terms of the Platonic dialogues. The fact that so many readers of the Circle's writings of the 1940s do not recognize the conscious abandonment of the Marxist theoretical tradition can be explained by the fact that their basic positions are not developed as criticisms of Marx. Their philological distance from his writings, maintained throughout the various development periods of the Circle's theory, of course do not aid the reader in recognizing the break with Marxist theory once it had been made. A critique of Marx from the perspective of *Eclipse of Reason* was developed for the first time by pupils of Horkheimer and Adorno.[39] But this break remained unrecognizable in subsequent years also because Horkheimer and, especially, Adorno maintained a Marxian form of argumentation. Arguments in *Dialectic of Enlightenment* are often based on Marx's theory of value. The Circle's break with Marxist theory is revealed only by the complete shift in the significance of Marxist theory within the total context of the Circle's theory. The law of value is, for Marx, the fundamental principle of capitalist development, whereas, for Horkheimer and Adorno it is only one principle among many principles of social integration by means of instrumental reason—albeit a principle specific to bourgeois society. Other principles of integration include the principle of predication in the mathematical sciences, the principle of totality in late capitalist forms of authority, the pressure to conform produced by the culture industry, and the biographical pressure threatening the identity of individuals.[40] To this synchronic relativization of the law of value corresponds a diachronic one, as when, in subtle analyses, Horkheimer and Adorno present the modern act of exchange as a secularized form of a magic offering (1944:47; 1972:49), or when Horkheimer, in his explication of the concept of reification, traces the formalization of reason back to the very beginnings of the organized use of tools, no longer viewing it, like Marx, as a cognitive consequence of abstract value in bourgeois society.

Relation of Philosophy to Science

In their writings of the 1940s, Horkheimer and Adorno identify the positive, specialized sciences and their philosophical legitimation—positivism—with their application (however mediated this may be) in productive technology. The classical Marxist argument, that scientific labor forms one aspect within the process of the socially organized appropriation of nature ("critical" theory distinguished itself from "traditional" theory by reflecting precisely on this aspect), is now turned against the positive sciences themselves. Scientific theory—in the emphatic sense of the word—has never existed because theory up to the present day has never been anything more than extended technological "praxis," an instrument for the appropriation of nature. Horkheimer and Adorno view strategies of scientific learning as technical tools in intellectual form; such strategies are technologies for the control of nature, simply in a different aggregate state. The conditioning of the objects of knowledge for the experimental techniques of the natural (and social) sciences, as well as the logical and mathematical formalization of all available categories, merely repeats, in the sphere of science, instrumental conditioning of natural objects for the self-reproduction of the species.

This is the basis of their mistrust of theory informed by the specialized sciences—something that had previously been promoted by the materialism of the early 1930s. As if to recall this fact, the *Dialectic of Enlightenment* is introduced with the following words:

Even though we have observed for many years that, in modern institutionalized science, the great discoveries are paid for with a continuing decline in theoretical culture [*Bildung*], we nonetheless believed that we could keep up with the institution well enough, that our efforts might be restricted to the critique or development of the ideas put forth by the specialized disciplines. We were to concern ourselves, at least thematically, with the traditional disciplines: sociology, psychology, and epistemology. The fragments brought together in this book show, however, that we had to give up this confidence. (1944:1; 1972:xi)

Horkheimer's and Adorno's mistrust (significant for their metatheoretical orientation from 1940 onward) of all specialized scientific disciplines made necessary a redefinition of the relation of philosophy to science. Whereas the materialist period considered philosophy the integrating medium of interdisciplinary theory construction (and sought, programmatically, the unification of philosophy and science), and, whereas the Critical Theory period took Marx's economic critique as the orienting, paradigmatic unity of philosophy and the specialized sciences, in this third period philosophy is a mental preserve, a critical island, an encapsulation resistant to the instrumentalistic *Zeitgeist*. Philosophy defines its role as one of resistance to the spirit of the specialized sciences:

In contrast to its administrators, *philosophy* denotes thought, to the extent that thought does not capitulate to the prevailing division of labor, nor allow its tasks to be dictated by this division. The status quo is coercive not only by means of physical violence and material interests but also by means of overwhelming suggestion. Philosophy is not synthesis, nor the fundamental science, nor even the executive science, but rather the effort to resist suggestion and the resolve toward intellectual and substantive freedom. (1944:217; 1972:243)

Utopia

The materialism period of the early 1930s understood itself as a theoretical support for revolutionary struggle. Its utopian point of reference was the socialization of the means of production. This reference point was made more abstract in the period of Critical Theory. Utopia was no longer "depicted"; thus the position once occupied by research on planned economy was now occupied by the transcendental reflection on both utopian and praxis-guiding goals.

In the third period of theory construction, all belief in the possibility of revolutionary social change had been abandoned. Nor was the object of theory any longer the development of capitalist societies, together with all their accompanying cultural and political problems. The object now was the process of man's confrontation with nature in general. Utopian reflections could thus no longer be based on the revolutionary reorganization of capitalist societies. The concept of utopia as an orientation for political action was already once diminished in 1937, through its "transcendentalization"; in the 1940s this diminution becomes explicit. Any utopian thoughts contained in the Circle's writings of this period are merely reflections on the conditions for the possibility of a nontechnical, noninstrumental relation to nature. Since there has never existed any other kind of relation—or, at least, a relation that is empirically and historically identifiable—the utopian reflection contained in *Dialectic of Enlightenment*, *Eclipse of Reason*, and *Minima Moralia* can only assume a form symbolizing a fantasy situated in pre-history, that is, graphic images of a relation to nature in which self-preservation would be separated from the oppression of nature. The content of such images, exiled to the collective unconscious of the species, is, for Horkheimer and Adorno, an identifiable symbolization such as the lotus-eaters in the *Odyssey* (1944:58; 1972:62), the Near Eastern custom of flower-eating, fruit-gathering in primitive cultures, or blind, purposeless somatic pleasure (Adorno 1951:72). Adorno himself develops and reflects on such an image in *Minima Moralia*:

Rien faire comme un bête, floating on water and peacefully gazing into the sky, being "and nothing more, with no further definition or content," might take the place of process, or act, of satisfaction—and in this way truly fulfill the promise of dialectical logic: to culminate in its origin. (1951:208; 1974:157)

In addition to these utopian reflections as imaginations of a nonexploitative relation to nature, certain writings, notably *Minima Moralia*, contain the foundations for an epistemology of utopian contents. Their basic idea can be succinctly characterized by the quotation with which Adorno introduces, programmatically, his 1945 sketches, which form part of *Minima Moralia*:

When everything is bad
it must be good
to know the worst. (1951:103; 1974:83)

Utopian images originate dialectically in the most negative aspects of a reality experienced as fate. In the aphorism entitled *"Zum Ende"*

[Finale], Adorno views the task of philosophy as this paradoxical form of reflecting on utopia:

The only philosophy that can be responsibly practiced in the face of despair is the attempt to contemplate all things as they would appear from the standpoint of redemption. . . . Perspectives must be fashioned that displace and estrange the world, that reveal its lacerations and cracks as indigent and distorted as they will appear in the messianic light. To gain such perspectives without caprice or violence, but entirely from a felt contact with objects—this and this alone is the last task of thought. It is the simplest of all things, since the situation calls imperatively for such knowledge, indeed, because the consummate negativity, once seen for what it really is, crystallizes into the mirror-writing of its opposite. (1951:333f.; 1974:247)

According to this postulate, utopian thought would have the task of decoding in fascist social relations the "mirror-writing" of the good society, the task of analyzing fascism as the negative foil of a society to be anticipated in utopian form. According to Horkheimer and Adorno,

The horror of fascism is the lie that, though manifest, continues to be. Although this lie allows no truth against which it might be measured, the truth appears negatively in the fantastic dimensions of the absurdity of the lie. Only if they are completely deprived of the faculty of thought can the undiscerning be kept from this truth. (1944:186; 1972:208)

Summary

Historical and Political Experience

We have distinguished three areas within the totality of the Frankfurt Circle's historical and political experience: (a) the German labor movement, (b) the development of socialism in the Soviet Union, and (c) the development of fascism in Germany and of authoritarianism in late capitalist societies.

(a) The labor movement's demise at the end of the Weimar Republic was the most significant experience undergone by the Circle; and up to 1945 the Circle based its reflections on its own political biography upon this experience. Yet in the late 1930s and in the 1940s, reference to this experience became less specific and increasingly sweeping and general. Whereas in the beginning the Circle's theory construction was characterized by a relatively detailed analysis of KPD and SPD policies—in writings synchronous with the historical context they discuss—from the apocalyptic perspective of 1944, the political orientation and structural organization of all German and European socialist parties are identified with each other in wholesale fashion.

(b) This assessment of socialist politics was influenced, among other factors, by an appraisal of socialism in the Soviet Union. In the Circle's early writings one finds a critical solidarity with Soviet policy. In Horkheimer's and Marcuse's programmatic writings of 1937 this skeptical, wait-and-see attitude is replaced by critical rejection, though a rejection that cannot be clearly ascribed to particular contemporary events within

Soviet politics. Without mentioning the USSR by name, the authors use the course of the Russian Revolution to demonstrate that nationalizing the means of production constitutes only a negative precondition for the creation of a socialist society. The writings of the 1940s criticize Stalinism openly and severely. Horkheimer places the Bolshevik social system in the proximity of a fascist social order, though without explicitly formulating the totalitarianism thesis.

(c) Not until the 1940s did the Institute study national socialism in a comprehensive and systematic way. Marcuse and Pollock had already formulated by 1934 the thesis that fascism is the political form most appropriate to developed monopoly capitalism. This theory established the temporal framework in terms of which the era of the National Socialist state was viewed. January 1933 did not appear to the Frankfurt Circle to be the caesura that we today see it to be. The theory of the Circle viewed the last years of the Weimar Republic and the first ones of national socialism as a continuum. This assessment did not change much until about 1940, when it was developed and refined in "The Jews and Europe." Correspondence from the years 1937 to 1940 reveals a presentiment, as yet theoretically undeveloped, of an apocalyptic tendency permeating fascism. In the philosophical writings of the 1940s the fascist era then becomes the historical point of reference for a comprehensive theory of culture and history. At the same time the numerous, empirically oriented monographs on cultural, political, legal, and economic aspects of the National Socialist system were, for the most part, left unedited; within the Circle, however, their significance for a comprehensive theory of fascism remained controversial.

Theory of the Theory-Praxis Relation

The Subject and Addressee of the Theory

A classical theme of the socialist intelligentsia is that the proletariat is itself the subject and bearer of revolutionary theory. This theme found its ultimate expression in Lukács's thesis of a speculative identity between proletarian class consciousness and Marx's theory. Horkheimer first broke away from this tradition of the socialist intelligentsia by psychologizing the theory of class consciousness. Apparently this too was untenable; the Institute's own survey of blue-collar and white-collar workers indicated that only a small portion of the German proletariat could be ascribed to the analytical category of "revolutionary type."

Henceforth the Frankfurt Circle's self-understanding is characterized by the conviction, increasingly radicalized in the course of the 1930s, that the proletariat's class consciousness could no longer be mediated with the theoretical work of revolutionary intellectuals. The theoretician could no longer feel himself existentially bound to the proletariat; if he is bound at all, then it is only through his moral decision. To be sure, the proletariat remains the addressee of the theory. The "objective" interests imputed to the proletariat constitute the criteria by which the intellectual can measure the relevance of his work. In the Critical Theory writings of the late 1930s, the Frankfurt Circle's tendency to marginalize itself in its relationship to the proletariat is heightened. Horkheimer sharply criticizes the principle of a "Luxemburgian" intelligentsia; a materialist theory tailored to the proletariat's situation must of necessity be realized even against manifest proletarian consciousness. The proletariat is simply no longer the subject of a theoretical orientation adequate to its historical situation. The role for the subject of revolutionary theory is reassigned in 1937. The position once occupied by the proletariat now comes to be occupied by the "subjects of critical activity." They may be characterized through their marginalization not only in authoritarian societies but also in proletarian mass organizations. Marginality is in general the condition for the possibility of work in political theory. The "subjects of critical activity" are not clearly identified. Several very pointed remarks by Horkheimer in letters and essays would suggest that he identified himself and his coworkers with the potential subject of historical truth.

The writings of the 1940s take as evident the notion that the late capitalist culture-industry and the fascist propaganda apparatus have made it entirely impossible to develop class consciousness of any political significance. The proletariat then could not, even in the most mediated sense, be the subject of theoretical orientation. Indeed, even the marginal groups are no longer mentioned as the authentic agents — under the historical conditions established by the authoritarian states — of revolutionary theory. Now only politically isolated, organizationally unaffiliated individuals are capable of theoretically advocating collective interests. According to their own self-understanding, the Frankfurt

Circle, or at least Adorno and Horkheimer, lost sight of any real addressee for their theoretical work.

Theory and Praxis

In the early 1930s, Horkheimer repeatedly insisted that the "best possible" social theory attainable through existing scientific means constitutes an unconditional presupposition for successful political struggle. Accordingly he attributed the force for revolutionary change only to those political groups for whom a theoretical orientation had become the primary, practical orientation. At the same time he argued for separating the scientific development of theory from practical politics: Political praxis can no longer provide the sole principle for theoretical verification. Indeed, the conditions for the possibility of revolutionary change in a historical situation might be determined according to theoretical criteria; yet such theoretical findings would not guarantee the success of political action based upon them. A theory could be scientifically "correct" even if those who oriented themselves upon it were defeated in political struggles. Horkheimer and Marcuse emphasized this point against the background of the National Socialist seizure of power.

The programmatic essay of 1937 contains the single linkage between theory and praxis within the entire period here under consideration. Here, Horkheimer presents the relation between critical intelligentsia and proletarian class as a "dynamic unity" guaranteeing that the intellectuals' radical self-marginalization with regard to the proletariat occurs in the proletariat's objective interest.

The writings between 1937 and 1940 were centrally concerned with a critique of a threshold of indifference—a normative supposition of all bourgeois science—sharply dividing science and politics. Critical Theory, on the contrary, proceeds, in terms both of its research program and of its critique of ideology, from the assumption that decisions of a political nature are inherent in the cognitive instrumentarium of science. The normative obligation to orient political action is based on the assumption that science is only one moment in the process of social labor. As a part of this process, it is obliged to reflect upon the political organization of the process. The complex theory maintaining this relationship between theory and revolutionary praxis was developed continually until about 1938; the writings of the 1940s abandon it. Horkheimer and Adorno maintain in their programmatic writings that the success of a theory whose praxis lay in its capturing the masses is hindered by the proletariat's integration into the late capitalist context of domination. Conditions within the public sphere brought about by the culture industry and by fascist propaganda allow Adorno and Horkheimer to formulate the political role of theory only negatively, providing a reflected critique of the shortsighted political instrumentalization of theory.

Theoretical Position

Defining a Theoretical Position

We chose to call the Circle's theoretical orientation in the early 1930s materialism. This name signifies more than simply membership in an anti-idealist tradition of theory. The Circle's identification with materialism went hand in hand with its specific stylization of it in the course of the theory's development. This stylization of the old European materialist tradition is characterized by the assumption that a continuous materialist position has existed since antiquity, that its content has varied through time, but its critical, enlightening function has at any given period always been the same. The current form of this position is Marx's (correctly interpreted) "theory of society." But even this theory becomes obsolete because of changed historical and social conditions. This emphasized relativism—based on the actual contents of theories and not on their political function—is aimed against Hegel's philosophy of identity. The Circle criticized its problematic nature as an epistemology, but even more so its identification of subject and object (in the context of a philosophy of history), seen as implicitly containing the ideological tendency to substitute in place of the historical process some kind of supersubject. This critique was directed not only at Lukács but also at the hypothesization of collective identities as perpetrated by the bourgeois philosophies and, in a narrower sense, by the prefascist philosophies of the Weimar Republic.

The concept of Critical Theory was introduced in 1937 in the programmatic essay "Traditional and Critical Theory." On the one hand, this was simply a new name introduced by Horkheimer and Marcuse for the Marxist theoretical tradition; on the other hand, it was the name of the Circle's own theoretical orientation, ultimately demonstrating the Circle's claim to represent the authentic intentions of the Marxist tradition. Traditional theory is the negative complement to Critical Theory. By *traditional theory*, Horkheimer means theory construction in all modern, theoretical endeavors oriented according to the natural sciences. It is characterized by a rigid division between the scientific object and the contemplative subject. Critical Theory, on the contrary, maintains that both the subject and the object of scientific activity are socially constituted. The objects and structures of relevance for research can be adequately understood only in the context of the process of social reproduction. Critical Theory's obligation to political reflection also follows from its self-understanding. Its political task is to prepare theoretically for the "rational organization of the social labor process."

In the 1940s the Circle's collective, general orientation no longer had any concise, programmatic name; its identity became vague as it ceased basing itself on any theoretical tradition, be it old European materialism or Marxism. What the theory defined as its adversary in the 1940s now assumed universal dimensions: The object of critique became the Western rationalist tradition in general, from its origins in early history up to the fascist present. Horkheimer's and Adorno's writings of the 1940s are concerned with the process of active confrontation with nature in general—thematically presented in terms of universal history and painted in very broad strokes. The critique of the technological, instrumental domination of nature is the core issue uniting all specialized analyses and specific arguments. The totalization of political authority in fascism, the maiming of individuality, the authoritarian disciplining of all forms of cognitive orientation through the culture industry and propaganda—these are the observable consequences of a reason directly instrumentalized for the purpose of domination.

Relation to Marxism

In the early 1930s the Frankfurt Circle considered Marx's "economic theory of society" the contemporary form of the old European materialist tradition as interpreted by Horkheimer. But this identification with and within Marx's theory is an identification neither with Marx's work as philologically extant in 1932 nor with the history of its dogmatic influence in the Second and Third internationals. Instead, it implies adjusting Marx's theory to the conditions of late capitalism—an adjustment only briefly mentioned in the texts, but one imputed to be feasible. The most palpable revision of the theory consisted in a reconceptualization, formulated by Erich Fromm and accepted by the entire Circle, of the base-superstructure model that integrated portions of psychoanalytic theory into historical materialism.

Essays written between 1937 and 1939 almost directly identify the Circle's theory construction with the Marxist theory tradition. Critical Theory is an artificial name for this tradition and at the same time marks a critical act by which the Circle tried to make itself independent of this tradition. Horkheimer and Marcuse distinguish Critical Theory from its distortions in social democracy and Bolshevism, identifying it as a guiding principle and standard, enduring through time and with an interest solely in the contemporary adequacy of Marx's theory. Yet it is characteristic that this strong concern with the historically adequate reformulation of Marxist theory remains the Circle's program. Suggestions about necessary revisions are confined to an explication of the concept of critique and to hints of a changed relation between base and superstructure in late capitalism.

In the writings of the 1940s, Horkheimer, Adorno, Pollock, and Löwenthal leave the Marxist theory tradition. The theory is no longer concerned with capitalism as the contemporary political form of social production. A theory of society becomes a philosophy of history, concerned with the world-historical drama of man's active confrontation with nature in general. Pollock's and Horkheimer's theory of fascism abandons the Marxist interpretive schemata of the 1930s. The concept of critique is no longer oriented on the paradigm of Marxian economic critique. Horkheimer and Adorno do not make this break explicitly but retain Marxian formulations (e.g., the theory of value) and arguments.

Philosophy and Science

The program of the materialism period of the early 1930s was the "unification of philosophy and science." This program is expressed in an interdisciplinary organization of research in which philosophy played the role of a problem-sensitive, integrating medium for the specialized sciences. The specialized sciences were to provide an empirical corrective to philosophy. The clear distinction between these reciprocal functions—based on Marx's distinction between "research" and "presentation"—disappears in Horkheimer's writing about 1935. In the programmatic essay of 1937, as well as in later contributions by Horkheimer and Marcuse based on it, the intended relation between philosophy and specialized science is immediately identified with the relation as found in Marx's economic critique. Horkheimer presents this relation as if Marx had interpreted classical bourgeois political economy as an ensemble of "abstract" knowledge from various scientific disciplines, all of which attain genuine scientific status only through their presentation (*Darstellung*) in a philosophical (meaning here critical-dialectical) manner. The philosophical interpretation of Marx's economic critique undertaken by Horkheimer and Marcuse is a reaction to the "New Economism"—whether or not Marcuse and Horkheimer mean by this the social-democratic theoretical tradition or Bolshevik economic policy remains unclear.

This tendency toward "re-philosophizing" the Circle's entire theoretical orientation becomes increasingly radical in the essays of the late 1930s and in the 1940s. Finally, in the *Dialectic of Enlightenment*, all inquiry within the specialized disciplines is identified with their technical and social application, hence is discredited as "positivist," "instrumental," and so forth. Against this "instrumental" *Zeitgeist*—concretely exemplified by the specialized sciences—philosophy should encapsulate itself as the mental preserve of a buried intellectual culture. Symptomatic for this (implicit) determination of the relation between philosophy and specialized science is the Institute's research policy. Indeed, the comprehensive research on fascism and the *Studies in Prejudice* employed empirical and specialized scientific methods. And yet, for example, Adorno's empirical studies and his philosophical reflections written at the same time are, to a startling extent, unmediated.

Utopia

The Frankfurt Circle's utopian point of reference in the early 1930s was still identical with its empirical, political orientation; thus it constituted a concrete utopia. It aimed at a revolutionary overthrow of the private control of the means of production and a complete economic reorganization along the lines of a planned economy. The Institute's comprehensive research on planned economy—which was undertaken in the years 1930–1934 and expressly sought to provide a scientifically informed orientation for action—again illustrates the way in which concrete utopia was understood.

Apparently influenced by political and economic developments in the Soviet Union, the utopian point of interest is displaced, beginning about 1935 and then quite clearly in the programmatic writings on Critical Theory, by a philosophical questioning of interests that could guide a revolution in capitalist economic organization. Marcuse and Horkheimer now decline to delineate "utopia," to give any substantive determination to the anticipated utopian society. The utopian goal is "transcendentalized." Now the moral qualification of the transcendental bourgeois subject provides the paradigm for a social form to be sought through revolution. Hence—and by contrast to the Circle's position until the early 1930s—no empirically identifiable social group can be considered the bearer of utopian goals. Instead, utopian conceptions are much more likely to be products of the transcendentally conceived bourgeois individual, of his "imagination" or "fantasy."

The writings of the 1940s abandon all reference to the revolutionary reorganization of capitalist relations. Against the background of a philosophy of history critical of technology, as developed in the *Dialectic of Enlightenment*, utopian reflections assume the form of graphic conceptions of a human relation to nature in which the reproduction of the species would cease to imply the domination of nature. The connection between utopian imagination and the political orientation of action has been severed.

Structural Change in Political and Historical Experience

"Das Wahre ist das Ganze"—Hegel
"Das Ganze is das Unwahre"—Adorno

A systematic study of the entire process of theory construction between 1930 and 1945 reveals, first of all, a transformation of the structure of experience. This process begins with the cognitive ideal of a scientifically methodological, transsubjective experience—in the form of an analysis of society as a totality realized through the organization of research. This program for a social theory is based on the maxim of "concrete totality" and assumes an unproblematic openness, that is, a receptivity to the "objective" interests of the proletariat. Indeed, the program's authors no longer simply assume a speculative unity of an analysis of the totality (realized through research methodology) and (an idealistically stylized) proletarian experience, as Lukács does in *History and Class Consciousness*. Nevertheless, early Critical Theory still stands within the broken tradition, maintaining a unity of proletarian experience and Marxist scientific method. The goal of addressing social theory to a proletariat in the process of its revolutionary emancipation, and the program of analyzing society as a totality were introduced together, and they disappear together.

In the 1940s this scientifically methodological, transsubjective form of experience is confronted by an intuitive-individualistic type of ex-

perience critical of science. Now *totality* no longer means a methodologically reflected reconstruction of social reality. The concept of
negative totality later introduced by Adorno stands for the quality of
history as a hermetic context of domination that became reality in
the period of fascism. In view of this interpretation, the truth value
of propositions about experience is no longer guaranteed by their
scientific organization, but solely by the reflected subjectivity of the
"lonely" intellectual completely marginalized in an authoritarian society.

From the perspective of the sociology of knowledge, the process by
which the Circle transformed its theory formation in its self-reflection
is characterized by its own self-marginalization (radicalized to the point
of self-elimination) in relation to potential political agents. Whereas
at the beginning of the 1930s (still in a phase of critical receptivity)
the theory was based on the experience of the proletariat (stylized
objectivistically), Critical Theory as of 1937 is characterized by the
marginality of intellectuals (in the form of small groups) in relation to
the proletariat. In the 1940s the theory's designated bearer was the
"lonely individual." At the level of the Circle's self-understanding, this
self-marginalizing process may be seen as a process of withdrawal in
reaction to the integrating tendency of the objective historical totality.

The medium of the theoretical understanding of this negative
totality—which became reality in the fascist period—is no longer scientific work in individual disciplines. This cognitive process of knowledge is now organized according to political interests that have already
been integrated into the authoritarian context of domination. The
specialized sciences have lost all critical potential. The bearers of Critical
Theory thus marginalized themselves in terms of their self-understanding, not only in relation to authoritarian society and the proletariat
(the latter having long since been integrated into the former) but also
in relation to socially recognized science. This distance from academ-
ically institutionalized science, now beyond all mediation, is expressed
by the way in which the image of the adversary increases in magnitude
with the passage of subsequent periods. The Circle began with a
critique of the Weimar Republic's prefascist ideologies. In 1937, Critical
Theory attacked "traditional" science, that is, the ideal of all bourgeois
scholarship; in 1944 its adversary was nothing less than the entire
Western rationalist tradition.

The cognitive medium for criticizing the negative totality—which
in the meantime has become reality—is exclusively philosophy, though

not in the sense of academic philosophy. Rather, philosophy is presented as a rhetorical-moral capacity. Only "lonely" intellectual individuals are able to develop this faculty, and its articulation is capable of liberating a language maimed by domination. Hence, philosophy itself becomes a kind of moral-political praxis; philosophy is a specific attitude, not a scientific discipline.

This moral pragmatization of philosophy complements an important political decision to make theory construction less pragmatic—for the latter distances itself from all groups that could become agents for the theory (a distancing to the point of extinguishing all political claims) and strongly criticizes all attempts to instrumentalize theoretical reflection for political action. This political de-pragmatization of theory is also expressed by the theory's loss of utopian images capable of guiding political action. The somewhat more concrete utopian orientation of the early 1930s—toward reorganizing the economy along the lines of a planned economy—is followed in 1937 by a transcendental reflection on the human interests for the sake of which socialism should be realized. In the 1940s, when the *Eclipse of Reason* was written, there remains only an antirealistic, archaic imagination of an alternative relation of man to nature.

We cannot here attempt to answer the question whether the moments of the process in which the Frankfurt Circle transformed its theory construction can be viewed as symptomatic for the way in which the socialist intelligentsia worked out its experiences in the fascist era. These moments are:

the transformation of the structure of experience itself;

the self-marginalization of the bearers of the theory;

the increasing distance from academic scholarship;

the moral pragmatization of individual philosophical reflection; and

the decreasing pragmatic-political importance of the theory as a whole.

The extent to which the Frankfurt Circle's working through of its historical experience (which was crucial to forming its theory) is generalizable can be determined only by a wide-ranging political history of ideas, employing the methods of a sociology of knowledge at the methodological and material level of the present study. Only a rich field of comparative case studies using concepts elaborated from the sociology of knowledge, together with a detailed study of sources, would be able to accomplish what would otherwise be possible only in a journalistic manner: to reflect once again on the theoretical adequacy of the way in which the Frankfurt Circle worked through its historical experience in theory.

Notes to Part I

1. Cf. Karl Mannheim's concept of *soziologische Zurechnung* in his article "Wissenssoziologie" in Vierkandt (1959:677).

2. These concepts are borrowed from Berger and Luckmann (1966).

3. This argumentation was suggested by Hans Blumenberg's theory of epochal transformation. Cf. Blumenberg (1966:29–35; 1983:457–482).

4. See Horkheimer (1972c:44).

5. Fromm (1980).

6. See Neumann (1968:74).

7. Weber (1969). Wolfgang Abendroth disagrees with this pronounced interpretation, in *Ein Leben in der Arbeiterbewegung* (Frankfurt/M., 1976).

8. Fischer (1948) provides a good account of this.

9. Conversation with Max Horkheimer in Nürnberg, March 1973.

10. One gets this impression by comparing Horkheimer's aphorisms in *Dämmerung* (1974a) with Abendroth's recollections quoted above.

11. See Jurinetz's point of view on psychoanalysis in *Unter dem Banner des Marxismus*, vol. 1 (1925).

12. See Pollock (1932:27).

13. Conversation with Horkheimer, March 1973.

14. See Rosenberg (1961).

15. Cf. Walter Holzhauer's excellent study, *Karl Kautskys Werk als Weltanschauung* (1972:101ff.).

16. Compare, as a concise documentation, Walter Benjamin's letter to A. Cohen of 6 February 1935, in Benjamin (1966, vol. II:645).

17. See Bracher (1974, vol. I:114ff.).

18. That the second line of the following quotation refers to 1933 is made quite clear by a letter from Marcuse to Horkheimer, dated 26 November 1935 (Pollock Archive).

19. Compare Leo Löwenthal's program for a materialist aesthetics (1934:342); also P. L. Landsberg's "materialist sociology" (1933:402) and Fromm's program for a "materialist" social psychology (1932a:28-54).

20. See Marx's short sketch of the history of modern materialism in his *The Holy Family*, chap. 6, sec. 3.

21. Compare as a relevant documentation Josef Revai's review of Lukács's *History and Class Consciousness*, in Furio et al., *Geschichte und Klassenbewusstsein heute* (Amsterdam, 1971:180-190).

22. Compare their emphatic characterization in Horkheimer (1935a:7ff.).

23. This connection will be fully considered in part II of this book.

24. See Lukács, "What Is Orthodox Marxism?", in *History and Class Consciousness* (1971:1-26).

25. For a concise discussion of this, see Horkheimer (1932a).

26. These suggestions will be examined in detail in part II of this book.

27. See Bracher (1974, vol. II:251).

28. The most informative texts by renegades are Arthur Koestler's *Der Pfeil ins Blaue* (1953), Hede Massing's *Die grosse Täuschung* (1967), Alfred Kantorowicz's *Deutsches Tagebuch* (1971), and Franz Borkenau's *The Spanish Cockpit* (1963).

29. See Radkau (1971).

30. See Benjamin (1966, vol. II:747, 776).

31. For example, Pollock's letter to Horkheimer dated 7 September 1937 (Pollock Archive).

32. Quotation from Fest (1976, vol. I:150).

33. See the excellent study by Kurt Kliem, "Der sozialistische Widerstand gegen das Dritte Reich dargestellt an der Gruppe 'Neu Beginnen' " (1957).

34. See Radkau (1971:157-163).

35. See the recollections of his then-wife Hede Massing, *Die grosse Täuschung* (1967).

36. See Korsch (1941-1965).

37. *Eclipse of Reason* is based on a lecture course given by Horkheimer in the winter of 1944-1945 at Columbia University.

38. Habermas (1971).

39. Above all by Jürgen Habermas and Albrecht Wellmer.

40. See Dubiel (1973:53ff.).

II

Dialectical Presentation and Interdisciplinary Research

Theory Construction and Research
Organization in the Institute for
Social Research after 1930

Introduction: On the Methodology of Interdisciplinary Research

We now turn to an examination of the organization of the Institute for Social Research in the early 1930s, which we shall approach in terms of the methodology of interdisciplinary research. As we will see, early Critical Theory represents one of the few cases in which interdisciplinary research is reflected throughout a group's philosophy of science, methodology, and organization.

The "disciplinary crisis"—that is, the costs and consequences of extreme specialization, the differentiation and isolation of scientific disciplines, and, based on this, the postulate of the need for interdisciplinary reorganization—is a common theme of academic discussions and moralizing cultural criticisms of science. Yet this theme is never reflected upon within science itself. Though at first glance this may appear to be a contradiction, it is not. For if the diagnosis behind the suggested therapy of interdisciplinary research is correct, then the crisis of the disciplinary structure of scientific inquiry is less and less capable of becoming a theme of reflection in the ensemble of diversified directions of research in the individual disciplines.

This makes analysis of the problem difficult, and we, too, can hardly demonstrate the correctness of our approach. Since it is impossible to gain an overview of the total context of the problem, because of restrictions of space and the specificity of our interest, we have decided to start with three (initially arbitrary) perspectives:

1. The transformation of the relationship between philosophy and the positive sciences.

2. The dialectic of the internal and external generation of problems.

3. The transformation of the relationship between science and society.

(1) From the lofty view of a secular intellectual history, the crisis of the structuring of science into separate disciplines appears as a tension between the extreme degree of specialization in inquiry within the individual sciences, on the one hand, and the presence, in secularized format, of the medieval unity of science, on the other. A good indicator of the overlapping of the demands of specialized science and holistic metaphysics as forms of knowledge is the decline in this century of the claims of philosophy to integrate all the sciences. The richest form of philosophy as a comprehensive science is Hegel's system, in which philosophy is the organon of reason that orders the merely particular determinants of "understanding"—that is, the individual research findings of the disciplines—in a reconstruction of the object of knowledge. With the exception of a specific reception within the materialist tradition of theory, the character of philosophy as comprehensive science has disintegrated along with Hegelian philosophy, even if, to this day, the reputation of philosophy within the academic world is fed by an appearance of retaining its integrative function. At the same time, bourgeois philosophy had already been reduced to a transcendental critique of knowledge in the form of neo-Kantianism and to an analytical-linguistic reflection on the conditions of formation of scientific concepts in logical positivism. Although the countermovement represented by *Lebensphilosophie*, phenomenology, and existential ontology guarded against the Hegelian claim to be a science of the totality, it did so only at the cost of a metaphysical ignorance and arrogance toward institutionalized scientific inquiry. Today we are confronted by the fact that all philosophical stimuli for theory construction within scientific disciplines have been integrated into the specialized sciences and to a significant degree have also become independent of systematic philosophy. In the work of Foucault, Lévi-Strauss, Chomsky, and Piaget it can be shown that the specialized sciences now stimulate philosophy, and not vice versa.

In the tradition of materialist theory this development took a different path. In his fragmentary suggestions for a theory of dialectical presentation, Marx appropriated Hegel's critique of the limitations of the kind of knowledge provided by the specialized sciences. His program was a materialist, unified science in which the treatment of the most general results would remain the province of philosophy. It is, in fact, the case that even his critiques of economics do not fall under the heading of any current discipline; this expresses not only his dialectical methodology but also the disciplinary structure of a broad, undifferentiated science of the state within which philosophy, jurisprudence, economics, sociology, and also, in part, the cultural sciences formed a seamless whole.

In the development of Marxist theory into the scientific socialism of early social democracy, the Marxist critique of idealist philosophy was restricted to an antiphilosophical materialism that, like the natural scientific materialism of the late nineteenth century, saw the advancement of science solely in terms of the accumulation of positivistic, specialized knowledge.

The reception and transformation of the Marxist conception of science within the Bolshevik tradition of theory is, by contrast, characterized by a philosophical tutelage of the specialized sciences. As a comprehensive theory of history and nature, dialectical materialism represents a materialist metaphysics that provides a dogmatic philosophical framework for all the results of the specialized sciences. In point of fact, the unity of the sciences *is* a problem for dialectical materialism but not for its official, theoretical-political self-reflection.

The Marxist, immanent critique of the shift in the relative significance of philosophy and the specialized sciences, which occurred within the various institutionalized forms of Marxism, was developed by intellectuals who were totally lacking in political influence. This trend is evident in an incipient form in Georg Lukács's *History and Class Consciousness*, in a pronounced form in the work of Karl Korsch, and in its most reflected, albeit unsystematic, form in Max Horkheimer's work of the early 1930s.

(2) If, from the perspective provided by research on science, we today look for the causes of the disciplinary crisis, we are confronted by a tangled complex of intrinsic and extrinsic factors. In the first place, in the last few decades the quantitative growth of science has been exponential.[1] This growth can be seen within the cognitive structures of science as an internal differentiation of basic disciplines into subdisciplines and, within these, into autonomous research complexes. It can also be seen in the synchronic as well as diachronic expansion of the competition of paradigms, in the creation of hierarchies of reflective levels, and in the intradisciplinary differentiation between

didactic literature, foundational literature, and literature oriented to applications. Linked to causally restricted external growth, this development of internal structures is itself exponential. Within almost all disciplines it has led to an unsurveyable pluralization of horizons of relevance. It has now become impossible to determine the relationship between two or more disciplines—even with respect to the same object—with the same degree of plausibility that is standard in communications among specialists. But this does not arise as a problem within such sciences as theoretical physics or foundational research in mathematics, which are characterized by the internal generation of problems whose criteria of relevance can be derived from the cognitive structures of the science. It is a widely held assumption in scientific research that, while natural scientific disciplines may originate in response to some external, usually technical problem, they quickly, in the course of their theoretical development, reach a cognitive level at which they determine their own further development. Thus, only at a highly elaborated level of development and under specific circumstances do they once again become receptive to externally induced problems.[2] The social sciences, on the contrary, are, in all stages of their theoretical development, open to externally defined problems. Our thesis is that the fragmentation of the sciences into disciplines, as well as the largely unguided intradisciplinary specialization, becomes a problem only if, as a consequence of the increasing social recognition of scientific information, the external generation of problems begins to dominate the internal generation. The reason for the contemporary relevance of interdisciplinary reorganization is the unrelatedness of the disciplinary structure of the universities and research institutes, on the one hand, and the problem structures imposed on them from the outside, on the other—in short, the tension between the process in which science is socialized and the institutional structures of its research enterprise.[3]

(3) The argument for an interdisciplinary approach can best be demonstrated in terms of the external factors in its favor. Socially relevant and politically urgent problems, such as health care, city and regional development, and the humanization of the work place, seldom fall within the competence of any one discipline; indeed, they often fall into an interdisciplinary no-man's-land.[4] Whether the question at hand is state sanctioning of the professionalization of disciplines, the technological development and utilization of basic scientific knowledge,

or the activity of scholars in joint planning and especially in providing systematic scientific advice and consultation in the political sphere, again and again it can be observed that the direct mediation of the fragmented scientific enterprise with the logic of problems governed by the reality of social action demands the transformation of its model of cognitive and institutional organization. It was not by chance that, in one of the first systematic reflections on the consequences for science of its increasing role in political consultation, Harold Lasswell discussed the reform of the structure of academic disciplines.[5]

We maintain that most of the initial steps toward interdisciplinary research can, roughly, be gathered into two groups: (a) a theoretically presuppositionless, externally generated, multidisciplinary approach; (b) a cognitively integrated, interdisciplinary approach generated in a process internal to science.

(a) The multidisciplinary approach covers a large proportion of the research projects currently labeled interdisciplinary. As a rule, these are less often initiated by scientific institutions than by some problem external to science. This type of research is, in theory, presuppositionless, in the sense that it does not even attempt an adequate integration of the disciplines involved. Instead, given a problem that exceeds the boundaries of any single discipline, theories, methodologies, and research techniques are simply amassed one after another. Already in the initial step a compact, extrascientific formulation of the problem is, in the course of its scientific reconstruction, analyzed and diversified according to the standards of the independently defined disciplines and the paradigms, models, and research methods valid in those disciplines at the given time. In this process of reconstruction the compact problem of schizophrenia, for example, is broken down into a loose aggregate of smaller problems, such as the demographic distribution of its frequency (epidemiology), the patterns of familial socialization that generate schizophrenia (microsociology, family sociology, psychoanalytic theory), the role of heredity (genetics), and the suspected biochemical and endocrinological processes. The concluding report of an imaginary, multidisciplinary research on the problem of schizophrenia would certainly give the impression that the results of the smaller problems had been placed next to each other without connections. The practical, politically orienting value of such a study for the preventive reorientation of psychiatric care, for example, would be extremely small. For in this type of multidisciplinary research, one systematically operates independently of the fact that the constitution of problems — within science, and diversified into disciplines — does not flawlessly reflect the extrascientific constitution of the problem. The externally predefined problem, which science can adequately treat only by integrating its various, disciplinarily diversified orientations, is spectrally dissected in an arrangement of interdisciplinary perspectives.

The described type of multidisciplinary research thus offers hardly any possibilities of solving the disciplinary crisis. Of course, in demonstrating, with regard to identical problems, the dissociation of the canon of academic subjects, this type of research vividly exemplifies the crisis.

In the case of multidisciplinary research projects, initial efforts at integration have been largely restricted to the establishment of such technical research instruments as documentation centers, data banks, and communications systems. Certainly those didactic concepts point to a future in which participation in multidisciplinary research processes are built into the curricula of graduate schools.[6] The organized participation of young scholars in multidisciplinary projects with a didactic intention is undertaken in the hope that transdisciplinary perspectives develop more or less haphazardly in the scholarly growth of creative individuals. The presence of interdisciplinary competences in a single person (as represented in sociology by Max Weber, Scheler, and Adorno, for example) should be systematized in the form of an interdisciplinary reorganization of the process of scientific socialization.

(b) The impetus to the type of interdisciplinary approach that we call cognitively integrated and consider to be induced within the sciences themselves does not, as in the last case, come from social demands for scholarly services. Rather, it is strategically generated more or less without planning and ex post facto by a particular discipline itself. This intradisciplinarily induced interdisciplinary approach is more or less incidental to the successful attempt to transfer to a neighboring discipline the model theories, methodologies, and standards of research that have become established paradigms in a particular discipline. Such processes of interdisciplinary homogenization would already be complete if the plurality of disciplines were no longer organized in terms of their methodologies, but rather in terms of their subject matter. From the perspective provided by the history of science, "metaphysical," model-theoretical, or methodological attempts to reunify scholarly disciplines—which, since the late nineteenth century, have worked against processes of differentiation into disciplines—are tremendously complicated processes that can be adequately presented only in detailed historical material.

Dialectical materialism is the most prominent attempt at a metaphysical reunification of the sciences. It is a theory encompassing the laws of nature and history and—at least in terms of its own claims— comprehends all results of the particular sciences. The most famous attempt within the history of science—albeit one that had no consequence—of a reunification of scientific disciplines on a methodological basis was the neopositivist *International Encyclopedia of Unified Science*. Its claim to universality was signaled by, among other things, its explicit identification with the French Encyclopedists. All recent attempts in functionalism, structuralism, game theory, and especially cybernetic systems theory can be seen as model-theoretical approaches to the reunification of science, attempts to develop conceptions of comprehensive theories. Current tendencies toward such model-theoretical reunification may be seen in attempts to found a theoretical form of "genetic structuralism" uniting general evolution theory, generative grammar, Piaget's developmental psychology, and a reinterpretation of historical materialism.

Yet this type of interdisciplinary approach, generated within science itself, has the disadvantage of being unreceptive to externally generated problems. This is a decisive disadvantage, since—as we have shown— the need for interdisciplinary research, as well as the generation of questions that can only be solved interdisciplinarily, is imported into scientific institutions. Interdisciplinary approaches internal to science take the form of a supradisciplinary homogenization of intradisciplinarily successful models and methods, and thus perpetuate the tendency of cognitively guided sciences to measure the relevance of questions solely in terms of the applicability of their array of cognitive instruments. Thus we now need to develop organizational forms whose cognitive and institutional structures could adequately respond to the external generation of problems.

We maintain that the systematic deficiencies in the types of interdisciplinary research described above—the ultimately additive arrangement of the results of research in the various disciplines in response to an identical, externally predefined problem in the case of (a), and the insufficient cognitive receptivity to external definitions of problems in the case of (b)—could be overcome through a supra-disciplinary organizational form that begins with, but then systematically integrates, the theoretical, technological, and methodological elements available from the various disciplines.

An organization that had as its goal a true synthesis of the disciplines would never be satisfied with the compounding arrangement of the results of individual disciplines. Fragmentary paradigms of two aspects of such an interdisciplinary and transdisciplinary program are available. First, although it is extremely difficult to make systematic, its methodology is present in the Marxian and Hegelian theory of dialectical presentation. Second, its organizational form was present in the Frankfurt Institute for Social Research, however implicit it may have remained, in the first years of Horkheimer's directorship; this was a form that also employed a method of dialectical presentation.

The Institute's program in the early 1930s consisted of "interdisciplinary"[7] social research. Its research method of comprehensive disciplinary organization was based on Horkheimer's approach to the theory of dialectical presentation as developed in Hegel and Marx. Such a theory proceeds from the conviction that the explanatory power of the knowledge provided by the specialized scientific disciplines is limited a priori; in its analyses its objects of historical and social knowledge are dissected according to the limits and forms of thematization specific to particular disciplines. In contrast, the method of dialectical presentation consists mainly in the reception, integration, and over-coming of disciplinary analysis. Although dialectical presentation employs the data as well as the analytic, model-theoretical, methodological, and technical elements of such analysis, it synthesizes them in a procedure Marx called *presentation* (in contrast to disciplinary *research*). By such synthesis the developed theory achieves an integral picture of "concrete" reality.

Without substantial interpretive effort we can show that the inter-disciplinary research methods introduced by Horkheimer (in his in-augural address as director of the Institute for Social Research) are based on the fundamental distinction between research and presentation. This research method gave philosophy the role of an integrating medium sensitive to the problems of the disciplines, while the disciplines adjudicated questions of specification, correction, and verification. The distinction between research and presentation, which Horkheimer identified with that between disciplinary analysis and philosophical construction, formed the organizational research substructure for his colleagues' scientific inquiry. The substructure consisted in the differentiation of cognitive roles according to the function of research and presentation, with these functions interrelated within the research process itself. This organizational research structure can be easily identified in the Circle's structure: Horkheimer systematically claimed the function of presentation for himself, while his colleagues were assigned the role of providing material from the various disciplines.

Our interest in reconstructing this context is not an interest in group biography or historiography, even though our goal of an exemplary, in-depth analysis can be realized only by means of the greatest possible historical and philological knowledge of the case as offered by the most recent research on the literature and documentation. Instead, this investigation is presented as a case study that, by drawing upon material dealing with the history of science, considers the methodological and organizational conditions necessary for interdisciplinary research.

We would characterize this stylization of the historical material as follows. We systematically assume that Horkheimer understood his ideas about a theory of "dialectical presentation," scattered throughout his early essays, as a methodological reflection on the interdisciplinary research done by his colleagues. This direct correlation between actual research practice and group and organizational structure, on the one hand, and Horkheimer's theory of dialectical presentation, on the other, is exaggerated by purely historical standards. According to the recollections of Leo Löwenthal, Herbert Marcuse, and Erich Fromm, the "dialectical" form of theory construction postulated by Horkheimer and the research practices of the group assembled around him were in fact less mediated than our somewhat forced interpretation suggests.[8]

Since our interest is not historiographical, we have not provided exact dates of publication, nor do we note when and for how long the correlation between organizational research practices and forms of theory construction was unambiguously observable, and when it became vague. We did this more precisely in the first part of this book. One can say, roughly, that the interdisciplinary program really mattered only in the first years of Horkheimer's directorship. The turn to a philosophical discrediting of every form of disciplinary knowledge, with which Critical Theory in general came to be identified, began in the mid-1930s.

Our discussion is organized as follows: We begin by reconstructing, from programmatic statements by Horkheimer, the project of a social research or social science that goes beyond the boundaries of any one discipline. This is followed by a presentation of the relationship between a philosophical-theoretical orientation, and an orientation within a particular discipline, in the philosophy and sociology of the Weimer Republic. Using Horkheimer's reflections (oriented on Hegel and Marx) upon a theory of dialectical presentation, we will develop the structure of the form of theory construction on which the Circle's research practices were based. Through an analysis of the cognitive and social structure of the way in which research was organized, the attempt will then be made to identify this basic structure in the Circle's own research practices. Finally, the abstracted results will be related to our guiding perspective — the methodology of interdisciplinary research.

The Program of the Institute
for Social Research

In January 1933, when Horkheimer assumed the directorship of the Frankfurt Institute for Social Research, he delivered an address entitled "The Present Situation of Social Philosophy and the Tasks of an Institute for Social Research." Here, he introduces the Institute's research program under his directorship with a critique of the most influential social philosophies of the time. After a brief overview of the pertinent theses of neo-Kantianism, Othmar Spann, Max Scheler, and Nicolai Hartmann, among others, Horkheimer maintains in wholesale fashion that all these social philosophies suffer from a central weakness: They are merely assertions and professions of conviction, insufficiently founded in method and in the specialized sciences:

It is precisely in this dilemma of social philosophy—to treat its object, the cultural life of man, merely in terms of *Weltanschauung*, assertions, professions of belief; and to distinguish the social teachings of Auguste Comte, Karl Marx, Max Weber, and Max Scheler more as an act of belief than as true, false, or problematic theories. In this dilemma we see the weakness that must be overcome. (1972c:39)

Horkheimer contrasts this with the natural sciences, for which physics serves as a paradigm. Despite varying theoretical concepts, physics does not tend to develop concepts of reality supported merely by statements of conviction, "because here concrete research of the object functions as a corrective" (1972c:39). Against this view one could maintain that, in social research, this dual postulate of theoretical speculation, on the one hand, and empirical work, on the other, corresponds to the division of labor between social philosophy or theoretical sociology, on the one hand, and empirically oriented branches of sociology, on the other. Yet Horkheimer wants to suggest that the division of labor now practiced is based on a theoretically inadequate determination of the relation between academic sociology and social philosophy:

The relation between philosophical disciplines and the corresponding disciplines of the specialized sciences should not be thought of in such a way that philosophy would appear to deal with the important problems and, in the process, to develop its theories, its own concepts of reality, and its absolute systems—all unassailable by natural science—while empirical research, by contrast, appears to make long, boring, very specific inquiries that fragment into a thousand specific questions and ultimately end in the chaos of specialization. (1972c:40)

Horkheimer thus holds the unmediated coexistence of philosophical theory and the empiricism of the specialized sciences responsible for the decisive weakness of contemporary science. And he postulates a form of research that would be characterized by a systematic intertwining of philosophical-theoretical work with the empirical research of the specialized sciences:

In this conception, the empirical scientist views philosophy as a perhaps pleasant, but nonetheless fruitless (because uncontrolled) exercise, while the philosopher emancipates himself from the empirical scientist because he thinks he cannot wait for him with his broadly conceived conclusions. This view is now overcome by the notion of an ongoing dialectical interpretation and development of philosophical theory and empirical-scientific praxis. . . . Chaotic specialization will not be overcome by undertaking poor syntheses of the results of specialized research; on the other hand, unrestrained empirical studies will not be achieved by attempts to eliminate the theoretical element contained within it. Rather, they are overcome only when philosophy, as a theoretical intention oriented toward the universal and essential, is able to give an animating impulse to specialized research, while at the same time it is sufficiently open to the world to allow itself to be influenced and changed by the course of concrete studies. (1972c:41)

This proposal is then expressed in a programmatic formulation succinctly outlining the Frankfurt Circle's interdisciplinary themes, interests, and orientations integrating theory and empirical material:

What matters today, and I am surely not alone in this opinion, is to organize investigations on the basis of current philosophical problems that unite philosophers, sociologists, economists, historians, and psychologists in an ongoing research community that can do together what in other disciplines one individual does alone in a laboratory, what genuine scientists have always done: pursue those questions aimed at the view of the whole, using the most refined scientific methods; reformulate questions in the course of work as demanded by the object; make more precise and develop new methods without losing sight of general considerations. (1972c:40)

Horkheimer's concern is not to reorganize *all* of scientific culture along the lines of a model. When he speaks of integrating philosophy with empirical research, and of an orientation transcending the boundaries of individual disciplines, he means "social research," the scientific thematization of society. In Horkheimer's programmatic understanding (not always identical with current usage), social research is not, like sociology, simply one discipline among others. Social research is concerned with socially relevant problems, even when this relevance is only indirect. For this reason sociology and social research do not, according to Horkheimer, coincide:

Social research does not coincide with sociology as a scientific discipline. For although it aims, like sociology, at understanding society, the objects of its research also extend to nonsociological areas. Yet what sociologists have themselves achieved or stimulated in the interest of their own science in economic, psychological, or historical areas completely corresponds to the meaning of this concept. (1932a:11)

Horkheimer's programmatic use of the term *social research* is related to our contemporary term *social sciences*: If taken in a sufficiently general sense, it embraces all of the disciplines represented by particular scholars within the Frankfurt Circle—sociology, social philosophy, economics, jurisprudence, the study of literature, the study of culture, and political science. With his concept of social research, Horkheimer meant more than simply some social-scientific superdiscipline to be developed within the institution of science. Rather, the Institute's work was aimed at a "theory of contemporary society as a whole":

The term "social research" does not propose to draw in new borders on the map of the sciences—a map that seems very questionable today anyway. Research in the most diverse areas and at the most

diverse levels of abstraction—which is what this term means here—
is united by the goal of furthering the theory of contemporary society
as a whole. (1932a:I)

The extent to which this research program was decisive for the
Circle's self-understanding, even when it was no longer practiced so
resolutely, is shown by a book advertisement written by Walter Benjamin in which, from the perspective of 1938, he recalls the group's
principle of cognitive integration. In an article for the magazine *Mass
und Wert* he describes the Frankfurt Circle:

The group spoken of here was formed during the German Republic,
around the Frankfurt Institute for Social Research. It cannot be said
that they all had the same academic background. The director of the
Institute, Max Horkheimer, is a philosopher, and his closest co-worker,
Friedrich Pollock, an economist. They are joined by the psychoanalyst
Fromm, the economist Grossmann, the philosopher Rottweiler [Ador-
no's pseudonym], who is equally a music aesthetician, the historian
of literature Löwenthal, and several others. The idea in terms of which
this grouping took place is the idea that "the study of society can be
developed today only in the closest possible cooperation with a number
of disciplines, above all economics, psychology, history, and philosophy." (Benjamin 1972:519)

The Program in the Context of
the History of Science

The Philosophical Critique of Science and the Neopositivist
Critique of Philosophy in the Weimar Republic

Horkheimer takes the unmediated coexistence of philosophical speculation and theory-blind empiricism, deplored in his inaugural address
as symptomatic of the situation of contemporary sociology, to be
simply one example of a general dissociation of philosophy from the
specialized sciences. Horkheimer finds his view confirmed in the philosophical critique of science in the 1920s and in the contemporary form
and philosophical justification of science. He maintains that the last
years of the Weimar Republic were characterized by the Institute's
relationship to empirical-analytical science, which took the form of
two divergent, extreme, and mutually exclusive positions. One position
(*Lebensphilosphie*, romantic spiritualism, materialist and existentialist
phenomenology), consists in the philosophical discrediting of all formal
academic knowledge. The other position, radically opposed to the first,
is neopositivism, which recognizes the dominant form of empirical,
scientific knowledge at any given time as the single source of truth.

(a) Ludwig Klages, Oswald Spengler, Max Scheler, Martin Heidegger,
and other philosophers of the 1920s were united in their skepticism
of the claim of empirical-analytical science to possess some kind of
orienting power for social or biographical-existential reality. Klages's
book, with its revealing title *Der Geist als Widersacher der Seele* [The mind
as a hindrance to the soul] (1931), attempts to reinstate inferior forms

of knowledge represented by magic and superstition; the author maintains that they provide a higher capacity for human orientation than does scientific knowledge. Spengler's *The Decline of the West* (1918) was one of the central texts for the conservative intelligentsia within the humanities until the advent of the Third Reich; human understanding, Spengler maintains, "deadens insofar as it knows." Spengler recommends replacing scientific knowledge with prescientific intuition. He maintains that a high valuation of science is characteristic of regressive, "overly cultivated" cultures; that world views seeking to provide themselves with a scientific foundation characterize cultural decline; and that socialism as a "scientific *Weltanschauung*" ushers in the end of Western civilization. In his wartime writings, Max Scheler criticized the Anglo-Saxon tradition of science from the perspective of *Lebensphilosophie*. His postwar philosophical writings have certainly enriched the special sciences, in such areas as the psychological theory of experience, the sociology of knowledge, and anthropology, yet his postwar metaphysics remained captive to the idea of "life": As the sole ontological reality, it resists a priori its apprehension through the specialized sciences. In his book of 1929, *Der Mensch im Zeitalter des Ausgleichs* [Man in the age of adjustment], Max Scheler interpreted the irrational tendencies of the time as a reaction "against the excessive intellectuality of our fathers" (1929:45). Heidegger's existential analysis of Dasein in *Being and Time* (1927) is marked by a disdain of scientific knowledge. His *Existenzphilosophie* (as well as that of Jaspers) claims that the fundamental ontological structures that it identifies as its philosophical object have primacy over the empirical research of the specialized sciences. For Heidegger, too, scientific knowledge (though not technical knowledge) has no orienting value for either society or the individual.

In Horkheimer's "Remarks on Science and Crisis" (1932), in which he discusses the Weimar Republic's politically significant identity crisis, the antiscientific positions mentioned above flow together to form a cultural syndrome:

The causes of the present crisis are concealed in part because precisely those forces that work toward a better organization of the human situation—above all, rational scientific thought itself—are made responsible for the crisis. There are those who would allow the growth and cultivation of reason to recede behind "spiritual" development; there are those who would discredit critical understanding, to the extent it is not needed by industry, as the decisive source of authority.

The doctrine that human reason is an instrument valuable only for the goals of daily life, that it should remain silent on the great problems, that it should clear the field for the more substantial forces of the soul—such a doctrine distracts from a theoretical treatment of society as a whole. The struggle of modern metaphysics against scientism reflects in part these broad social movements. (1932a:2; 1972b:4)

(b) The strict alternative to *Lebensphilosophie*'s critique of empirical science is the tradition of positivism or empiricism. Such names usually characterize the epistemological generalization of the modern, natural-scientific ideal of knowledge, particularly as represented in the philosophies of Hume and the French Encyclopedists. The rise of this modern formulated ideal of knowledge coincides with the formation of bourgeois society; it characteristically supports all judgments in methodically controlled sense experience and sharply rejects all metaphysics. According to this ideal of knowledge, the propositions of theology, aesthetics, ethics, and politics are "incapable of truth." Modern natural science originates in part in confrontation with the metaphysical pretensions of scholastic theology. Horkheimer maintains that the philosophical self-reflection of modern natural science is characterized by an ahistorical adherence to this adversarial posture toward medieval theology:

The task, unconcerned with extrascientific considerations, of registering facts and determining the regularities existing between them, was originally formulated as a partial goal of the process of bourgeois emancipation in critical confrontation with the scholastic impediments to inquiry. But by the second half of the nineteenth century this definition had already lost is progressive meaning; indeed, it limited science to the registration, classification, and generalization of decisions, making no distinctions between the insignificant and the essential. (1932a:3; 1972b:5)

The positivist ideal of knowledge—which Horkheimer identified as the ideological self-consciousness of scientific inquiry oriented toward the natural sciences and splintered into various disciplines—was renewed and more radically formulated by the Vienna Circle and logical positivism. This epistemological orientation (also characterized as neopositivist) is distinguished from the earlier form of positivism particularly by its reflection upon the logical and analytical-linguistic conditions for the observation and description of natural processes. It made concrete, and formulated more sharply, the older positivist critique of metaphysics: All propositions can be discredited as "metaphysical" that fail to satisfy the restrictive conditions for verification by means of a physicalist language of observation. Accordingly, there is no such thing as the human *sciences*, and philosophy can continue solely as the study of the logic of our language; philosophy is now nothing more than the reflective form of the natural-scientific formation of concepts. Within a science unified by physicalist language,[9] philosophy no longer enjoys the status of an independent discipline. The theories of the early Wittgenstein, of Carnap, Russell, Reichenbach, Schlick, and others, have no theoretical standard or principle that goes beyond physicalist language:

Empiricism denies that thought can evaluate observations and the way in which science combines them. It assigns supreme intellectual authority to accredited science, the given structure and methods of which are reconciled with the status quo. For the empiricist, science is a mere apparatus for arrangement and rearrangement of the facts, regardless of which particular one it selects from among the infinity of facts; it is as if the acts of selection, description, recognition, and combination were, in this society, free of interpretation and orientation. (Horkheimer 1937a:15; 1972b:144–145)

The Relation of Theory to Empirical Research in Contemporary Sociology

The antirationalism of Weimar philosophy also had its counterpoint in the philosophical periphery of the academic sociology of the time. Many reviews in the last issues of the *Grünberg Archiv* and in the first two issues of the *Zeitschrift für Sozialforschung* assume a critical stance toward representatives of the social-philosophical critique of rationalism such as Weber, Troeltsch, Sombart, and Freyer, among others.

Horkheimer and his co-workers were not particularly well acquainted with the formal academic sociology of the Weimar Republic. For this reason we will only briefly outline the relation of theory to empirical research in the sociology of that time.

The relation between theoretical and empirical orientation in the sociology of the 1920s cannot be compared with the contemporary relation between sociological theory and empirical social research, between "hyphenated sociology" and general sociology.

In the 1920s social scientists did in fact systematically apply statistical-empirical methods. Yet the technical level was far below comparable studies of the time done in America and England.[10] And knowledge gained through statistical-empirical means was not accorded much significance compared to historical research, social philosophy, and the scientific treatment of social-welfare policies. Symptomatic in this connection is the critique by Leopold von Wiese of Paul Lazarsfeld's well-known study, *Die Arbeitslosen von Marienthal* [The unemployed in Mariental], in which von Wiese takes offense at Lazarsfeld's method of considering only those results that he can statistically verify.[11]

Nor can one speak of a differentiation between specialized sociology and general sociology at the end of the 1920s. If one looks at the reports of sociological conferences held in 1926, 1928, and 1930, one is struck by the fact that the big names of the sociology of the time (von Wiese, Vierkandt, Spann, Tönnies, Oppenheimer, among others) are unsystematically strewn among almost all of the chapter meetings. Although areas of special concentration, such as ethnology, sociology of art, political sociology, and methodology, had been established, almost all of the scholars mentioned worked simultaneously in a number of disparate areas. This unsystematic distribution of interests offered no basis whatsoever for a division of labor providing the structure for a variety of sociologies, each with a specific area.

The discussion within the Weimar sociological community concerning the relation of theoretical to empirical sociology was ignited primarily by the concept of "sociography." The field of sociography, also called empirical sociology, refers to the program of an inductive kind of social research, empirically and analytically oriented, which sought to apply the survey techniques of demography and epidemiology — already widely practiced — to all possible objects of sociological research. The creater of the concept of sociography — the Dutchman R. Steinmetz — even developed a "sociographic" sociology in contrast to a "pure," or "theoretical," sociology.[12] At the Fifth German Sociological Conference in Vienna in 1926, Steinmetz presented the program of an inductive, empirically and analytically oriented social research. Tönnies developed this in his book *Statistik und Soziographie* (1929), and at his initiative an independent subgroup for sociography was founded at the 1930 sociology conference in Berlin. At the center of their discussion stood the Steinmetzian doctrine of "theoretical" sociology on the one hand and sociography on the other. The establishment of empirical sociographic sociology as an independent discipline, championed by Steinmetz, was criticized by almost all participants. Nevertheless, its supporters could point out that with his metaphor of "mother country versus colony," Steinmetz too was suggesting a mutually fruitful interaction between theory and empirical work. Just as the colony furnished the mother country with raw materials, so would sociography offer raw materials that, after having been theoretically refined, would constitute the problematic of sociography.[13] This suggestive metaphor implies an imperialistic claim to power of theory over empirical material; that it was more than just a rhetorical element is shown by the fact that even sociographers sharply criticized the theory-free empiricism of American social research of the time.[14]

Mention should also be made of the way in which the relation of a theoretical to an empirical orientation was viewed by certain theories of science maintained by the sociology of the time. The fronts of these (apparent) alternatives were even less distinct in the Weimar Republic than they are in contemporary sociology. If we disregard Otto Neurath, a decidedly "positivistic" sociology existed only in what the opponents of a positivist sociology imagined as the "enemy." These opponents of positivism were sociologists and social philosophers who wanted to create a humanistic sociology from the perspective of a completely heterogeneous theoretical orientation. These theorists alone preserve for us today the suggestive stylization of their contemporary methodological positions. In 1926 Vierkandt wrote the essay "The Overcoming of Positivism in Contemporary German Sociology,"[15] in which he criticizes the application of all inductive, empirical-analytical methods in sociology and recommends phenomenological intuition as an alternative. As proponents of this orientation he names Spann, Freyer, Spranger, and Troeltsch. At the Fifth German Sociological Conference in Vienna in the same year, a controversy developed when Othmar Spann suggested that Leopold von Wiese's sociology was, in terms of its own concepts, oriented toward natural science. This controversy was subsequently interpreted—even if in the process violence was done to certain details—as a controversy between theoretical and empirical-analytical sociology.[16] Yet, not until Otto Neurath's *Empirical Sociology* of 1931 did this adversarial image, the "positivist" sociology as anticipated by Vierkandt and Spann, correspond to anything concrete. Neurath understood sociology as a subdiscipline of a physicalist unified science and postulated a natural-scientific methodology.

It was only after the 1934 emigration to America that the Frankfurt Circle confronted a predominantly empirically oriented social research. The *Zeitschrift für Sozialforschung* seldom criticized the type of social research widespread in the United States. Until the outbreak of the war, the German authors of the *Zeitschrift* continued to orient themselves on the political and scientific culture of the Weimar Republic. As a consequence, they were quite isolated within the American scholarly community until the end of the 1930s. It is significant that the well-known controversy between Lazarsfeld and Adorno, which is rightly understood as a controversy between the American and German traditions of research, did not occur until the late 1930s.[17]

The *Zeitschrift* contains only one essay that deals openly and critically with the empiricist orientations of American social research of the time. Written by the American historian Charles Beard, the essay, "The Social Sciences in the United States" (1935), closely approximated the Frankfurt Circle's probable views. According to Beard, the central problem of American social research is to provide a theoretical synthesis of the results of detailed empirical research:

For the moment American scholarship runs in its historical course. Its statistical and factual studies have produced materials and work of immense value to future thought and use. . . . But efforts of American scholars to bring to pass a social synthesis by the application of the empirical methods have come to a dead end. . . . (1935:64)

Gumperz's analysis of the Hoover Report was a critique of American social research that was more direct but equally suggestive. The study, "Recent Trends in the USA," of the general situation of American society was initiated by President Herbert Hoover in 1932; it was massive in both conception and cost. Julian Gumperz remarked in the *Zeitschrift* that the inability of American social researchers to realize a theoretical-interpretive synthesis of the empirical-statistical material was brought into high relief when viewed against the study's claim to represent a comprehensive social analysis:

The report abstracts American society from the historical movement and environment, in terms of which alone it can be understood, and replaces the historically oriented movement with a mere juxtaposition of statistics. The sociological concept of trend, by allowing qualitative factors to sink in a homogeneous sea of statistics, tends to dissolve sociology into statistics. . . . Here, the fact that qualitative analysis cannot be replaced by a purely quantitative analysis is proven once again. . . . (1935:228, 225)

Gumperz's critique of the Hoover Report well documents the impression of American social research held by the emigres around Horkheimer: Its empiricism, blind to all theory, sharply contrasted with the over-burdening of Weimar sociology with philosophy.

We have seen that the contact, following emigration, with American social science—which represented the radical antithesis to German sociology's philosophical quality—only reinforced the impression of the necessity, expressed in Horkheimer's inaugural address of 1931, of redefining the relation between philosophy and the specialized sciences. This exposure to American social research only further under-scored the urgency with which Horkheimer appealed, as early as 1931, for a "dialectical interpenetration and development of philosophical theory and individual scientific praxis" (1972c:40).

Theoretical and Historical Background

In this chapter we reconstruct Horkheimer's stylization of Hegel's and Marx's theory of dialectical presentation. I shall not discuss how Horkheimer's interpretation is related to the general discussion and reception of dialectics at that time (which was heavily influenced by Lukács).

The concept of integrating philosophical theory into the research methods of the specialized sciences—put into practice through the project for an interdisciplinary social science—originated in Horkheimer's reconstruction of the intentions of Marxist and Hegelian dialectics. His essay "The Controversy over Rationalism in Contemporary Philosophy" (1934b) discusses the dialectical method developed by Hegel in the context of his critique of Kant; it "is the essence of all intellectual means of making fruitful the abstract moments achieved in the faculty of understanding for the image of living objects." (1934b:20)

The Hegelian logic is founded on the notion that in the act of thinking every object of knowledge does not remain formally identical with itself but, rather, because of its immanent "contradictory nature," attempts to go beyond itself and thereby transforms its identity and boundaries. Hence a form of knowledge that did no more than apply the static potential of formal logical categories cannot adequately grasp the object's self-movement. This is why knowledge itself must be much more like a process; within this process, particular judgments are valid only as provisional phases through which the process of knowledge proceeds. The criterion of "truth" is no longer the adequate correspondence of a particular judgment to a delimited sphere of objects. Rather it is the process of knowledge itself, which passes through all preliminary acts of judgment, claiming to be complete within itself: *"Das Wahre ist das Ganze"* [The truth is the whole]. Hegel conceives of this process of knowledge metaphysically, as the process of self-reflection by a theologically conceived supersubject that frees itself from its quality of being an object; only through a reflection that recovers this objectivity does it come into its own.

The Hegelian identity of object and concept is, however, a metaphysical presupposition. In the process of knowing in true "science," Hegel proceeds from the empirical difference between concept and object. Philosophy's task is to overcome this difference, to realize the speculative unity of thing and concept. In the circular process of spirit's self-reflection, speculative philosophy is the locus of reconciliation of object and logical concept, where the object is "brought to the level of the concept." In thus performing its role, speculative philosophy utilizes in a specific way the "preliminary determinations" of the specialized sciences.

The significance of the Hegelian "dialectic" for the sciences depends on the significance of the objects of science that, unlike in theology or aesthetics, do not yet by themselves achieve the speculative identity of a reflecting subject and a scientific object. Rather, this identity must first be developed by the reflecting subject. For Hegel this is expressly the case in his *Philosophy of History*, whose object must be brought to the level of the concept first through the narrative work of the historiographer and then through the synthesizing work of the philosopher. The passage that Horkheimer repeatedly quotes in this context reads:

Empirical science prepares the empirical material for the dialectical concept, so that the dialectical concept can receive it ready for use. The process of the origination of science is different from its process in itself when it is complete, just as the process of the history of philosophy differs from that of philosophy itself. . . . The development of the empirical side had been . . . the essential condition of the Idea, so that it can reach its full development and determination. (Hegel 1896:176)

Fundamental to Hegelian dialectics is the presupposition that the results of specialized-scientific research are dependent on the philosophical reflection that "sublates" them. Hegel illustrates this not only in terms of the relation between historiography and philosophy of history; according to Hegel, natural philosophy's role in relation to physics—a typical specialized science—is to bring the analytical and empirical findings of physics to the level of the concept:

The material prepared out of experience by physics is taken by the philosophy of nature at the point where physics has brought it, and reconstitutes it without any further reference to experience as the basis for verification. Physics must therefore work together with philosophy so that the universalized understanding which it provides can be translated into the concept by showing how this universal, as an intrinsically necessary whole, proceeds out of the concept. (1970:201)

Although, according to Hegel, the positive or specialized sciences do reach "the ground of the concepts," they cannot accomplish the complete realization of science as such—as the "Idea," as a "system." Just as historiography furnishes every philosophy of history with material, so does physics furnish the material for natural philosophy. But the course of mind or spirit is not itself able to affect the material content of the specialized sciences. Horkheimer maintains that for Hegel, the the results of the empirical sciences are significant only as examples; this, says Horkheimer, does not correspond to Hegel's self-understanding, but certainly to the way in which Hegel expressed his philosophy. The findings of empirical research enter into the presentation as an application; they are a specific demonstration of the course of the idea. The autonomy of the idea, of mind or spirit—speculative philosophy's independence from the reality studied from the empirical perspective—is expressed in the speculative identity, postulated by idealist dialectics, of concept and content. Hegel goes so far as to attribute to the act of reflecting upon a historical process, or to the act of reflecting upon the realm of empirical objects itself, the character of a subject. He then substitutes this imaginary subject of the historical process, or of the empirical realm, with the Idea. Hegel's philosophy concludes in the identification of the process of reflection with the empirical process; and it completely subsumes the latter under the former.

Marx concisely summarizes this basic cognitive figure:

For Hegel, the process of thinking, which he even transforms into an independent, self-sufficient subject and then calls the "Idea," is the demiurge of the real world, and the real world is merely the external, phenomenal form of the "Idea." (1974:27; 1906:19)

In his critique of this identity in the afterword to *Kapital*, Marx restricts his discussion to its political implications—namely, that it mystifies social relations that are essentially historical. The critique of Hegel's identity of the reflective process with the empirical process—as well as the materialist assertion of their nonidentity—is, says Horkheimer, the precise point of difference between idealist and materialist dialectics. He describes this point of difference as follows:

This view presupposes the idealist principle that concept and being are in truth one and the same, that full and complete knowledge therefore is only attained in the pure medium of spirit. . . . Materialism maintains on the contrary that objective reality is not identical with thought, and that it can never be reduced to thought. As much as thought seeks in its own elements to reproduce the life of the object, and thus to adapt or conform the object, thought nonetheless is not, at the same time, the object conceived (unless in the case of self-observation and reflection—and really not even there). (1935b:334; 1978:419)

But with respect to scientific method, idealist and materialist dialectics are structurally identical. They are identical in that they both differentiate between an analytical and a synthetic level in the scientific process. What Hegel calls the empirical side, which "prepares the empirical material," corresponds to what Marx called research; Hegel's "dialectical concept," which "takes up" this empirical material, corresponds to Marx's "presentation." Marx describes the relation between the two levels as follows:

Research must appropriate the material in detail, analyze its different forms of development, and trace out their interconnection. Only after this has been accomplished can the actual movement be correspondingly presented. If this proves successful and the life of the material is now ideally reflected, it may appear as if it were an a priori construction. (1974:27; 1906:19)

Hegel considers the cognitive act complete when the philosopher has so prepared the "empirical material" that it finally conforms to the Idea, "so that it can reach its full development and determination." Hegel means scientific development in the form of a unilinear movement from the specialized sciences to speculative generalizations. The "Idea" subsumes the findings of specialized scientific research:

The materialist dialectic is . . . fundamentally distinct from the Hegelian dialectic. By developing dialectical principles, and even more by giving special examples of dialectical presentations, Hegel demonstrated how analytically won concepts can be rendered fruitful for the conceptual reconstruction of living processes. Yet he maintains that there is in fact only one single process, containing within itself all concepts as its moments; and he maintains that the philosopher can grasp and present this process, this "concrete entity," the "one," in final form. (Horkheimer 1934b:24)

By contrast, the method of materialist dialetics is characterized by a reciprocity in the relation between philosophical speculation and empirical research. Marx's economic critique unites philosophy with the specialized sciences both in its stated objectives and in their realization; in Hegel's idealist dialectics, speculative philosophy merely subsumes the results of the specialized sciences.

Marx made few remarks, at least in his economic writings, that were explicit reflections on his methodology as interpreted by Horkheimer: the corrective and specifying function of empirical-analytical "research" in the specialized sciences, compared to the synthetic function of "presentation." Throughout the early writings, as well as the economic works, there are critical references to the Hegelianizing tendency (e.g., that of Bruno Bauer) "to develop empirical relations out of the concept," the tendency toward "methods of establishing connections merely conceptually."[18]

The epistemological principle of concrete totality characterizes the epistemological maxim upon which the idealist as well as the materialist dialectic is based. According to this principle, an object of knowledge is never perceived as an isolated object abstracted from its larger context, but rather always in terms of a totality given, at least latently, together with the object. The identity of an object of knowledge is doubly determined: through the context of interdependence to which it belongs, and through the position that it occupies within this context. For Hegel, as for Marx, the concept of the "concrete" characterizes the relation between an object of knowledge and the context of interdependence. The theoretical reconstruction of a sense object, of a historical event, of a scientific fact, or of the legal facts of a juridical case can be described in Hegel's terminology as concrete only to the extent that this reconstruction is related to the totality of the phenomenon's context. Similarly, for Marx research on one element of the capitalist mode of production—such as competition among individual capitalists—becomes concrete only insofar as it is related to the totality of the capitalist reproduction process.

The epistemological principle of concrete totality avoids the scholastic debate between nominalism and conceptual realism. The totality has no existence without the particular that refers to it, and the particular can be determined only in terms of its position within the total context. The movement of dialectical knowledge from part to whole, from particularity to totality, from essence to appearance, and vice versa, is not a closed, circular movement.[19] The first step in the dialectical process of knowledge consists in the conceptual anticipation of the completely empty and chaotic totality. The dialectical construction of theory begins, according to Horkheimer, with empty, global definitions—for example, with the description of capitalist wealth as an "immense collection of commodities." In a second step an element within this total context is defined. This "positionless," "free-floating" definition is, in a third step, related back to the totality, which for its part becomes increasingly focused and more precise through these differentiations of its internal structure. At the same time, by this differentiation, the context embodying the analytically defined or identified details can be specified with increasing precision. In the course of the dialectical process of knowledge, the reference to totality and the determination of detail thus "comment" on each other reciprocally, until a complex theoretical structure has been developed.

Dialectical theory-construction is thus conceived differently from the forms of analytical theory-construction. The latter assumes, even on a methodological level, that complex phenomena are merely the relations between details that are organized serially. Dialectical theory-construction is also conceived differently from synthetic speculative forms of theory that "deduce" particular determinations from general concepts. Horkheimer describes the "peculiarities of dialectical thought" as "the effort,"

not to line up attributes alongside each other, but rather, through analysis of each general characteristic, to show with regard to the particular object that this generality, when taken exclusively, contradicts the object—and that, in order to be properly understood, it must also be related to the contrary property and finally to the entire system of knowledge. From this follows the principle that every insight is to be regarded as true only when viewed in connection with the whole body of theoretical knowledge. (1935b:350; 1978:432–433)

The essence of our thesis is this: Horkheimer always understood these basic reflections upon problems of dialectical epistemology in the methodological terms of the Circle's interdisciplinary research. Accordingly he reads Hegel's dictum, coined as a criticism of Kant, that the "understanding merely draws distinctions" as a demand on the specialized sciences to become conscious of their limited ability of presentation:

The specialized sciences provide only the elements for a theoretical construction of the course of history. . . . The formation of concepts within physics, the definition of life processes in biology, the general description of an instinctive drive, the presentation of the typical mechanism of inflation or of capital accumulation, as well as other results of the specialized sciences, do not of themselves constitute an adequate presentation of human activity in dead and living nature, but rather its precondition. (1934b:22)

For research practice this means that the empirical-analytical sciences— quite to the contrary of their self-understanding—are not at all so constituted as to adequately reflect the structure of reality. For their results are "abstract"—in the sense of both everyday speech and philosophical discourse. They offer a kaleidoscope of the research findings of an empirical science fragmented into a multiplicity of disciplines; at most these findings can be synthesized one after another, that is, untheoretically, to appear as a trustworthy and action-orienting reproduction of reality. Horkheimer also emphasized that the weakness of orientation in the particular sciences is compensated for in bourgeois consciousness through unscientific metaphysics. Scientism and the metaphysical creation of meaning are, he maintained, complementary symptoms of an identical pathology.

Certainly a scientific undertaking such as Horkheimer's programmatically proclaimed "materialist" social theory—which expressly takes into account the analytical and empirical findings of the specialized sciences, combining them into a complex structure by means of dialectical theory-construction—better reflects the structure of a reality understood in terms of a historical process. The form of dialectical theory-construction "tries to place analytically achieved concepts in relation to one another, and reconstruct reality through them" (1935b:351; 1978:433). Thus it lends to the particular sciences' analytical concepts and empirical findings a presentational and orienting value that they, of themselves and in a merely compound arrangement, do not possess.

Horkheimer considers Marx's method in *Kapital* to offer the decisive paradigm for such a methodology:

Since a concept plays a determinate role in the dialectical construction of an event, it becomes a dependent moment within a conceptual whole possessing more characteristics than merely the sum of all the concepts it has assimilated into itself. Of course this whole, the construction of a particular object, can only then be realized in a manner adequate to existing knowledge if the concepts are interpreted in the sense that belongs to them in the systems of the individual sciences, within the systematic inventories of scientifically based definitions (insofar as it is a question of concepts for which special branches of science exist). In *Kapital*, Marx introduces the fundamental concepts of classic English political economy: exchange value, price, labor time, and so on, in accordance with their precise definition. All of the most progressive definitions drawn from scientific practice at that time are employed. Nevertheless, these categories acquire new functions in the course of the presentation; they contribute to a theoretical whole whose character contradicts the static perspectives in terms of which these categories were first developed, in particular their uncritical use in isolation. Materialist economics as a whole is placed in opposition to the system of classic economics, and yet the former has taken over individual concepts of the latter. (Horkheimer 1935b:355–356; 1978:437)

Alfred Schmidt maintains that Horkheimer was among the first to appreciate the methodology of the critique of political economy (particularly its differentiation between research and presentation) as the principle of construction of *Kapital*.[20] This may be so. It is certain, nevertheless, that Horkheimer was not particularly interested in an exegesis of Marx—as indicated by the scant number of relevant philological references he made. Other than what has already been cited, and in addition to suggestions never realized, one finds only in the essay "Traditional and Critical Theory" arguments that might, in a rather exaggerated interpretation, be described as an exegesis of Marx. We maintain that Horkheimer's interest in the logic of scientific analysis represented by the critique of political economy was an interest in the form of science embodied in this critique.

Under the historical conditions of scientific inquiry in the 1930s, the phrase "accounting for the analytical findings of the particular sciences" could no longer mean to incorporate critically the concepts of classic bourgeois, eighteenth-century economics. When Horkheimer spoke of the "materialist unification of philosophy and specialized science," he spoke at a moment in the history of science in which, out of the broad, unitary discipline that in the eighteenth and nineteenth centuries constituted the study of politics, the disciplines of economics, jurisprudence, sociology, and political science had been differentiated, a psychoanalytically oriented psychology had been developed, and the humanities had been constituted and had already come into conflict with the cognitive ideal of the natural sciences. Yet the relevant texts by Horkheimer contain no precise answer to the central question of how, under the conditions mentioned, this particular form of science is still to be realized. More specifically, they provide no answer to the "how" of dialectical construction or the "how" of presentation of empirical-scientific research findings.[21] In these passages he occasionally recalls the old Aristotelian argument that the historiographer needs not only knowledge of the relevant events but also poetic imagination as well—that is, an ability that resists scientific control. The answer to the question concerning dialectical construction precedes Horkheimer's theoretical writings—namely, in the idea of placing the research apparatus of the well-equipped Frankfurt Institute for Social Research in the service of research of the kind represented by the critique of political economy (as understood by Horkheimer).

The Theory of Dialectical Presentation and Research Organization

The Frankfurt Institute's fundamental principle of research organization appeared, in our (for systematic reasons) idealized and stylized retrospective, as follows. The differentiation (characteristic of dialectical method) between the levels of research and presentation was realized in actual research practice. Research and presentation were functions within the research process that—although related to each other as stages in a process—were nonetheless separated in actual procedure. *Research* and *presentation* were defined as social roles within a context of research organized in terms of a division of labor. Those co-workers who performed the role of presentation had the function of:

(a) defining the problem in a general, "philosophical" way,

(c) integrating with other disciplines those theory concepts still bound to particular disciplines,

(e) integrating empirically confirmed hypotheses into interdisciplinarily generated supertheories, and

(g) formulating, in certain cases, the conclusions drawn from the findings. Those co-workers who performed the role of research had the function of:

(b) making the general, philosophical formulation of the problem more specific by "translating" it into the terms of the specialized sciences,

(d) making interdisciplinary concepts of theory workable, and planning and developing empirical research, and

(f) testing the hypotheses, now integrated into a supertheory, on the analytical, the methodological, and the technical (measurement) standards of the specialized sciences.

Figure 1 shows clearly the division between the two levels of research and presentation; the line drawn point by point from (a) to (g) traces the succession of individual steps and reveals the interaction within the role system. By using fragments of the Frankfurt Circle's theory development as examples, we will illustrate this process. As in the diagram, lowercase letters mark stages in the research process:

(a) With the conceptual apparatus proper to him, the philosopher deplores the fact that under the conditions of capitalist society, man does not make his own history with will and consciousness.

(b) The economist transforms this philosophical lament into the terms of his own science, into studies in crisis theory and planned economy.

(a) The philosopher further criticizes the bourgeois philosophy of history, claiming that its explanation of historical processes is based on an anthropological conception of man as an unchanging being. The philosopher challenges this position with the thesis—expressed in terms of social philosophy—of the socioeconomic variance of psychic structures. The social psychologist (b) then "translates" this thesis into the terms of a psychoanalytically based, materialist social psychology.

(c) Thus the philosopher's general definition above might be "translated" or "specified" within the context of the historical phenomenon of the dispossession of the middle classes in the Weimar Republic, and the consequent changes in socialization patterns. If the philosopher makes claims about this historical situation, he then orients himself through social-psychological and economic analyses. The decisive role of presentation—as here performed by the philosopher—is to treat concepts and hypotheses of organizationally and cognitively distinct disciplines in such a way that they can be related to each other with respect to a central theme.

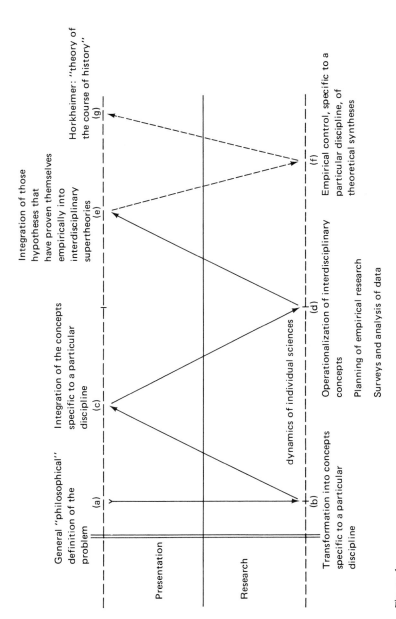

Figure 1
Research and presentation in the program of the Institute for Social Research.

(d) From these theory concepts (integrated at the level of presentation) are derived hypotheses that are informed by all of the analytical and empirical findings of the specialized sciences. These hypotheses are then collectively and empirically tested as an ensemble of studies.

(e) They are then integrated, at the level of presentation, into a comprehensive theory that (f) must be continually justified against the analytical, methodological, and technical standards of the particular disciplines.

We have derived the basic structure of the Frankfurt Circle's research process from programmatic texts and then systematically stylized it in our reconstruction. We will now identify this structure in the Circle's published studies. It is our intention not only to verify or falsify a hypothetical supposition but also to differentiate this highly formalized structure in terms of its actual operation, and thereby to examine its capacity to be transformed into practical research. This perspective will then be reconsidered in a final summary.

We shall identify this structure in the Frankfurt Circle's research process through an anlysis of the *Zeitschrift für Sozialforschung*, the *Studies on Authority and the Family*, the general cognitive structure of its research, the structure of internal communications, and the differentiation of roles within the group. We shall then turn to institutional factors external to, but significant for, the development of the Circle's theory.

The Cognitive Structure of the Organization of Research

In attempting to identify the idealized research structure of figure 1 in the *Zeitschrift für Sozialforschung* and in *Studies on Authority and the Family*, we immediately run up against a problem. Horkheimer's program for an interdisciplinary "social research" conceives of the following as a unity: (a) the reorganization (along interdisciplinary lines) of the specialized sciences (now fragmented into disciplines) within the medium of philosophy and (b) the integration of philosophy and the specialized sciences. This leads to such distortions as a methodologically vague concept of the empirical side. Sometimes he considers empiricism an attribute, not of a research method, but merely of a direct, pretheoretical approach to an object. He thus often overlooks the degree to which the work of philosophical reflection has long been integrated into the specialized sciences themselves.

For our analysis it follows that the two moments—the (horizontal) interdisciplinary integration of the specialized sciences and the (vertical) integration of specialized science and philosophy—are to some extent dissociated and hence must be weighted differently in the texts to be analyzed.

We begin with an analysis of Circle texts in the first three issues of the *Zeitschrift*, in which the moment of horizontal integration dominates. We then analyze *Studies on Authority and the Family*, in which the moment of vertical integration is prominent. This difference results from the fact that the *Zeitschrift* was conceived primarily as a platform for theoretical studies, while *Studies on Authority and the Family* was an empirically oriented project.

The following interpretation goes against the usual pattern of interpreting Critical Theory, which implicitly assumes that it can be explained only in terms of the intellectual biographies of the individual workers. We, on the other hand, proceed from the fact that, at least for the period discussed in this book, the theory production of each worker considered was structurally entwined with that of the other co-workers.

The Zeitschrift für Sozialforschung

We shall analyze the structure and the process of mutual interaction of theory concepts and proposed explanations. This we shall do in terms of the content of individual Zeitschrift articles (in the first three issues only), with the following question in mind: To what extent to the individual contributions form an interdisciplinary whole?

Figure 2 shows schematically the structure of these processes of mutual influence. The arrows represent the direction of the "influence," and the half circles represent in each case the particular object area within which individual contributions were, despite thematic differences, integrated. Authors' names stand for their Zeitschrift essays in the issues analyzed here. We will explicate the diagram in the following discussion.

In his book Anfänge der bürgerlichen Geschichtsphilosophie [The origins of the bourgeois philosophy of history], Horkheimer criticizes the early bourgeois political philosophers Machiavelli and Hobbes, maintaining that their explanation of the course of history is based on a conception of a constant, unchanging human nature. This perspective overlooks the fact "that the psychical and physical elements determining human nature are part of historical reality" (1930a:29). The historical and social contingency of psychical nature is the theme of a lecture, entitled "History and Psychology," delivered before the Frankfurt Kant Society and subsequently published in the Zeitschrift für Sozialforschung. Here, Horkheimer sets forth a program "to characterize the role appropriate to psychology in terms of a theory of history fully informed by the most recent developments in the social sciences" (1932b:125). He includes an analysis of historical materialism in the context of a critique of bourgeois philosophies of history in terms of their ignorance of psychical factors that influence history. He maintains that historical materialism's assertion of the primacy of the economic base, and its

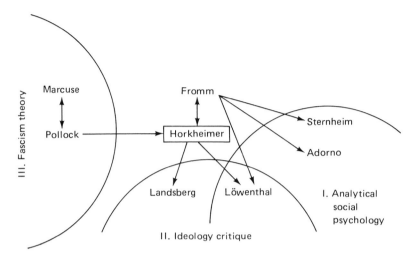

Figure 2
Patterns of influence in the work of the Institute for Social Research.

thesis of the superstructure's one-way dependence on this base, must be complemented by a social psychology:

> To the extent that we do not know how structural changes in economic life transform all aspects of an individual's life—by means of the given psychological disposition of individuals from the various social groups— the doctrine of the dependence of the psyche upon economic life contains elements that strongly prejudice their hypothetical value for explaining the present. (1932b:134)

Horkheimer argues for a social psychology that utilizes the findings of political economy and deals with the psychical forms that express economic forces:

> Psychology will thus have to advance to these deeper-lying psychical factors by means of which economics determines human beings. (1932b:135)

He refers in a note to Erich Fromm's attempt to develop, on a psychoanalytic basis, just such a social psychology.

In the essay "On the Method and Function of an Analytical Social Psychology" (1932), Fromm proceeds from the psychoanalytic premise of the plasticity of the sexual drive, its capacity for being transformed and displaced. Against the research undertaken at the same time by Freud's student Wilhelm Reich, Fromm maintains that this theory (which Freud developed specifically for the psychology of the individual) can be applied to mass phenomena. Fromm's attempt to "consistently apply to social phenomena the method of analytical social psychology" is part of a program defined by Horkheimer in terms of a psychoanalytic refinement of political economy:

Analytical social psychology seeks to understand the instinctive apparatus of a group, its libidinous and largely unconscious behavior, in terms of socioeconomic structure. (1932a:34; 1970:116)

Social-psychological phenomena are to be understood as processes of active and passive adaptation, on the part of the instinctive apparatus, to the socioeconomic situation. In certain fundamental respects, the instinctive apparatus is a biological given; but it is highly modifiable. The primary formative factors are economic conditions. The family is the essential medium through which the economic situation exercises its influence on the individual psyche. The task of social psychology is to explain the shared, socially relevant psychic attitudes and ideologies—and especially their unconscius roots—in terms of the influence of economic factors on libidinal drives. (1932a:40; 1970:121)

This plan—even though it was developed more broadly in the social-psychological part of *Studies on Authority and the Family*—was never expanded beyond programmatic remarks. It nonetheless provides us with what was to have been exemplified within this framework: the "translation" or specification of a philosophical problem (in this case formulated by Horkheimer) into social-scientific terms.

   This project, worked out between Horkheimer and Fromm, of an analytically oriented and materialistically based social psychology was surely the chosen paradigmatic core of the Circle's theoretical orientation in the early 1930s. This program offers problem-solving potential for a great number of interdisciplinarily generated questions, even in articles, even in articles whose subject matter was only remotely relevant.

   In his essay "On the Problem of Organizing Leisure Time" (1932), Andries Sternheim provides empirical material toward a theory that would differentiate between various uses of leisure time—material drawn from investigations of the Geneva-based International Labor

Office. He maintains that a theoretically satisfactory solution to the problem posed can be provided only by an analytical social psychology:

The study of particular ways of using leisure time—a study applying the analytic, social-psychological methodology—will provide us with information about the psychological preconditions of the origin, continued existence, and eventual decline of certain types of free time. . . . (1932:355)

What counts, more so in the use of leisure time than anywhere else, is the extent to which man's instinctive drives and intellectual needs are . . . already completely satisfied in the labor process itself. . . . Analytical social psychology stands before a large task. (1932:348)

Adorno argues similarly in the context of research on the effects of so-called light music:

But as long as the social dialectic and the analysis of instinct structure remain juxtaposed—discretely, or one complementing the other—the concrete influence of light music cannot be understood; for as long as this remains a task for the analysis of specialized sciences, which, like proper systematic bourgeois science, work in isolation from each other, it only affirms one of the most questionable disjunctions within bourgeois thought: that between nature and history. (1932a:378; 1978:164)

According to Löwenthal, a materialist social psychology would also provide a key to the solution of numerous problems in the study of literature. It alone could define the role that psychology might play in the study of literature.

One has misunderstood the theory [i.e., the materialist understanding of history] if one would ascribe to it the belief in culture's direct derivation from the economy; indeed, it is a misunderstanding to maintain simply that this theory attempts to deduce the basic aspects of cultural and psychical formations from a certain economic structure. What this theory really attempts to do is demonstrate the significant extent to which the conditions of human life—in all its forms, hence in literature as well—are mediated. This is where psychology finds a quite secure place within the study of literature. . . . (1932:94)

We find a similar relation between the theoretical-philosophical formulation of a problem and its "translation" or specification into terms of a specialized science in the relation between Horkheimer's foundational ideas on ideology critique and Löwenthal's attempt to apply these ideas to material drawn from the history of literature. In *The Origins of the Bourgeois Philosophy of History* and "A New Concept of Ideology?" (1930b), Horkheimer emphasizes—by criticizing the sociology of knowledge of his contemporary, Karl Mannheim—that the theory of ideology demands more than just the demonstration of the historical and social dependence of theoretical processes. On the one hand, one must bear in mind that historically prominent theoretical achievements can be measured only against the standards of the science of the time; on the other hand, the analysis of the politically and socially harmonizing, stabilizing functions of ideologies is indispensable—as is, therefore, the critique of ideology:

The insight that a theory is historically determined is in no way identical to the proof that the theory is ideological. To show this, one must provide the complicated proof of its social function. (Horkheimer 1930b:74n)

Löwenthal appropriates this postulate of ideology critique in his essay, "On the Social Situation of Literature":

In the social explanation of the superstructure—and not simply in social theory in general—the concept of ideology assumes a decisive role. For ideology is a content of consciousness, a content that has the function of concealing contradictions and of replacing knowledge of social antagonisms with the appearance of harmony. To a large extent the study of the history of literature is research on ideologies. (1932:95)

In his contributions to the *Zeitschrift für Sozialforschung* Löwenthal then develops this program of utilizing ideology critique in the study of literature. Whether he attempts, in an essay on Conrad Ferdinand Meyer, to explain Meyer's affinity with the ideology of the large landowners and the industrial and military leadership in the Wilhelminian Reich (1933), or whether, in a study of the reception of Dostoevski in prewar Germany (1934), he investigates the prefascist potential of the petit bourgeois and dispossessed middle-class readers of Dostoevski, in all cases he is concerned with analyzing an ideology's functional capacity—using material drawn from the history of literature—for politically stabilizing and harmonizing class relations.

Horkheimer's relation to Paul Ludwig Landsberg also reveals the relation of reciprocal influence—already described in the relationship between Fromm and Löwenthal—between the conceptual thematization of a problem and its subsequent "translation" or specification in terms of a specialized science. Like Löwenthal, Landsberg understands his scholarly work as ideology critique. His essay, "Race Ideology and Race Science (1933)," is based on Max Horkheimer's definition of ideology. In Landsberg's formulation:

As for the concept of ideology—we would certainly not identify the ideologue with, for example, the deceiver. To say that a particular doctrine is ideological is to say that its origin and its evidence for its adherents are essentially based, not upon experience, but upon a social function, upon influence on society and its struggles—all of which is expected of it. (1933:388)

Landsberg cataloged the characteristics of racist ideology in the writings of the forefathers of the National Socialist race ideology (Gobineau, Lapouge, Chamberlain) and their contemporary representatives in Germany (Lenz, Günter, and Scheman). He challenged these suggested characteristics with the thesis of "materialist sociology" (1933:402): that class differences are economically, not racially, determined, and that whatever biological differences might in certain cases be identified constitute a belated consequence of class situation—and not the other way around. During the National Socialist racial madness, the primary function of the serious study of race must be the "destruction of ideology"; under contemporary conditions the scientific study of races must be "ideology critique."

The interaction between the philosophical articulation of a problem and its subsequent specification in terms of a specialized science, as well as the differentiation in terms of a specialized science of the general and speculative formulation of a problem, describes the relationship between Horkheimer and Pollock as well as between Pollock's co-workers, Kurt Mandelbaum and Gerhardt Meyer. The relation of influence between Horkheimer and Pollock, however, was not entirely reciprocal. Horkheimer profited more from Pollock than Pollock from Horkheimer. Prior to 1930, Horkheimer formulated the postulate of reorganizing society along the lines of a planned economy in complete philosophical generality—as the "sublation of the blind mechanism of many competing single wills" and "the planned regulation of life processes in the common interest" (1930b:88ff.). But his introduction four years later to the essay by Mandelbaum and Meyer, "On a Theory of Planned Economy," was not a philosophical text but rather a general summary of economic results (cf. Mandelbaum and Meyer 1934:228).

Within the circle of co-workers, Pollock had the role of studying possibilities for reorganizing—along the lines of a planned economy—West European capitalist countries shaken by the world economic crisis. In his essay of 1932, "The Present Situation of Capitalism and the Outlook for a New, Planned Economic Order," Pollock argues for the replacement of "limited planning" as practiced by monopolies with thoroughgoing state planning. Yet his consideration of the conditions for the possibility of a planned, economic, new order in West European societies does not go beyond particular questions (bookkeeping in socialism, freedom in consumption, guiding technological development). In their essay Mandelbaum and Meyer systematize and further differentiate the basic ideas developed by Pollock in his first two essays.

Not until the end of the 1930s did the Institute conduct systematic research projects on fascism or German national socialism. Yet the central thesis—which all later discussions, up to Neumann's *Behemoth*, simply applied and refined—was formulated quite early: that fascism is merely a continuation of economic liberalism employing different means, and that it is the political form corresponding to the bourgeois society of monopoly capitalism. This thesis was first formulated by Pollock in his 1933 essay, "Remarks on the Economic Crisis." In 1934 Marcuse added to the thesis in an intellectual-historical analysis. The thesis of the affinity and continuity between late liberalism and fascism—which Pollock developed in economic terms and Marcuse in terms of a critique of ideology—was accepted and articulated by Horkheimer, most radically in his 1939 essay, "The Jews and Europe." The following quotations demonstrate that the Circle's fascism theory, as developed between 1933 and 1935, was the product of several minds. After listing all the obvious objections to a system-immanent, economic overplanning, Pollock remarks:

But should the difficulties in the capitalist system continue to worsen, then these obstacles, too, will probably be overcome, in the interest of saving the system—even if it takes terrible struggles to accomplish this. Such a reorganization of economic methods would necessarily be accompanied by a complete transformation of society's political organization. Events of the past few years have demonstrated the nature of those political forms corresponding to monopoly capitalism. (1933:349)

In his 1934 essay, "The Struggle against Liberalism in the Totalitarian View of the State," Marcuse develops the thesis that fascism's objections to elements of the liberal idea of society camouflage fascism's fundamental recognition, indeed affirmation, of late capitalism's economic structure. Using the Italian theorist of fascism, Gentile, and his application of the leader ideology to the entrepreneur, Marcuse demonstrates the ideological and practical affinity between late liberalism and fascism. As he concludes his discussion of the liberalist *Weltanschauung*:

A rough sketch of liberalist social theory has shown that it contains many elements of the totalitarian notion of the state. Taking the economic structure as a point of reference, we see an almost unbroken continuity in the development of the social theory. We shall here assume some prior knowledge of the economic foundations of this development. (1934:174; 1968:18)

Then, in a note, he refers to the 1933 essay by Pollock.

Horkheimer uses this thesis on fascism in his introduction to Mandelbaum and Meyer's essay "On a Theory of Planned Economy":

The internal affinity between this harmonious metaphysics, ignoring as it does all social differences, and a totalitarian notion of the state has made it easy for the representatives of decisive branches of industry and for many politicians—who at one time subscribed to liberalism—to make the ideological transition from liberalism to capitalist statism. . . . [He refers in this context to Marcuse's text.] People do not have to choose at all between a liberalist economy and a totalitarian organization of the state—since the one necessarily flows into the other. . . . (Horkheimer 1934c:230)

We thus find a high degree of interdependence between *Zeitschrift* articles that varied widely in subject matter. There were no essays by members of the inner circle that were not mediated by other *Zeitschrift* articles.

This relation of interdependence can now be described more precisely. The individual essays cannot be subsumed under any single, homogeneous *tertium comparationis*. Instead, their integration was effected—as figure 2 makes clear—in terms of three different theory concepts:

1. Sternheim, Adorno, and, to an extent, Löwenthal define their own methodology as an "analytical social psychology"—a methodology to be further developed.

2. Löwenthal and Landsberg characterize "the critique of ideology" as the programmatic form of their work.

3. Pollock and Marcuse converge—one from an economic perspective, the other from intellectual history—in their thesis on liberalism and fascism.

Each of these three media of interaction operates at a different level. The analytical social psychology functions as a general methodology, ideology critique is a unifying theory form, and the thesis relating fascism to liberalism represents a commonly accepted preliminary finding. In all three media of integration Horkheimer's role is more or less central. Fromm developed the concept of an analytical or materialist social psychology, but it was Horkheimer who encouraged its use within the Circle; Horkheimer developed ideology critique as a scientific form in his critique of Karl Mannheim, and he drew and formulated the conclusions to Pollock's and Marcuse's contributions to a theory of fascism.

Studies on Authority and the Family

The structure of the Circle's theory after 1930 can be seen quite clearly in *Studies on Authority and the Family*, published in 1936. This volume documents studies initiated immediately after Horkheimer's assumption of the directorship. They are well suited to our purposes, since they form the single instance in which (for the period examined here) the program of integrating philosophical theory and empirical method was tested in a collective project. Horkheimer states that *Studies on Authority and the Family* was planned as the first project to realize the program articulated in his inaugural address in terms of content as well as in terms of methodology and research technique. Horkheimer indicated this in his introduction by quoting his own inaugural address:

After the preliminary studies indicated that this theme was theoretically significant and that at the same time it could be started with promising empirical means, we made a common effort "to reformulate questions in the course of work as demanded by the object, to make more precise, to develop new methods and yet not to lose sight of the larger whole." (p. ix)

At the same time Horkheimer himself relativizes the claim that *Studies on Authority and the Family* realized the interdisciplinary social research program integrating theory and empirical research. He considered the work to be in large measure "preliminary," in part because of historical circumstances (emigration), and in part because of the time-consuming nature of the development of dialectical theory. For

the range of questions treated by the studies will attain their true meaning only in a comprehensive theory of social life — in which these questions are embedded. (p. vii)

Studies on Authority and the Family was published as no more than a "report on work in progress." The structure of this work is nonetheless basically clear.

The division of labor within the project was as follows:

Part I (Editor: Horkheimer)
Theoretical Sketches
General Section (Horkheimer)
Section on Social Psychology (Fromm)
Section on the History of Ideas (Marcuse)
Section on Economics (Pollock, never completed)

Part II (Editor: Fromm)
Surveys
(a) on blue-collar and white-collar workers
(b) on sexual mores
(c) of experts on authority and the family
(d) of youth on authority and the family
(e) of unemployed on authority and the family

Part III (Editor: Löwenthal)
Sixteen individual studies and eight overviews of the latest relevant literature, including materials on the relation between the state of the economy and the family; the debates of the German National Congress in 1919 on family policy; authority and the family in German fiction after the First World War.

In the general section of part I, Horkheimer develops the problem systematically. After presenting his materialist theory of culture, he introduces the concept of authority that is to be used in explaining a certain aspect of the economically deprived classes—namely, their tendency toward adaptation—in terms of their social circumstances. Horkheimer's theme is the classic-specific forms in which authority is generated within the family.

Marcuse wrote the theoretical-historical introduction to Horkheimer's systematic development of the problem. Marcuse traces how the relationship between authority and family is represented in the teachings of Luther, Calvin, Kant, Hegel, Marx, and counterrevolutionary theoreticians. Fromm's social psychology section contrasts sharply with these two somewhat philosophical reconstructions of the problem's relevance. The theoretical passages in Fromm's section—concerning superego formation, *Angst*, and repression—reveal a marked concern with the extent to which his assumptions are operable. Fromm discusses, for example, forms in which authoritarian behavior appears, and he develops types of correlation between forms of authority and membership in a particular class. Fromm's theoretical sketch in this section is thoroughly consistent with the introduction he wrote to the second, empirical part of the studies. Pollock's economic section was never completed. His preliminary studies, in which he discusses the relevant literature, appeared as a review in the *Zeitschrift* (1933:131).

Even though the majority of the investigations hardly went beyond the stage of collecting the completed questionnaires, it is nonetheless interesting to observe the connections between the first (theoretical) part and the empirical part. In the general section of part I, Horkheimer discusses the problem of how the father's authority role within the family—based on his economic function of provider—is subject to fluctuations in the economy (pp. 70ff.). He maintains the thesis that, in times of long-term mass unemployment, a transformation in the father's authority position within the family will be found throughout society. This assumption was translated into a study on the influence of unemployment on family structure, and particularly on the father's position of authority. Fromm reports that this project (survey e), undertaken in the Geneva and Paris branch offices, never got beyond the "pretest" stage (p. 233).

Nevertheless, there are interconnections between the theoretical and empirical parts, both thematically and with regard to evaluation techniques. Those portions of the questionnaire supervised by Fromm—which analyzed the interviewee's psychic structure—did not evaluate by means of generalization or type construction. Rather, data on personality structure were interpreted in light of the types developed by Fromm in the social psychology section of part I. Fromm wrote:

From the totality of the answers to each particular, complete questionnaire, we tried to deduce the character structure of the respondent, and to compare these structures with each other (structural statistics). . . . Although this type construction should be influenced by, and continually differentiated in terms of, the study's empirical material, these types cannot be won exclusively through classification; rather, they presuppose a developed psychological theory. The authoritarian-masochistic character, which we attempted to outline in the social psychology section of this volume, provides an example of a theoretically founded structure type. (p. 235)

In his essay, "Psychoanalytic Characterology and Its Significance for Social Psychology," published in the *Zeitschrift* (1932), Fromm made further contributions to a theoretically based typology with an empirical intention.

Part III contains sixteen individual studies, published only in extracts, on specialized problems—sociopolitical, juridical, and economic. These studies were supplemented by eight overviews of the recent literature on the state of the international discussion. The individual studies and overviews were commissioned pieces—paid expert opinions—mainly by scholars outside the Institute from all parts of Europe. According to Horkheimer, the studies were to provide "expert information and quick orientation for [Institute's own] co-workers"; they served as "aids, proofs, and explanations to the essays of part I" (p. iv). Horkheimer asserts that this intended, processslike relation—of mutual interaction between the theoretical formulation of a problem and its "translation" into terms of empirical science—existed between parts I and III. In the case of part III, the term *empirical* is to be understood, not in the sense of a methodology of empirical social research, but as case studies:

A whole series of such scientific information is the product of an extended correspondence between a particular expert and the Institute; after a preliminary report on the theme had been submitted, the report would be expanded and refined on the basis of inquiry. Hence there are two or three different versions of many of the contributions. (p. iv)

Leo Löwenthal, who supervised part III, told me that this had indeed been the case. The information contained in these sixteen individual studies and eight literature reports, however, can no longer be completely identified within the texts; at most this can be done at certain points. For example, it seems quite clear that Horkheimer's remark on the connection between the Chinese cult of ancestors and the widespread agrarian mode of production (p. 16) was based on information provided by Karl August Wittfogel. Similarly, Erich Fromm's remarks on the ambivalent relation of anarchism to authority (p. 131) seems to me to have profited from Hans Meyer's report on the current literature, entitled "Authority and the Family in the Theory of Anarchism" (p. 824). The fact that the individual studies and literature reports were not cited, even though the theoretical sketches utilized their information, again indicates that they were conceived merely as working material and not as independent studies. Consequently the relation between parts I and III—unlike that between parts I and II— was such that a large part of the mass of information could not be considered at all, and hence the empirical chaos was never theoretically mastered.

With regard to a mutual interaction between a problem's theoretical statement and its empirical verification (specification), and vice versa, we thus see that the extent to which the empirical researches were theoretically conditioned or preformed with respect to their organization and evaluation technique was much greater than the extent to which theoretical consequences were drawn from the empirical findings. Apparently because of lack of time, money, and personnel, most of the surveys were never even evaluated or the findings published. According to Erich Fromm this was the case for the Institute's earliest and best-known study, the "Revolt of the Blue-Collar and White-Collar Workers," with which the Institute began during the Weimer Republic.[22]

Analysis of the Circle's Cognitive Structure

We can analyze the group's cognitive organization with the concept of a disciplinary matrix, with which Kuhn (1962) refined his concept of paradigm. Using the idea of a disciplinary matrix, Kuhn differentiated cognitive levels, thereby allowing for a more precise determination of the cognitive levels of a scientific paradigm. Musgrave (1971) and Weingart (1974) have further differentiated these levels.

Using these differentiations we shall outline the cognitive organization of the Circle's work, naming those cognitive stages and levels (which served at the same time to integrate the group socially) as follows:

(a) a thematic that was binding for all,

(b) common fundamental epistemological and social-ontological assumptions ("metaphysics"),

(c) the same orientation within a certain policy on theory and within a certain theoretical tradition,

(d) a heuristics of problem-solving and argumentation, common to all of the authors, and

(e) a common orientation on Horkheimer's role of determining the cognitive framework (i.e., an orientation on "paradigmatic"writings).

(a) The contributions by individual members of Horkheimer's group were united by a general scientific objective—namely, cultural science. The term *cultural science* is not to be understood in opposition to the treatment of "fundamental problems"; rather, *culture* should be understood as a category of totality equally comprehending (in the terminology of the 1920s) the spheres of "material" and "intellectual" culture. Broadly put, cultural science analyzes the forms in which "material" culture is related to "intellectual" culture, the economic base to ideological forms of consciousness—though not in the sense of the economic determinism maintained by the theoreticians of the Second International, which did not consider forms of culture, meaning, and knowledge as possible objects of scientific study. What later came to be called Critical Theory distinguished itself from economic determinism by conceptualizing base and superstructure in a more differentiated manner: by integrating psychoanalysis and historical materialism; by taking into account the relative autonomy of cultural forms of development (such as legal, scholarly, and artistic skills); and, finally, by making an interdisciplinary study of particular cultural spheres. Horkheimer formulated as a question the theme that was to "guide the Institute's collective work":

The question [is one] of the connection between society's economic life, the individual's psychical development, and changes within various cultural spheres understood in a narrower sense, to which belong not only the so-called intellectual contents of science, art, and religion but also law, mores, fashion, public opinion, sports, recreation, life-style, and so forth. . . . (1972a:43)

(b) Horkheimer formulates the epistemology and methodology implicit in all the Circle's studies and articles as the "unifying principle" in terms of which the Circle's interdisciplinarily organized social research presents itself:

It seeks knowledge of all social processes and therefore presupposes that, beneath the chaotic surface of events, a structure of influential forces, capable of being grasped conceptually, can be recognized. (1932a:i)

This basic assumption—that studying society in terms of the category of totality is possible and necessary—is not only a social-philosophical postulate. It is equally—and in distinction to the positivistic self-understanding of disciplinary science—the implicit premise that studies within any individual discipline can achieve adequate assertions about social structures only in cooperation with other disciplines. For Horkheimer and his co-workers the picture of society developed in theory may not be an amalgam of individual problems to be studied within a particular discipline. Society may be analyzed solely in terms of the cognitive maxim of the "concrete totality."

(c) In the first part of this book we showed how almost every individual contribution by a Circle member—essays oriented within a particular discipline—was set in the context of certain theory policy (materialism from 1932 to 1937, Critical Theory from 1937).

In his materialism essays from 1933 and in his essay "Traditional and Critical Theory" (1937), Horkheimer deals with this coordinated orientation (binding for all Circle members). For the most part it meant the identification of an article with a certain theoretical tradition. This process took the form of dogmatically introducing the construct of a "materialist" (and later "Critical Theory") tradition, and then arguing that the Circle's theoretical activity represented the most advanced form of each of these constructs.

The extent to which this general framework of theoretical orientation was mediated by research in particular disciplines varied greatly, according to the degree to which individual studies were in agreement with or merely external to the theoretical policy of the Institute. For example, Pollock's studies on crisis theory and the planned economy cannot be clearly assigned within this policy. Renaming the materialist theoretical policy Critical Theory affected the actual content of Löwenthal's studies no more than if Löwenthal had identified his work as progressive bourgeois sociology of literature. On the other hand, Fromm's early work on a materialist social psychology, which sought to synthesize psychoanalysis and historical materialism, is inconceivable without Horkheimer's discussion of the materialist content of Freudian theory.

(d) In almost all of the Circle's studies, ultimately the same argumentative heuristic is maintained despite the great diversification of themes and disciplines; it can be characterized only abstractly. It refers to the awareness—one might call it dialectical—that the semantics of concepts and of notions of theory are constituted in the movement of historical process. Pollock's anticritique of the liberalist critique of the New Deal, Adorno's critique of the fiction of naive immediacy in the late-capitalist culture industry, Marcuse's theory of fascism as the political form most adequate to advanced monopoly capitalism, Fromm's critique of "tolerance" in the self-understanding of bourgeois theoreticians—all these arguments take the form of demonstrating that the level of legitimation is either contemporary or not contemporary with the social structure on which it is based. Time and again the discipline-specific arguments of Circle members hinge on the historicity and social dependence of patterns of explanation and legitimation. In Hegelian language, this might be described as a consciousness of both an object's unity with and difference from its concept in the continually changing course of history.

(e) For the period of theoretical work studied here, there exists no single text (or group of texts) that might be considered a model for successful problem-solving which others in the Circle could have followed. This is because the Circle was split into disciplines. There are no comprehensive standards for problem-solving in philosophy, economics, psychoanalysis, sociology, or music theory, but rather only texts in which Horkheimer brought to bear his prerogative of deciding matters of administration, theory policy, and analytical framework. Reference texts for this prerogative can be identified.

One of these texts is Horkheimer's inaugural address of 1930, in which he outlines the Institute's program with regard to methodology and themes. To a lesser extent this holds true for his materialism essays of 1933 and for "Traditional and Critical Theory," together with an appendix (1937), where Horkheimer determines the Circle's theoretical orientation with "paradigmatic" clearness.

The Social Structure of the Organization of Research

An analysis in terms of the sociology of knowledge of significant cases in the history of science is plagued by several difficulties related to information on relevant social structure. Even in exceptionally well-documented cases, the historian cannot even begin to reach a level of information comparable to what he might easily attain as a participant-observer. Even in-depth interviews with surviving participants cannot compensate for this deficit. It is especially true of those involved in scientific endeavors that they tend to interpret themselves in their autobiographical reflections in light of the history of their own intellectual development, narratively distorting the earlier stages by viewing them from a personal perspective.

The Circle's Structure of Communication

The few published letters (for example, by Walter Benjamin), the unpublished letters to which I had access, Paul Kluke's and Martin Jay's excellent studies, as well as the interviews I conducted, do indeed fit together to form a concise configuration that can be roughly characterized as the structure of a group process and that as such can be applied to the cognitive structure of the group's work. This configuration is determined by Max Horkheimer's institutionally as well as cognitively dominant position. As a significant documentation of the nature of this position we need cite only one passage from a letter Pollock sent in September 1937 to Horkheimer, then living in Paris:

Social Structure of the Organization of Research

Table 1
Quotations (and self-quotations) in articles published in the *Zeitschrift* by members of the inner circle of the Institute for Social Research (quoters are in columns, quotees in rows)

	Horkheimer	Pollock	Löwenthal	Fromm	Adorno	Marcuse	Benjamin	Total[a]
Horkheimer	(13)	1	3	2	2	17	3	28
Pollock	—	(3)	—	—	1	1	—	2
Löwenthal	—	—	(1)	—	1	1	—	2
Fromm	4	—	—	(6)	—	—	—	4
Adorno	—	—	—	—	—	—	—	0
Marcuse	4	—	—	—	—	(3)	—	4
Benjamin	—	—	—	—	1	—	(1)	1
Total[a]	8	1	3	2	5	19	3	41

a. Excluding self-quotation.

Today we had our first plenary session, about which (L) will inform you in detail. When you're not there the group makes a very sorry impression indeed. I have pondered the remarkable extent to which you can achieve something with these very weak persons when taken individually. . . . (Pollock Archive)

There are many similar remarks in other correspondence; indeed, this sentiment is expressed—even if not so sharply—by almost all of the Circle's members. In interviews all former members recalled Max Horkheimer's formally as well as informally central position, which created a structure of communication something like a star. I examined this quantitatively by analyzing reciprocal quotations among Circle members in their *Zeitschrift* articles. I must emphasize, though, that I share all the prejudices against this research method, which is widespread in the Anglo-Saxon sociology of knowledge.[23] The merely quantitative perspective of this method fails to appreciate the often subtle act—quided by a certain theoretical orientation—of quotation. One might make this method more sophisticated by introducing qualitative aspects, distinguishing, for example, between "confirming" and "critical" quotations. In the present instance it was possible to dispense with this qualitative differentiation in the pattern of citation. All quotations recorded in table 1 are of a "positive" character: They refer to parallel texts by Circle members supporting, confirming, or expanding the thesis of the author making the quotation. This analysis takes into account all editions of the *Zeitschrift für Sozialforschung* but not all of the authors who published in the *Zeitschrift*; it is limited to those writers who can be considered as having belonged to the inner circle. In the table, the vertical column indicates who quoted whom and how often; the horizontal column indicates who was quoted by whom and how often.

The low rate of reciprocal quotation is surprising. It clearly indicates that the Frankfurt Circle was not an "invisible college."[24] Rather, it was a "visible college" in which the interdependence between a number of texts did not need to be indicated *post festum* by their authors quoting one another; from the start the texts were collectively planned and each was considered in relation to the others before final editing and publication. Moreover, in evaluating the numbers one must take into account the fact that the authors varied greatly in their level of quotation. Marcuse, for example, frequently quotes authors from the Circle as well as non-Circle authors, whereas Adorno seldom cites others, either inside or outside the Circle, and Fromm and Pollock, although they frequently quote others, rarely quote their Circle colleagues. The rate of self-quotation is naturally difficult to interpret— at least as evidence that, insofar as the growth of their knowledge is cumulative, the authors thereby drew more on their own personal interdisciplinary learning experiences than on an exchange of information with colleagues. This will be explained below in an analysis of the relation between the Circle's acts of internal and external quotation.

The fact that Horkheimer was quoted seven times more often than the next most frequently quoted Circle author indicates clearly, despite all the inadequacies of quotation analysis, the prominent position Horkheimer occupied within the group.

Even a cursory overview of the number of quotations of non-Circle authors shows that there were many more external quotations than internal ones. Examples are offered by essays in the second volume of the *Zeitschrift*. The ratio of external to internal quotations is, in Horkheimer's "Materialism and Metaphysics," 61:0; in Löwenthal's "Conrad Ferdinand Meyer's Heroic Conception of History," 40:1; and in Pollock's "Remarks on the Economic Crisis," 55:3. The relation between internal and external citation clearly shows that the Circle did not isolate itself from the larger scientific community, as is so often the case for innovative paradigm groups. In their articles, Circle members quote almost exclusively texts drawn from their own discipline. Fromm, for example, cites exclusively texts by Freud and

Freudians, whereas Pollock quotes only texts on economic research and on the theory of planned economy, and Löwenthal cites only texts drawn from the study of literature. Freud and Marx are quoted by all Circle authors, yet so unsystematically that this purely quantitative observation does not by itself provide any further insights.

In interviews, Max Horkheimer, Leo Löwenthal, Herbert Marcuse, and Erich Fromm all stated expressly that the process of discussion preceding the publication of essays in the *Zeitschrift* was extraordinarily intensive—indeed, that no single article appeared without having been ratified by the entire Circle. The numerous cross-references, intertwined with the texts themselves and not adequately identified by means of quotation analysis, bear witness to this fact. There is only one essay whose ratification process is documented in published texts, namely, Walter Benjamin's "On Several Motifs of Baudelaire" (1939).[25] Whether the degree of mutual intervention in the text proposals submitted by individual authors was the rule or the exception could not be clearly deduced from what the interviewed authors said. A reading of the Institute's correspondence (kept in the Pollock Archive) suggested that the degree of mutual critique present in the Benjamin case was not at all unusual. An essay by Adorno on Husserl, for example, was criticized much more sharply and bluntly—and subsequently was not published. Pollock, Löwenthal, and Marcuse opposed the article to the extent of intervening directly with Horkheimer.[26]

I gather from the correspondence that not all texts were discussed with equal intensity. Some were immediately accepted, others were criticized only superficially. The discussion was always intensive in the case of essays whose theses might touch on the group's outward, political presentation.[27]

The authors interviewed offered differing characterizations of the degree of equality in the criticism made by the various participants and affecting editorial decisions. One interviewee said that Horkheimer reserved to himself the final editorial decision on articles, and that he occasionally exercised this right. The correspondence suggests that this was indeed the case. The decisive role played by Horkheimer in the editing of essays, even when he was on trips, is suggested by a telegram sent by Pollock to Horkheimer in 1937:

Grossmann has inquired about essay for *Zeitschrift*—Marcuse rather perplexed apparently because of his essay—Could you send quidelines—(8 September 1937, Pollock Archive)

Role Differentiation within the Circle

The basis for a discursive egalitarian group structure—that is, for an optimally equal chance for each member to assume the relevant cognitive roles—was not developed because of the variety of disciplines represented. The variety of disciplinary backgrounds was indeed desired and closely bound to the Institute's program under Horkheimer's directorship.

Documents as well as discussions with former Institute members clearly indicate that, above and beyond all cognitive role differentiations, there were also differentiations of administrative and technical roles. Max Horkheimer clearly held the leading cognitive role. During the entire period from 1928 to 1941, Friedrich Pollock held the leading administrative role.[28] Because of his experience in editorial work and in the technical aspects of publishing, Leo Löwenthal was the managing editor for the Institute's publications.

Other than Horkheimer's leading cognitive role, provided for in the Institute's statutes, the differentiation of technical and administrative roles within the Circle was not codified but arose out of informal decisions. In this context Leo Löwenthal remarked (in a conversation) that the Circle had always been at pains to avoid overinstitutionalizing its operation.

The cognitive differentiations in roles cannot be overlooked. Friedrich Pollock was the Circle's political economist. Together with his co-workers Gerhardt Meyer and Kurt Mandelbaum, he represented a type of political economy that, although it understood itself politically in Marxist terms, is methodologically linked to bourgeois political economy. His intensive research on Soviet planned economy, with which he quickly made a name for himself, was less influential within the Circle than were his studies of the early 1930s on theories of planned economy and on crisis theory.

Leo Löwenthal was the Circle's literary scholar. He applied the program for ideology critique enunciated by Horkheimer to material drawn from literary scholarship.

In addition to his work at the Institute for Social Research, Erich Fromm held the position of *Lektor* at the Psychoanalytic Institute in Frankfurt. His essays on an analytical social psychology were designed to serve as central elements in the Circle's social theory.

Herbert Marcuse did not join the Circle until 1932. Like Horkheimer, he was a philosopher. In the initial years he was by far the Circle's most productive critic and reviewer. It is likely that this was his assigned function. But even later the philosopher Marcuse was clearly, in significant contrast to the philosopher Horkheimer, the Circle's specialist on strictly philosophical questions.

Theodor W. Adorno studied philosophy, music, psychology, and sociology. After earning a doctorate under L. Cornelius, he studied composition with Alban Berg in Vienna. The manuscript he wrote as a candidate for a *Habilitation*—never submited, and recently republished—indicates quite early a detailed knowledge of psychoanalytic theory. Other publications show that, in addition to his extensive knowledge of philosophical, psychoanalytic, and music theory, around 1930 Adorno was also thoroughly acquainted with the social-scientific literature. In terms of the breadth of his reading, and his ability to absorb and synthesize material, Adorno was the most interdisciplinary Circle member. It is all the more striking, then, that—with the exception of reviews and contributions to some of the *Zeitschrift*'s last issues— Adorno restricted himself to essays on the aesthetics of music. The fact also confirms our impression that all co-workers other than Horkheimer were to represent particular disciplines.

These men constituted the Circle's inner group. In a larger sense, though, the Circle included the sinologist Karl August Wittfogel, the economist Henryk Grossmann, the historian of science Franz Borkenau, the cultural philosopher Walter Benjamin, the sociologists Andries Sternheim and Paul Ludwig Landsberg, and several others.

In relation to all these co-workers Horkheimer clearly occupied the leading cognitive position. Still, his contributions betray his philosophical origins, even though political-economic and psychoanalytic elements begin to appear as early as 1934 in some of his texts. That he clearly remained bound to his origins in academic philosophy does not mean that he lacked the competence to fulfill the integrative function of his role. If what Marx called presentation was to become the methodological program of interdisciplinary organization, then surely it would have to proceed from that formal academic discipline distinguished from other disciplines by its integrative powers. In Horkheimer's time this was surely the discipline of philosophy.

The qualitative singularity of his central position is expressed in the nature of his *Zeitschrift* contributions. His role, bound to his highly visible position, was to determine policy on theory and to represent that policy in the public sphere. This is indicated not only by the fact that he was Institute director and *Zeitschrift* editor, and hence that all editorial and programmatic texts came from his pen. Up to 1937 each issue began with his contribution; for many co-workers, Horkheimer's essays represented the point of thematic unification—in their argumentation heuristic and the orientation of their theory. The premises of the Circle's policies on politics and scholarship—which went far beyond the content of any particular article—find their most significant and thorough expressions in Horkheimer's contributions. These are the premises that again and again reformulate the Circle's historical and political identity throughout the various phases of its development.

The *Zeitschrift*'s function as the stage for the group's work clearly indicates that the cognitive differentiation of roles described above stood in the service of a theoretical program integrating the group and transcending each individual's research. The criterion for selection of contributions for publication was not a diffuse, socialist pluralism of theory or purity of scientific standards, but rather the adequacy of each contribution to form integrating moments of a "theory of society," the program to be developed. In explicating the programmatic term *social research* [*Sozialforschung*] in the title of the journal, Horkheimer remarks:

The term *social research* does not propose to draw in new borders on the map of the sciences. Research in the most diverse areas and at the most diverse levels of abstraction—which is what this term means here—is united by the goal of furthering the theory of contemporary society as a whole. (1932:I)

That this formulation of a program referred exclusively to the Circle's own paradigm and not to theories developed outside the Circle is made clear in an editorial note in which Horkheimer, looking back from the perspective of 1937, reflects upon the Circle's publication policy:

As the journal was taken over by the house that published it as of the autumn of 1933 [Felix Alcan, Paris], the possibility suggested itself of making the journal available to all valuable scholarly work within the humanities that, because of events elsewhere, could no longer be published. The parameters of our journal, however, were simply too narrow. We therefore decided to continue a philosophical tradition insofar as the selection of articles would be governed (other than by scientific adequacy) above all by the type of thought and the orientation of interest. The most significant articles from the various disciplines should develop and bring to bear a common philosophical view. (1937d:i)

Thus the journal was in fact the "organ" or platform for presenting the Circle's development of theory. It was an organ in the sense that the contributions of Horkheimer, Fromm, Adorno, Löwenthal, Pollock, Marcuse, and occasionally those of Walter Benjamin, Grossmann, and Wittfogel, among others, combined into a certain gestalt, which can be considered the still indistinct, early form of a programmatically envisaged "theory of society."[29]

Conditions Determining the Institutional Framework

Although we possess little information about the internal structure of the Institute for Social Research at the University of Frankfurt am Main during the Weimar Republic, what we possess is nonetheless significant. Paragraph 3 of the Institute's statutes (published in 1925) very briefly states the rights of the Institute director: "The administration in scholarly matters is the duty of the director." The sentence is followed by general descriptions of the director's relation to the donor foundation, the Society for Social Research, and to the university; these descriptions determine the director's sole right of decision in scholarly questions. Carl Grünberg so interpreted the statute as to expand "downwards" the principle of the director's absolute autonomy: In his decisions the director should also be autonomous in relation to his scholarly co-workers. In contrast to the comparable social-scientific research institute in Cologne—under the collective direction of Christian Eckert, Leopold von Wiese, Max Scheler, and Hugo Lindemann—the Institute for Social Research was governed by the administrative principle of the preeminent position of a sole director:

A further difference from similar institutions is the manner in which the Institute director's position and the extent of his responsibility is defined. The administration of other research institutions is usually organized collectively; that of ours, however, is entrusted to a single person. Here we have established, so to speak, the *dictatorship of the director*. (My emphasis; Grünberg 1924:7)

This autocratic administrative structure is based on the goal of realizing a "unity of problem formulation and problem-solving." Grünberg thus felt that

sharing the directorship at all, let alone with someone with a different outlook and methodology, is out of the question. (1924:7)

When Horkheimer assumed the Institute's directorship in 1930, he expressly continued—despite his accentuating various aspects of the research program differently—the autocratic administrative structure introduced by Carl Grünberg:

As I now, following the director's long years of illness, undertake to steer the Institute's works toward new tasks, I am thereby aided not merely by the experience of his co-workers and the collected literary riches but also by the Institute's statutes, which he largely established; according to these statutes the director, appointed by the minister, is "in all regards" completely independent and, as Grünberg used to say, there exists, in distinction to some collective arrangement, "the dictatorship of the director" (1972c:420)

He adds that the administrative structure adopted from Grünberg's directorship forms a good institutional precondition for his program for a synthesis of philosophical speculation and empirical research:

This will make it possible for me to use what he has created, at the very least to institute with my associates a dictatorship of planned work in the strictest common framework, concerning the juxtaposition of philosophical construction and empirical research in social theory. (1972c:42)

It thus becomes clear that Max Horkheimer's preeminent position—as demonstrated not only by numerous documents but also by an analysis of the use Circle members made of each other's texts and by an analysis of the content of the Circle's cognitive structure—was made possible and was strengthened by the Institute's internal structure.

In the following we would like to analyze the degree to which the Institute's relations to outside institutions influenced its internal structure. We will find that the larger institutional context within which the Institute existed—namely, the university administration and the Prussian Ministry of Education—had remarkably little influence on its internal structure.[30]

Even the earliest thoughts on founding an institute were characterized by a conception of a center "to exist side by side with the university," much like the existing Kiel Institute for International Economics, which was attached to the university but subject to the administrative prerogative, not of the university, but of the appropriate ministry. The Institute's independence was based on a grant by Hermann Weil, an Argentinian wheat dealer.

Hermann Weil was the father of Felix Weil, who must be seen as the Institute's actual organizational founder. Grants for scholarly institutions were not unusual in Germany. The University of Frankfurt, founded in 1914, was until the 1920s itself a "grant university"; that is, it was first made possible by, and subsequently supported by, grants from wealthy Frankfurt citizens. In the Institute's first years, from 1922 to 1924, the University of Frankfurt negotiated with the Prussian state over being integrated into the federal budget. According to Paul Kluke, this was an additional reason for the Institute's founders to seek a status of relative independence in relation to the university. Otherwise the Institute stood in danger of falling under the direct control of state policy regarding culture. The plan of "associating" the Institute with the university was surely based, in addition to pragmatic considerations, on the intention of profiting from the university's reputation. A purely private institute would never be influential within the scientific community. Kluke describes in detail the conflicts, particularly in the negotiations at the time of the Institute's foundation—between the founding society, presided over by Felix Weil, and the university administration—about the degree to which the Institute was to be autonomous. The regulation ultimately worked out under the supervision of the Prussian Ministry of Education provided that the Institute director must also occupy a full-time chair in the university's Department of Economic and Social Sciences. Hence the department had de jure influence over appointments to the directorship. De facto, the Society for Social Research, however, which in large measure was identical with the group of co-workers, was able, in the cases of both Carl Grünberg and Max Horkheimer, to install its choice over the department's preferences.[31] Over and above its legal connection to the Institute, the university had no further possibility of intervention. Precisely because of the director's complete autonomy, the university and the faculty influenced at most the atmosphere, but never the substance, of the Institute's research process.

Summary

In our reconstruction of the intertwining structures in the initial *Zeitschrift* issues we found such a high degree of interdependence between the disciplinarily diversified individual articles that any interpretation based on individual texts remains far below the level of the texts themselves, as is typical in the process of reception. The texts came to form *one* basic, theoretical configuration—not merely through progressive coordination, but by being integrated (Horkheimer's decisive achievement) within a medium constituted by an interdisciplinary problem-solving heuristic (analytical social psychology) and a unifying form of theory (ideology critique).

With regard to the relation of mutual interaction between the theoretical statement of a problem and its empirical verification and specification (and vice versa), our analysis of *Studies on Authority and the Family* revealed that the degree to which empirical research was influenced by theory (in terms of organization and evaluation technique) was far greater than the degree to which theoretical conclusions were drawn from the empirical findings. We also found that the empirical information provided by individual studies and by reports on the current literature was not systematically integrated into theory construction, beyond the consideration given in the theoretical section to specific points.

In reconstructing the general, cognitive organization of theory construction we found once again that the Circle was cognitively integrated through a common theme, methodology, and form of argument.

The common theme was social processes, thematized in terms of such totality categories as society, history, the course of history, and culture and were conceived of as a unity of material and ideational processes. The social process was the object of social philosophy. In the Institute's actual research process, however, programmatic mediation between the theme's philosophical statement and its empirical-scientific restatement remained unclear.

The *methodology* employed in all of the Circle's research—totality as an operating category—was, in the individual studies, at most implicit but not constitutive. The studies were more thoroughly integrated by being externally labeled in terms of a specific policy (materialism or Critical Theory).

The recurrence of the same general *form* of argumentation in almost all the disciplines represented was, though obvious, so bound to the materials of the particular discipline in each case that it was identifiable only at a high level of generality.

Our reconstruction of the Circle's communication structure clearly confirmed the impression left by biographical and documentary material. Institutionally *and* cognitively, Max Horkheimer occupied the dominant position within the Circle. In analyzing the social organization of the Circle's research work, as well as the patterns of quotation of authors inside and outside the Circle, we found that the members brought together a wide range of disciplines. The Circle's social organization was characterized by a differentiation of cognitive roles. This meant that not every member could play an equally influential role within the group, suggesting an overall structure in which a figure of cognitive leadership systematically integrated the various disciplines. This group structure was in turn based on the Circle's institutional substructure—on the "dictatorship of the director" that was anchored in the Institute's statutes and often invoked by Horkheimer.

Early Critical Theory distinguished, in its organization of research, between the levels of research and presentation—or more precisely, it defined research and presentation as roles related to each other linearly, within a research process organized within a division of labor.

In an initial step a problem—which the human subjects experience as a single, unitary problem, such as the crisis of family structures in the Weimar Republic—is broken down into partial themes specific to particular disciplines. This is the function of research roles. In a second step the role of presentation sythesizes several elements of this ensemble of partial themes into an integrated perspective (in terms of which questions can be framed). In a third step this developed, integrated perspective is reconnected with the role of research, that is, with the models, methods, and measuring techniques provided by the specialized sciences. This guarantees that the interdisciplinarily generated perspectives do not make themselves philosophically independent of the specialized sciences. This process of repeated interaction between research and presentation is continued until a highly complex theoretical structure has been established as the product of an organization of research whose elements—detailed differentiations, on the one hand, and a concern with the whole, on the other—influence each other.

The Frankfurt Circle's research program never got beyond the project stage; its implementation in research praxis remained incipient at best. To function, it would have to be freed from such disruptive contingencies as the personal union of the directorship with the role of presentation. In the case studied here, Horkheimer's presentational role was a function of a genius (ascribed to him by others or by himself) for organizing research. This direct amalgamation of institutional and cognitive authority made it impossible to determine, within the actual research process, whether successful cases of theory integration were expressions more of a fixed group-dynamic structure than of an intended methodology. For this reason, connecting the functions of research and presentation with permanently assigned roles within a division of labor is problematic in general. Within a group of highly qualified inquirers who combined competence in particular disciplines with the capacity to work both empirically and theoretically, role differentiation might be foregone, and it would be possible to achieve a differentiation of functions in each researcher's approach to the problem. But the more complex a particular theme, the more likely that functions will be distributed in a context of collective work. What disciplinary background would qualify particular researchers for the synthetic function of the role of presentation would have to be decided in terms of specific problems and projects.

When presenting interdisciplinary social research in his programmatic articles, Horkheimer always identified an interdisciplinary reorganization of the formal disciplines in the medium of philosophy with an integration of theoretical-philosophical and empirical work. He did not differentiate between the horizontal integration of the specialized sciences and the vertical integration of theoretical and empirical work in the specialized sciences. This lack of differentiation was based on considerations that are today recognized as false. Horkheimer had a naive concept of the empirical; he considered every scientific reference to sense objects as empirical. Yet from the perspective of contemporary history of science, what is empirical is not the sense object but its specific technical control. Moreover, Horkheimer had not yet realized that theoretical initiatives in the specialized sciences no longer came—and for some time had not come—from philosophy, but rather from the various disciplines themselves; and that philosophy, which stood in close relationship to the specialized sciences, had disintegrated into a loose ensemble of "hyphenated" philosophies. Hence, any notion of an interdisciplinary formation would have to ask whether the various discipline-specific proposals of theory were compatible with each other and receptive to conceptualizations foreign to any given discipline. Furthermore, one would have to determine whether there had been any generalizable developments in the relation between theory and the empirical *within* the particular specialized sciences— whether, for example, the empirical techniques revolutionized through electronic data processing were becoming increasingly independent and self-sufficient, hence indifferent to the scientific material under examination, or whether, following the critique of the increasing independence of quantitative techniques from all theory, there is a tendency toward generating experiential data specific to particular research objects.

One question remains central: Does the formation of a supertheory— effected through the systematic intertwining of theoretical and empirical research—in turn develop into an institutionally established discipline, a kind of superdiscipline? Or does it develop into a new philosophy that, under the conditions of extremely well-delineated specialized sciences, once again seriously raises its classical claim to being a universal science? We think this unlikely, since a new philosophy or an interdisciplinary superdiscipline could not begin at some posited null point, but would have to begin with the material established by that discipline which, at the state of contemporary science, had distinguished itself among the particular disciplines as the most receptive and as having the greatest integrative power. This would scarcely be the academic discipline of philosophy, which has either stagnated in its historical self-reflection or been absorbed by the specialized sciences themselves. Yet, for all other disciplines we would have to expect that the superdiscipline we imagined would simply be colonized and absorbed by the expansionist tendencies of already existing paradigms, thus leading precisely to what at the beginning we described as the increasing loss of differentiation between the disciplines through the transference of *intra*disciplinary models and methods to other disciplines.

Hence we consider it unlikely that an interdisciplinary organizational form would have a coherent history as a discipline. Its temporal form would surely be that of a discontinuous succession of large scholarly projects. Apparently Horkheimer still believed—as he wrote in his foreword to *Studies on Authority and the Family*—that the results of such projects would be cumulative and that they therefore balance out to a "theory of the course of history."

The boundaries of the identity of an interdisciplinary organization— with reference to the organization's self-appointed task—would surely change, and the relation of this sort of science to its object would therefore also change. Whereas the unity of the traditional specialized sciences was in large measure realized through the immanent history of each discipline, the structure of an interdisciplinarily organized science would be much more determined by the structures of the particular object of this science at any given time. Put in a slightly exaggerated way, there would no longer be sociology, psychology, jurisprudence, criminology, pedagogy, and so forth, but rather the science of juvenile delinquency within a concrete historical and social situation.

Surely the relation of such a science to society would also change. Because of the increased relevance of its questions and results, it would soon burst the academic boundaries of its scholarly activities. If only tendentiously, it might develop into a progressive moment within the consciousness of the society it studies. Precisely this was a central thought of early Critical Theory: The political relevance of scientific work (in addition to being oriented toward the interests of underprivileged social groups) should result from qualities inherent in the work itself. Any given scientific pursuit does not become political simply by being placed within the context of a political cause external to this pursuit, or through a misuse of the social recognition of scientific inquiry for the sake of a cause. What counts is the further scientific development at such a theoretical and methodological level, and in terms of such problem constellations, that the distance of science from politics becomes unacceptable by its own standards. The connection we described between the process of socialization of science and the demand for the interdisciplinary reorganization of its institutionalized practice proves that the area of indifference between science and society—in political terms, scientific "autonomy"—became possible through the loss of science's political relevance (a phenomenon essentially connected with its fragmentation into a multiplicity of subdisciplines) and through the insignificance of purely internally generated questions. Even the merely instrumental political application of scientific information, which we see today, can in part be deduced from the circumstances in which science functions as a consultant. This would be different in the case of an interdisciplinarily reorganized science. Precisely for this reason its organizational research development is not a problem that would remain external to its political consequences. Precisely because its results for actors in the political sphere are not irrelevant, it may not be excused from reflecting upon the form of its political utilization. Early Critical Theory was conscious of this. Its demand for politically oriented science and its work on an interdisciplinary "theory of society" were the two sides of one very complicated matter.

Notes to Part II

1. Price (1963: esp. 13–14).

2. According to the well-known "finalization thesis" of G. Böhme, W. an den Daele, and W. Krohn.

3. See Hentig (1972:20ff.).

4. In gerontology, for example, physicians, psychologists, sociologists, and demographers work in multidisciplinary cooperation without being able to cover the entire problem of aging. Compare de Bie (1973:59ff.).

5. See Lasswell (1951).

6. See Jantzsch (1970).

7. To apply the term *interdisciplinary* to Horkheimer's research program is an application *avant la lettre*; the term *interdisciplinary* first appears in the United States in the 1950s. It has since become so widespread and its approximate synonyms are so unwieldy that we did not think we could forgo its use.

8. Conversations in Berkeley and San Diego, December 1975.

9. Compare the "unified sceince" movement founded by Carnap and Reichenbach in 1930.

10. Such as the Lynds' famous "Middletown" studies and their reception in the contemporary urban sociology by A. Walter; compare Maus (1959) and Klages (1969:105–111).

11. For von Wiese's critique see *Kölner Vierteljahreshefte für Soziologie* 12 (1933–1934). Compare Lazarsfeld (1975:163).

12. R. Heberle, "Soziographie," in Vierkandt (1959:564).

13. Compare Steinmetz's lecture (without title) at the sociology conference in Vienna in 1926, in *Verhandlungen des V. Deutschen Soziologentages* (Tübingen, 1927), p. 217.

14. Compare R. Heberle's contribution in *Verhandlungen des VII. Deutschen Soziologentages* (Tübingen, 1931).

15. In *Jahrbuch für Soziologie (1926)*.

16. For example, Dunkmann (1928: esp. 1-10).

17. See Adorno (1969:123) and also Lazarsfeld (1975:199ff.).

18. See Marx (1974:368ff.).

19. Kosik describes this cognitive form with the suggestive metaphor "coil" [*Spirale*].

20. See Schmidt (1968:37).

21. The sole text in which the interdisciplinary program of social research (reconstructed from the theory of dialectical presentation) was expressly associated with the structure of its organizational realization is Horkheimer's inaugural address. In an allusion to Grünberg's autocratic principle of administration, which he took over, Horkheimer comments: "Thereby I will be able to use what he created, so as to establish, at least within the closest circle of my co-workers, a dictatorship of planned work on the juxtaposition of philosophical construction and empirical work in the study of society" (1972c:72).

22. Conversation with Erich Fromm in Locarno, November 1976; compare Jay (1976:148).

23. See the excellent article by Sklair (1972).

24. See Crane (1972).

25. See Adorno's letter to Benjamin of 20 November 1939, in Benjamin (1966, vol. 2:782ff.).

26. See Pollock's telegram to Horkheimer of 9 September 1937 (Pollock Archive).

27. Horkheimer's essay "Die Juden und Europa" (1939, for example, was very intensively discussed before its final editing.

28. According to Jay (1976:7) and Carlota Pollock (letter to the author), this was not particularly conducive to advancement in his career.

29. In a conversation with Jay (1976:46), Leo Löwenthal, too, maintained that the *Zeitschrift* clearly had the character of a platform.

30. This section has benefited from Paul Kluke's study, *Die Stiftungsuniversität Frankfurt am Main* (1972). In the chapter entitled "Das Frankfurter Institut für Sozialforschung," he presents the results of his minute research into the history of the Institute's origin. I owe this reference to Horst Baier.

31. See Kluke (1972:496).

Bibliography

Abbreviations

ARSP = *Archiv für Rechts- und Sozialphilosophie*
KZfSS = *Kölner Zeitschrift für Soziologie und Sozialpsychologie*
SPSS = *Studies in Philosophy and Social Science*
ZfS = *Zeitschrift für Sozialforschung*

Abt, Clark C., 1970. Analysis of the survey of interdisciplinary activities of teaching and research in American universities. OECD Document/CERI/HE/CP.

Adorno, Theodor W., 1932a. Zur Gesellschaftlichen Lage der Musik. *ZfS* 1. English: On the social situation of music. *Telos* 35 (1978):128–164.

———, 1932b. Review of Herbert Marcuse, *Hegels Ontologie und die Grundlegung einer Theorie der Geschichtlichkeit*. *ZfS* 1.

———, 1932c. Review of Oswald Spengler, *Der Mensch und die Technik*. *ZfS* 1.

———, 1933a. *Kierkegaard: Konstruktion des Ästhetischen*. Tübingen.

———, 1933b. Review of Hans Driesch, *Philosophische Gegenwartsfragen*. *ZfS* 2.

———, 1933c. Review of Nicolai Hartmann, *Das Problem des geistigen Seins*. *ZfS* 2.

———, 1936. Über Jazz. *ZfS* 5 (under the pseudonym Hektor Rottweiler).

———, 1938. Über den Fetischcharakter in der Musik und die Regression des Hörens. *ZfS* 7. English: On the fetish character in music and the regression of listening, in A. Arato and E. Gebhardt, eds., *The Essential Frankfurt School Reader* (New York: Urizen, 1978), pp. 270–299.

———, 1939a. Fragmente über Wagner. *SPSS* 8.

———, 1939b. On Kierkegaard's doctrine of love. *SPSS* 8.

———, 1941a. On popular music. *SPSS* 9 (with G. Simpson).

————, 1941b. Spengler today. *SPSS* 9.

————, 1941c. Veblen's attack on culture. *SPSS* 9. Reprinted in T. Adorno, *Prisms* (London: Neville Spearman, 1967; Cambridge, MA: MIT Press, 1981), pp. 73–94.

————, 1951. *Minima Moralia.* Frankfurt/M. English: *Minima Moralia* (London: New Left Books, 1974).

————, 1968. *Der autoritäre Charakter,* 2 vols. Amsterdam (with B. Bettelheim et al.).

————, 1969. Wissenschaftliche Erfahrungen in Amerika. In *Stichworte: Kritische Modelle,* vol. 2 (Frankfurt/M).

————, 1970. *Über Walter Benjamin,* edited by Rolf Tiedemann. Frankfurt/M.

————, 1973a. Der Begriff des Unbewussten in der transzendentalen Seelenlehre. In *Schriften,* vol. 1 (Frankfurt/M).

————, 1973b. Reflexionen zur Klassentheorie. In *Schriften,* vol. 8 (Frankfurt/M).

Arato, A., and E. Gebhardt, eds., 1978. *The Essential Frankfurt School Reader.* New York: Urizen.

Arendt, Hannah, 1951. *The Origins of Totalitarianism.* New York: Harcourt Brace.

————, 1976. Oranisierte Schuld. In *Die verborgene Tradition* (Frankfurt/M).

Banckhaus, Hans G., 1969. Zur Dialektik der Wertform. In Alfred Schmidt, ed., *Beiträge zur marxistischen Erkenntnistheorie* (Frankfurt/M).

Barnes, Barry, ed., 1972. *Sociology of Science.* Middlesex, England: Penguin.

Barth, Hans, 1961. *Wahrheit und Ideologie.* Frankfurt/M. English: *Truth and Ideology* (Berkeley, CA: University of California Press, 1976).

Beard, Charles, 1935. The social sciences in the United States. *ZfS* 4.

Ben-David, Joseph, 1971. *The Scientist's Role in Society: A Comparative Study.* Englewood Cliffs, NJ: Prentice-Hall.

Benjamin, Walter, 1934. Zum gegenwärtigen gesellschaftlichen Standort des französischen Schriftstellers. *ZfS* 3.

————, 1935. Probleme der Sprachsoziologie. *ZfS* 4.

————, 1936. L'oeuvre d'art a l'epoche de sa reproduction mecanisée. *ZfS* 5. English: The work of art in the epoch of mechanical reproduction, in *Illuminations* (New York: Harcourt, Brace & World, 1968).

————, 1937. Eduard Fuchs, der Sammler und Historiker. *ZfS* 6. English: Eduard Fuchs: Collector and historian, in A. Arato and E. Gebhardt, *The Essential Frankfurt School Reader* (New York: Urizen, 1978), pp. 225–253.

————, 1939. Über einige Motive bei Baudelaire. *SPSS* 8. English: On several motifs in Baudelaire, in *Illuminations* (New York: Harcourt, Brace & World, 1968).

————, 1955. *Einbahnstrasse*. Frankfurt/M. Partial English translation: One-way street, in *Reflections* (New York: Harcourt Brace Jovanovich, 1978).

————, 1965. *Zur Kritik der Gewalt und andere Aufsätze*. Frankfurt/M.

————, 1966. *Briefe*, edited by Gershom Scholem and Theodor W. Adorno, 2 volumes. Frankfurt/M.

————, 1968. *Illuminations*. New York: Harcourt, Brace & World.

————, 1969. *Charles Baudelaire: Ein Lyriker im Zeitalter des Hochkapitalismus*. Frankfurt/ M.English: *Charles Baudelaire: A Lyric Poet in the Era of High Capitalism* (London: New Left Books, 1973).

————, 1972. Ein deutsches Institut freier Forschung. In *Gesammelte Schriften*, vol. III (Frankfurt/M).

————, 1978. *Reflections*. New York: Harcourt Brace Jovanovich.

Berger, Peter, and Thomas Luckmann, 1966. Social Construction of Reality: A Treatise in the Sociology of Knowledge. New York: Doubleday.

Blumenberg, Hans, 1966. Die Legitimität der Neuzeit. Frankfurt/M. English: The Legitimacy of the Modern Age (Cambridge, MA: MIT Press, 1983).

Borkenau, Franz, 1932. Zur soziologie des mechanistischen Weltbildes. *ZfS* 1.

————, 1934. *Der Übergang vom feudalen zum bürgerlich Weltbild*. Paris.

————, 1940. *The Totalitarian Enemy*. London: Faber and Faber.

————, 1963. *The Spanish Cockpit*. Ann Arbor, MI: University of Michigan Press.

Bracher, Karl D., 1974. *Die nationalsozialistische Machtergreifung*, 3 volumes (with Gerhard Schulz and WR). Frankfurt/M.

Brandt, Willy, 1965. *Ein Leben für die Freiheit: Eine politishe Biographie* (with Richard Löwenthal and Ernst Reuter). Berlin/Vienna.

Brauer, Ludwig, 1930. *Forschungsinstitute* (with A. Mendelssohn-Bartholdy). Hamburg.

Breines, Paul, 1968. Herbert Marcuse and the New Left in America. In Jürgen Habermas, ed., *Antworten auf Herbert Marcuse* (Frankfurt/M).

Bullock, Alan, 1952. *Hitler. A Study in Tyranny*. New York: Harper.

Cerutti, Furio, et al., 1971. *Geschichte und Klassenbewusstsein heute: Diskussion und Dokumentation*. Amsterdam.

Crane, Diana, 1972. *Invisible Colleges: Diffusion of Knowledge in Scientific Communities*. Chicago: University of Chicago Press.

de Bie, Pierre, 1973. *Problemorientierte Forschung.* Frankfurt/M.

Dietrich, B., J. Perels, and Wolfgang Abendroth, 1976. *Ein Leben in der Arbeiterbewegung.* Frankfurt/M.

Dubiel, Helmut, 1973. *Identität und Institution.* Düsseldorf.

————, 1974. Dialektische Wissenschaftskritik und Interdisziplinär Sozialforschung: Theorie- and Organizationsstruktur des Frankfurter Instituts für Sozialforschung 1930ff. *KZfSS* 2.

————, 1975. Ideologiekritik versus Wissenssoziologie: Die Kritik der Mannheim'schen Wissenssoziologie in der kritischen Theorie. *ARSP* 2.

————, ed., 1975. *Stadien des Kapitalismus,* by Frederick Pollock. Munich.

Dunkmann, Karl, 1928. *Der Kampf um Othmar Spann.* Leipzig.

Eckert, C., 1921. Aufriss und Aufgaben des Forschungsinstituts für Sozialwissenschaften. *Vierteljahreshefte für Sozialwissenschaften* 1.

Eisermann, G., 1959. Die deutsche Soziologie im Zeitraum von 1918 bis 1933. *KZfSS* 11.

Enzensberger, H. M., n.d. Dossier: Revolutionstourismus. *Kursbuch* 30.

Fest, Joachim C., 1976. *Hitler,* 2 volumes. Frankfurt/M.

Fischer, Ruth, 1948. *Stalin and German Communism: A Study in the Origins of the State Party.* Cambridge, MA: Harvard University Press.

Fleming, Donald, 1969. *The Intellectual Migration: Europe and America, 1930–1960.* Cambridge, MA: Harvard University Press.

Frese, Jürgen, 1974. Prozesse im Handlungsfeld (manuscript). Bielefeld.

Fromm, Erich, 1931. *Die Entwicklung des Christusdogmas: Eine psychoanalytische Studie zur sozialpsychologischen Funktion der Religion.* Vienna.

————, 1932a. Über Methode und Aufgabe einer analytischen Sozialpsychologie. *ZfS* 1. English: In *The Crisis of Psychoanalysis* (1970), pp. 110–134.

————, 1932b. Die psychoanalytische Charakterologie und ihre Bedeutung für die Sozialpsychologie. *ZfS* 1. English: In *The Crisis of Psychoanalysis* (1970), pp. 135–158.

————, 1934. Die sozialpsychologische Bedeutung der Mutterrechtstheorie. *ZfS* 3. English: In *The Crisis of Psychoanalysis* (1970), pp. 79–83.

————, 1935. Die gesellschaftliche Bedingtheit der psychoanalytischen Therapie. *ZfS* 4. English: In *The Crisis of Psychoanalysis* (1970), pp. 1–29.

————, 1936. Sozialpsychologischer Teil. In *Studien über Autorität und Familie* (Paris).

————, 1937. Zum Gefühl der Ohnmacht. *ZfS* 6.

Bibliography

————, 1941. *Escape from Freedom.* New York: Farrar & Rinehart.

————, 1962. *Beyond the Chains of Illusion.* New York: Simon & Schuster.

————, 1970. *The Crisis of Psychoanalysis.* New York: Holt, Rinehart & Winston.

————, 1980. *Arbeiter und Angestellte am Vorabend des Dritten Reiches*, edited by Wolfgang Bonss. Stuttgart. English: *The Working Class in Weimar Germany: A Psychological and Sociological Study* (Cambridge, MA: Harvard University Press, 1984.)

Gitermann, V., 1976. Die russische Revolution. In *Propyläen Weltgeschichte*, volume 9/1 (Frankfurt/M).

Gouldner, Alvin, 1970. *The Coming Crisis of Western Sociology.* New York: Basic Books.

Grebing, Helga, 1966. *Geschichte der deutschen Arbeiterbewegung.* Munich. English: *The History of the German Labour Movement*, abridged translation (London: Wolff, 1969).

Grossmann, Henryk, 1929. *Das Akkumulations- und Zusammenbruchsgesetz des kapitalistischen Systems.* Leipzig.

————, 1932. Die Wert-Preis-Transformation bie Marx und das Krisenproblem. *ZfS* 1.

————, 1935. *Die gesellschaftlichen Grundlagen der mechanistischen Philosophie und die Manufaktur. ZfS* 4.

————, 1969. *Marx, die klassische Nationalökonomie und das Problem der Dynamik.* Frankfurt/M.

Grossmann, Henryk, and Carl Grünberg, 1971. *Anarchismus, Bolshewismus, Sozialismus.* Frankfurt/M.

Grünberg, Carl, 1924. Inaugural address at the opening of the Institute for Social Research at the University of Frankfurt/M on 22 June 1924. *Frankfurter Universitätsreden* 20.

Gumperz, Julian, 1932. Zur Soziologie des amerikanischen Parteiensystems. *ZfS* 1.

————, 1933. Recent social trends in USA: Gesichtspunkte zur Kritik des gleichnamigen "Report." *ZfS* 2.

Gurland, Arcadius, 1941. Technological trends and economic structure under national socialism. *SPSS* 9.

Habermas, Jürgen, 1971. *Philosophisch-politische Profile.* Frankfurt/M. English: *Philosophical-Political Profiles* (Cambridge, MA: MIT Press, 1983).

Hahn, Erich, 1974. *Materialistische Dialektik und Klassenbewusstsein.* Frankfurt/M.

Hegel, G. W. F., 1896. *Lectures on the History of Philosophy, vol. III.* London: K. Paul, Trench, Trübner.

————, 1958–1959. *Sämtliche Werke*, edited by H. Glockner, vols. 9 and 19. Stuttgart.

————, 1970. *Hegel's Philosophy of Nature*. London: Allen & Unwin.

Hentig, Hartmut von, 1972. *Magier oder Magister?* Stuttgart.

Hirschler, Eric, ed., 1965. *Jews from Germany in the United States*. New York.

Hobsbawn, Eric, 1963. *Primitive Rebels: Studies in Archaic Forms of Social Movement in the 19th and 20th Centuries*. New York: Praeger.

Holzhauer, Walter, 1972. *Karl Kautskys Werk als Weltanschauung*. Munich.

Horkheimer, Max, 1930a. *Anfänge der bürgerlichen Geschichtsphilosophie*. Frankfurt/M.

————, 1930b. Ein neuer Ideologiebegriff? *Grünberg Archiv für die Geschichte des Sozialismus und die Arbeiterbewegung* 15.

————, 1932a. Bemerkungen über Wissenschaft und Krise. *ZfS* 1. English: In *Critical Theory* (New York: Herder and Herder, 1972), pp. 3–9.

————, 1932b. Geschichte und Psychologie. *ZfS* 1.

————, 1932c. Hegel und die Metaphysik. In *Festschrift für Carl Grünberg zum 70. Geburtstag* (Leipzig).

————, 1933a. Materialismus und Metaphysik. *ZfS* 2. English: Materialism and metaphysics, in *Critical Theory* (New York: Herder and Herder, 1972), pp. 10–46.

————, 1933b. Materialismus and Moral. *ZfS* 2.

————, 1933c. Zum Problem der Voraussage in den Sozialwissenschaften. *ZfS* 2.

————, 1934a. Zu Bergsons Metaphysik der Zeit. *ZfS* 3.

————, 1934b. Zum Rationalismusstreit in der gegenwärtigen Philosophie. *ZfS* 3.

————, 1935a. Bemerkungen zur philosophischen anthropologie. *ZfS* 4.

————, 1935b. Zum Problem der Wahrheit. *ZfS* 4. English: On the problem of truth, in A. Arato and E. Gebhardt, eds., *The Essential Frankfurt School Reader* (New York: Urizen, 1978), pp. 407–443.

————, 1936a. Allgemeiner Teil. In *Studien über Autorität und Familie* (Paris).

————, 1936b. Egoismus und Freiheitsbewegung. *ZfS* 5.

————, 1937a. Der neuest Angriff auf die Metaphysik. *ZfS* 6. English: The latest attack on metaphysics, in *Critical Theory* (New York: Herder and Herder, 1972), pp. 132–187.

————, 1937b. Philosophie und kritische Theorie. *ZfS* 6.

————, 1937c. Traditionelle und kritische Theorie. *ZfS* 6. English: Traditional and critical theory, in *Critical Theory* (New York: Herder and Herder, 1972), pp. 188–243.

————, 1937d. Vorgang zum sechsten Jahrgang. *ZfS* 6.

————, 1938a. Montaigne und die Funktion der Skepsis. *ZfS* 7.

————, 1938b. Die Philosophie der absoluten Konzentration. *ZfS* 7.

————, 1939a. Die Juden und Europa. *SPSS* 8.

————, 1939b. The relation between psychology and sociology in the work of Dilthey. *SPSS* 8.

————, 1939c. The social function of philosophy. *SPSS* 8.

————, 1941a. Art and mass culture. *SPSS* 9. Reprinted in *Critical Theory* (New York: Herder and Herder, 1972).

————, 1941b. The end of reason. *SPSS* 9.

————, 1941c. Notes on Institute activities. *SPSS* 9.

————, 1941d. Preface. *SPSS* 9.

————, 1947. *Eclipse of Reason*. New York: Oxford University Press.

————, 1970. *Vernunft und Selbsterhaltung*. Frankfurt/M.

————, 1972a. Autoritärer Staat. In *Gesellschaft im Übergang*, edited by Werner Brede (Frankfurt/M). English: The authoritarian state, in A. Arato and E. Gebhardt, eds., *The Essential Frankfurt School Reader* (New York: Urizen, 1978), pp. 95–117.

————, 1972b. *Critical Theory*. New York: Herder and Herder.

————, 1972c. Die gegenwärtige Lage der Sozialphilosophie und die Aufgaben eines Instituts für Sozialforschung. In Werner Brede, ed., *Sozialphilosophische Studien* (Frankfurt/M).

————, 1974a. Dämmerung: Notizen in Deutschland. In Werner Brede, ed., *Notizen 1950 bis 1969 und Dämmerung: Notizen in Deutschland* (Frankfurt/M).

————, 1974b. *Aus der Pubertät: Novellen und Tagebuchblätter*. Munich.

Horkheimer, Max, and Theodor W. Adorno, 1944. *Dialektik der Aufklärung* (original title: *Philosophische Fragmente*). New York: Institute of Social Research. English: *Dialectic of Enlightenment* (New York: Herder and Herder, 1972).

Jantzsch, Erich, 1970. Toward inter- and transdisciplinarity in education and innovation. *Policy Science* 1:403–428.

Jay, Martin, 1973. *The Dialectical Imagination*. Boston: Little, Brown.

————, 1976. The extraterritorial life of Siegfried Kracauer. *Salmagundi* 31/32.

Jonas, Friedrich, 1968. *Geschichte der Soziologie*, vol. IV. Hamburg.

Kantorowicz, Alfred, 1948. *Spanisches Tagebuch*. Berlin.

————, 1964. *Deutsche Schicksale: Intellektuelle unter Hitler und Stalin*. Vienna.

————, 1971. *Deutsches Tagebuch*, 2 volumes. Munich.

Kirchheimer, Otto, 1939. Criminal law in National Socialist Germany. *SPSS* 8.

————, 1941a. Changes in the structure of political compromise. *SPSS* 9.

————, 1941b. The legal order of national socialism. *SPSS* 9.

————, 1964. *Politik und Verfassung*. Frankfurt/M.

————, 1967. *Politische Herrschaft: Fünf Beiträge zur Lehre vom Staat*. Frankfurt/M.

Kirchheimer, Otto, and George Rusche, 1939. *Punishment and Social Structure*. New York: Columbia University Press.

Klages, Helmut, 1969. *Geschichte der Soziologie in Deutschland*. Munich.

Kliem, Kurt, 1957. Der sozialistische Widerstand gegen das Dritte Reich dargestellt an der Gruppe "Neu Beginnen." Ph.D. dissertation, University of Marburg.

Kluke, Paul, 1973. *Die Stiftungsuniversität Frankfurt am Main*. Frankfurt/M.

Koestler, Arthur, 1940. *Darkness at Noon*. London: J. Cape.

————, 1945. The fraternity of pessimists. In *The Yogi and the Commissar* (London: J. Cape).

————, 1952–1954. *Arrow in the Blue*, 2 volumes. London: Collins.

König, René, 1971. *Studien zur Soziologie*. Frankfurt/M.

Korsch, Karl, 1941/1965. The fight for Britain, the fight for democracy, and war aims of the working class (1941). *Alternative* (April 1975).

————, 1966. *Marxismus und Philosophie*. Frankfurt/M. English: *Marxism and Philosophy* (London: New Left Books, 1970).

Kosik, Karel, 1967. *Die Dialektik des Konkreten*. Frankfurt/M. English: *Dialectics of the Concrete* (Boston: Reidel, 1976).

Krahl, Hans-Jürgen, 1971. *Konstitution und Klassenkampf: Zur historischen Dialektik von bürgerlichen Emanzipation und proletarischer Revolution*. Frankfurt/M.

Krauch, Helmut, 1970. *Die organisierte Forschung*. Neuwied/Berlin.

Krenek, Ernst, 1938. Bemerkungen zur Rundfunkmusik. *ZfS* 7.

Kuczynski, Jürgen, 1944. *Über die Unpraktischkeit des deutschen Intellektuellen*. London: Free German League of Culture in Great Britain.

Kuhn, Thomas, 1962. *The Structure of Scientific Revolutions.* Chicago: University of Chicago Press.

Landsberg, Paul, 1933. Russenideologie und Russenwissenschaft. *ZfS* 2.

Laqueur, Walter, 1967. *The Fate of the Revolution: Interpretations of Soviet History.* New York: Macmillan.

Lasswell, Harold D., 1951. The policy orientation. In H. D. Lasswell and D. Lerner, eds., *The Policy Sciences* (Stanford, CA: Stanford University Press).

Lazarsfeld, Paul, 1937. Some remarks on the typological procedures in social research. *ZfS* 6.

―――, 1975. Eine Episode in der Geschichte der empirischen Sozialforschung: Erinnerungen. In T. Parsons, E. Shils, and P. Lazarsfeld, *Soziologie autobiographisch* (Stuttgart).

Lazarsfeld, Paul, and Marie Jahoda Lazarsfeld, 1975. *Die Arbeitslosen von Marienthal.* Frankfurt/M.

Lefebvre, Henri, 1968. Marxian thought and sociology. In *The Sociology of Karl Marx* (New York: Pantheon).

Löwenthal, Leo, 1932. Zur gesellschaftlichen Lage der literatur. *ZfS* 1.

―――, 1933a. Conrad Ferdinand Meyers heroische Geschichtsauffassung. *ZfS* 2.

―――, 1933b. Zugtier und Sklaverei. *ZfS* 2.

―――, 1934. Die Auffassung Dostojewskis im Vorkriegsdeutschland. *ZfS* 3.

―――, 1936. Das Individuum in der individualistischen Gesellschaft: Bemerkungen über Ibsen. *ZfS* 5. English: In *Literature and the Image of Man* (Boston: Beacon Press, 1957), pp. 166–189.

―――, 1937. Knut Hamsun: Zur Vorgeschichte der autoritären Ideologie. *ZfS* 6. English: In *Literature and the Image of Man* (Boston: Beacon Press, 1957), pp. 190–220.

―――, 1964. *Literatur und Gesellschaft.* Neuwied/Berlin.

Löwenthal, Leo, and Norbert Guterman, 1949. *Prophets of Deceit: A Study in the Techniques of the American Agitator.* New York: Harper & Row.

Löwenthal, Richard, 1937. Zu Marshalls neoklassischer Ökonomie. *Zfs* 6 (under the pseudonym Paul Sering).

Ludz, Peter-Christian, 1976. *Ideologiebegriff und marxistische Theorie: Ansätze zu einer immanenten Kritik.* Cologne/Opladen.

―――, 1977. Ideologieforschung: Eine Rückbesinnung und ein Neubeginn. *KZfSS* 1.

Lukács, Georg, 1968. *Geschichte und Klassenbewusstsein*. Berlin/Neuwied. English: *History and Class Consciousness* (Cambridge, MA: MIT Press, 1971).

———, 1974. *Die Zerstörung der Vernunft*, 3 volumes. Berlin/Neuwied. English: *The Destruction of Reason* (London: Merlin Press, 1981).

Luxemburg, Rosa, 1970. Schriften zur Theorie der Spontaneität. In Günther Hillmann, ed., *Texte des Sozialismus und Anarchismus* (Hamburg).

Mandelbaum, Kurt, 1933. Autarkie und Planwirtschaft. *ZfS* 2 (under the pseudonym Kurt Baumann).

———, 1936a. Keynes Revision der liberalistischen Nationalökonomie. *ZfS* 5 (under the pseudonym Erich Baumann).

———, 1936b. Neuere Literatur über technologische Arbeitslosigkeit. *ZfS* 5.

———, 1974. *Sozialdemokratie und Leninismus*. Berlin.

Mandelbaum, Kurt, and Gerhardt Meyer, 1934. Zur Theorie der Planwirtschaft. *ZfS* 3.

Mann, Golo, 1958. *Deutsche Geschichte 1919–1945*. Frankfurt/M.

Mann, Klaus, 1966. *Der Wendepunkt: Ein Lebensbericht*. Frankfurt/M.

Mannheim, Karl, 1930. *Ideologie und Utopie*. Frankfurt/M. English: *Ideology and Utopia* (New York: Harcourt, Brace & World, 1936).

———, 1943. *Diagnosis of Our Time: Wartime Essays of a Sociologist*. London: K. Paul, Trench, Trübner.

———, 1964. *Wissenssoziologie: Auswahl aus dem Werk*, edited by Kurt H. Wolff. Neuwied/Berlin.

Marck, Siegfried, 1938. *Der Neuhumanismus als politische Philosophie*. Zürich.

Marcuse, Herbert, 1928. Beiträge zu einer Phänomenologie des historischen Materialismus. *Philosophische Hefte* 1.

———, 1929. Zur Wahrheitsproblematik der soziologischen Method. *Die Gesellschaft* 2.

———, 1932a. *Hegels Ontologie und die Grundlegung einer Theorie der Geschichtlichkeit*. Frankfurt/M. English: *Hegel's Ontology and the Theory of Historicity* (Cambridge, MA: MIT Press, forthcoming).

———, 1932b. Neue Quellen zur Grundlegung des historischen Materialismus. *Die Gesellschaft* 7/IX.

———, 1934. Der Kampf gegen den Liberalismus in der totalitären Staatsauffassung. *ZfS* 3. English: In *Negations* (Boston: Beacon Press, 1968), pp. 3–42.

———, 1936a. Zum Begriff des Wesens. *ZfS* 5. English: In *Negations* (Boston: Beacon Press, 1968), pp. 43–87.

———, 1936b. Ideengeschichtlicher Teil. In *Studien über Autorität und Familie* (Paris).

———, 1937a. Über den affirmativen Charakter der Kultur. *ZfS* 6. English: In *Negations* (Boston: Beacon Press, 1968), pp. 88–133.

———, 1937b. Philosophie und kritische Theorie. *ZfS* 6. English: In *Negations* (Boston: Beacon Press, 1968), pp. 134–158.

———, 1938. Zur Kritik des Hedonismus. *ZfS* 7. English: In *Negations* (Boston: Beacon Press, 1968), pp. 159–200.

———, 1939. An introduction to Hegel's philosophy. *SPSS* 8.

———, 1941a. *Reason and Revolution*. New York: Oxford University Press.

———, 1941b. Some social implications of modern technology. *SPSS* 9.

———, 1958. *Soviet Marxism*. New York: Columbia University Press.

———, 1965. Der Einfluss der deutschen Emigranten auf das amerikanische Geistesleben. *Jahrbuch für Amerikastudien* 10.

Marx, Karl, 1974. Vorrede zur zweiten Auflage des *Kapital*. In *Marx-Engels-Werke*, vol. 19 (East Berlin). English: Preface to the second edition of *Capital* (Chicago: C. H. Kerr,1906).

Massing, Hede, 1967. *Die grosse Täuschung*. Freiburg.

Maus, Heinz, 1959. Bericht über die Soziologie in Deutschland, 1933–1945. *KZfSS* 1.

Merleau-Ponty, Maurice, 1969. *Humanism and Terror*. Boston: Beacon Press.

———, 1973. *Adventures of the Dialectic*. Evanston, IL: Northwestern University Press.

Meyer, Gerhard, 1933. Neuere englische Literatur zur Planwirtschaft. *ZfS* 2.

———, 1934. Zur Theorie der Planwirtschaft. *ZfS* 3 (with Kurt Mandelbaum).

———, 1935. Krisenpolitik und Planwirtschaft. *ZfS* 4.

———, 1936. Authority and family in the theory of anarchism. In *Studien über Autorität und Familie* (Paris).

Molnar, Thomas, 1966. *Kampft und Untergang der Intellektuellen*. Munich.

Mommsen, Hans, 1974. Die sozialdemokratie in der Defensive: Der Immobilismus der SPD und der Aufstieg des Nationalsozialismus. In *Sozialdemokratie zwischen Klasenbewegung und Volkspartei* (Frankfurt/M).

Mullins, N. C., 1973. *Theories and Theory Groups in Contemporary American Sociology.* New York: Harper & Row.

———, 1974. Die Entwicklung eines wissenschaftlichen Spezialgebiets: Die Phagengruppe und die Ursprünge der Molekularbiologie. In P. Weingart, ed., *Determinanten wissenschaftlicher Entwicklung* (Frankfurt/M).

Musgrave, A. E., 1971. Kuhn's second thoughts. *British Journal of the Philosophy of Science* 22.

Negt, Oskar, 1974. Rosa Luxemburg: Zur materialistischen Dialektik von Spontaneität und Organisation. In Claudio Possoli, ed., *Rosa Luxemburg oder die Bestimmung des Sozialismus* (Frankfurt/M).

Negt, Oskar, and Alexander Kluge, 1972. *Öffentlichkeit und Erfahrung: Zur Organisationsanalyse von bürgerliche und proletarischer Öffentlichkeit.* Frankfurt/M.

Neumann, Franz, 1937. Der Funktionswandel des Gesetzes im Recht der bürgerlichen Gesellschaft. *ZfS* 6.

———, 1939. Types of natural law. *SPSS* 8.

———, 1944. *Behemoth: The Structure and Practice of National Socialism, 1933–1944,* second edition. New York: Oxford University Press.

Neumann, Sigmund, 1942. *Permanent Revolution: The Total State in a World at War.* New York: Harper and Brothers.

———, 1970. *Die Parteien der Weimarer Republik.* Stuttgart.

Nolte, Ernst, 1965. *Der Faschismus in seiner Epoche.* Munich.

Parsons, Talcott, 1975. Die Entstehung der Theorie des sozialen Systems: Ein Bericht zur Person. In T. Parsons, E. Shils, and P. Lazarsfeld, *Soziologie autobiographisch* (Stuttgart).

Plessner, Monika, 1964. Die deutsche "University in Exile" in New York und ihr amerikanischer Gründer. *Frankfurter Hefte* 19.

Pollock, Frederick, 1929. *Die planwirtschaftlichen Versuche in der Sowjetunion, 1917–1927.* Leipzig.

———, 1930. Das Institut für Sozialforschung an der Universität Frankfurt a.M. In L. Brauer and A. Mendelssohn, eds., *Forschungsinstitut,* 2 volumes (Hamburg).

———, 1932. Die gegenwärtige Lage des Kapitalismus und die Aussichten einer planwirtschaftlichen Neuordung. *ZfS* 1.

———, 1933. Bemerkungen zur Wirtschaftskrise. *ZfS* 2.

———, 1941a. Is national socialism a new order? *SPSS* 9.

———, 1941b. State capitalism: Its possibilities and limitations. *SPSS* 9.

————, n.d. Notes on European postwar economic problems. Pollock Archive (place of publication unknown).

Post, Werner, and Alfred Schmidt, 1975. *Was ist Materialismus? Zur Einleitung in Philosophie.* Munich.

Price, Derek de Solla, 1963. *Little Science, Big Science.* New York: Columbia University Press.

Pross, Helge, 1955. *Die deutsche akademische Emigration nach den Vereinigten Staaten, 1933–1941.* Berlin.

Radkau, Joachim, 1971. *Die deutsche Emigration in den USA: Ihr Einfluss auf die amerikanische Europapolitik 1933–1945.* Düsseldorf.

Rauschning, Hermann, 1938. *Die Revolution des Nihilismus: Kulisse und Wirklichkeit in Dritten Reich.* Zurich/New York. English: *The Revolution of Nihilism* (New York: Longmans, Green, 1939).

Riemer, Svend, 1959. Die Emigration der deutschen soziologen nach den Vereinigten Staaten. *KZfSS* 1.

Rosenberg, Arthur, 1961. *Geschichte der Weimarer Republik.* Frankfurt/M.

Scheler, Max, 1929. *Der Mensch im Zeitalter des Ausgleiches.* Berlin.

Schlesinger, Rudolf, 1938. New Soviet-Russian social research. *ZfS* 7, 8.

Schmidt, Alfred, 1968. Zum Erkenntnisbegriff der Kritik der politischen Ökonomie. In Walter Euchner and Alfred Schmidt, eds., *Kritik der politischen Ökonomie heute* (Munich).

————, 1974. *Zur Idee der kritischen Theorie.* Munich.

————, 1976. *Die kritische Theorie als Geschichtsphilosophie.* Munich.

Shakolsky, Leon, 1970. The development of sociological theory in America. In L. T. Reynolds and J. M. Reynolds, eds., *The Sociology of Sociology.* (New York: McKay).

Sherif, M., and C. W. Sherif, eds., 1969. *Interdisciplinary Relationships in Social Sciences.* Chicago: Aldine.

Shils, Edward, 1975. Geschichte der Soziologie: Tradition, Ökologie und Institutionalisierung. In T. Parsons, E. Shils, and P. Lazarsfeld, *Soziologie autobiographisch* (Stuttgart).

Shirer, William L., 1960. *The Rise and Fall of the Third Reich.* New York: Simon & Schuster.

Sklair, L., 1972. The political sociology of science: A critique of current orthodoxies. In R. Halmos, ed., The Sociology of Science (Sociological Review Monograph no. 18, University of Keele).

Skuhra, Anselm, 1974. *Max Horkheimer: Eine Einführung in sein Denken.* Berlin.

Slater, Phil, 1976. *Origin and Significance of the Frankfurt School: A Marxist Perspective.* London: Routledge & Kegan Paul.

Söllner, Alfons, 1976. Geschichtsphilosophie und Herrschaftstheorie: Eine kritische Analyse zur Wissenshaftsgeschichte der kritischen Theorie. *Philos. Jahrbuch der Görres-Gesellschaft* 83.

Spiegel-Rösing, I. S., 1973. *Wissenschaftstentwicklung und Wissenschaftssteuerung.* Frankfurt/M.

Stern, Carola, et al., 1974. *DTV-Lexikon zur Geschichte und Politik im 20. Jahrundert,* 3 volumes. Munich.

Sternheim, Andries, 1932. Zum Problem der Freizeitgestaltung. *ZfS* 1.

Stourzh, Gerald, 1965–1966. Bibliographie der deutschsprechigen Emigration in den Vereinigten Staaten 1933–1963: Geschichte und Politische Wissenschaft. *Jahrbuch für Amerikastudien* 10/11.

Tenbruck, Friedrich, 1975. Der Fortschritt der Wissenschaft als Trivialisierungsprozess. In R. König, ed., *Wissenschaftssoziologie* (special issue 18 of the *KZfSS,* Opladen).

Verhandlungen des V. Deutschen Soziologentages 1926 in Vienna, 1927. Tübingen.

Verhandlungen des VI. Deutschen Soziologentages in Zürich, 1929. Tübingen.

Verhandlungen des VII. Deutschen Soziologentages 1930 in Berlin, 1931. Tübingen.

Vierkandt, Alfred, et al., 1959. *Handwörterbuch der Soziologie.* Stuttgart.

Weber, Hermann, 1969. *Die Wandlung des deutschen Kommunismus: Die Stalinisierung der KPD in der Weimarer Republik.* Frankfurt/M.

Weingart, Peter, ed., 1972. *Wissenschaftssoziologie I: Wissenschaftliche Entwicklung als sozialer Prozess.* Frankfurt/M.

———, ed., 1974. *Determinanten wissenschaftlicher Entwicklung.* Frankfurt/M.

Wellmer, Albrecht, 1969. *Kritische Gesellschaftstheorie und Positivismus.* Frankfurt/M. English: *Critical Theory of Society* (New York: Herder and Herder, 1971).

Wiese, Leopold von, 1921. Zur Einführung: Die gegenwärtigen Aufgaben einer deutschen Zeitschrift für Soziologie. *Vierteljahreshefte für Soziologie* 1.

Wittfogel, Karl A., 1938. Die Theorie des orientalischen Gesellschaft. *ZfS* 8.

———, 1970. *Die natürlichen Ursachen der Wirtschaftsgeschichte.* Frankfurt/M.

Zelený, Jindrich, 1962. *Die Wissenschaftslogik bei Marx und das "Kapital."* Frankfurt/M.

Zweig, Arnold, 1947. *Der Typus Hitler.* Fanara.

Index

Index

DE